INTERN NATION

ROSS PERLIN is a graduate of Stanford, SOAS and Cambridge. His work has appeared in the *Washington Post*, *New York Times*, and the *Guardian*. He has written on forgotten histories and disappearing languages in the U.S., China and the former Soviet Union.

INTERN
NATION

How to Earn Nothing and Learn Little
in the Brave New Economy

Ross Perlin

VERSO

London • New York

This updated paperback edition first published by Verso 2012
First published by Verso 2011
© Ross Perlin 2012

1 3 5 7 9 10 8 6 4 2

Verso
UK: 6 Meard Street, London W1F 0EG
US: 20 Jay Street, Suite 1010, Brooklyn, NY 11201
www.versobooks.com

Verso is the imprint of New Left Books

ISBN-13: 978-1-84467-883-9

British Library Cataloguing in Publication Data
A catalogue record for this book is available from the British Library

Library of Congress Cataloging-in-Publication Data
Perlin, Ross.
  Intern nation : earning nothing and learning little in the brave new economy / by
Ross Perlin. -- Updated paperback ed.
     p. cm.
  Includes bibliographical references and index.
  ISBN 978-1-84467-883-9 (alk. paper) -- ISBN 978-1-84467-906-5 (alk. paper)
  1. Internship--United States 2. Internship programs--Economic aspects--United
States. 3. Interns--Economic aspects--United States. 4. Conflict of laws--United
States. 5. Experiential learning--United States. 6. Business and education--United
States. I. Title.
  HD58.7.P463 2012
  331.25'92--dc23

                              2012001190

Typeset in Minion Pro by MJ Gavan, Truro, Cornwall
Printed in the US by Maple Vail

For my parents, who taught me how and why to work.

… the processes of exclusion we are about to describe emerged at the end of an accumulation of micro-alterations, micro-displacements, involving an abundance of good will, with people who often believed that what they were doing was for the best.

—Luc Boltanski and Eve Chiappello, *The New Spirit of Capitalism*

Experience is the name everyone gives to their mistakes.

—Oscar Wilde, *Lady Windermere's Fan*

Contents

Preface: The Rules of the Game   ix

1.   The Happiest Interns in the World   1

2.   The Explosion   23

3.   Learning From Apprenticeships   43

4.   A Lawsuit Waiting to Happen   61

5.   Cheerleaders on Campus   83

6.   No Fee for Service   99

7.   The Economics of Internships   123

8.   Futures Market   145

9.   What About Everybody Else?   159

10. The Rise and Rebellion of the Global Intern   185

11. Nothing to Lose but Your Cubicles   203

Afterword to the Paperback Edition   225

Notes   235

Appendix A: Intern Bill of Rights   249

Appendix B: Internships and the Law   251

Acknowledgments   255

Index   257

The Rules of the Game

One steamy Saturday in late August—I must have been about seven years old—I opened a store. Like so many American kids, I wanted to play at business. With trays of Pillsbury cookies swelling in the oven, a pitcher of sickly sweet lemonade, and prices listed on a sign hand-drawn with Magic Markers, I was in business under the cherry trees. Soon I had my first bank account, urged on by a friendly dinosaur who promoted special accounts for kids. I longed to make the printed numbers in my little passbook go up, so I found work pulling up weeds in a neighbor's garden, sold off old toys and unwanted football cards, and begged my parents for advances and raises on my $1.20 weekly allowance. A few years later, I was following the daily jitters of the Dow Jones Industrial Average, mesmerized by the mysterious ticker symbols, by the idea of fortunes won and lost overnight. I still didn't know what work was really about, but I believed in following the rules, trying hard, and reaping the benefits. I believed in a simple equation: work brings rewards.

At college, people no longer asked, "What do you want to be when you grow up?" with a pinch of the cheek or a tousling of hair. From the lecterns I heard: *Do something meaningful with your life. Give back to those who are less fortunate.* From relatives, family friends, and assorted advice-giving adults, I heard: *Get paid to do something you enjoy.* From those a few years older than me: *It's a tight job market out there. Be flexible, control your own destiny.* And from the professionals, the career gurus sponsored by colleges and plunked down in the center of campus, I heard the nitty-gritty about résumés, networking, breaking into different industries and fields. And I had thought college was about road trips and reading Homer.

There was at least one thing they all agreed on: get an internship. And after years of avoiding the question—I spent the summers studying, traveling, and working "regular jobs"—I finally gave in to the pressure and got one. I was twenty-three, enrolled in a Master's program at the University of London, and I worried that my résumé was looking increasingly impractical.

In much of the developed world, the subtle, relentless pressure to do an internship is now simply part of being young. Already in the first years of high school they were a hot topic; I dimly understood that it was a privilege or a necessary humiliation, I wasn't sure which. Was it a real job, or just a dress rehearsal for a job? Why was it that scholarship kids worked in the cafeteria or shelved books in the library, while rich kids name-dropped their internships at prestigious companies, famous newspapers, high-minded nonprofits? A parent got them in, an uncle, a family friend, or perhaps it was just a casual word exchanged at the country club. I grew nervous that I was closing myself off from this loftier world of work—did my work experience as a camp counselor, a babysitter, or a tutor *count*? When I finally made the plunge and took an internship, I hoped to put a long-festering anxiety to rest. I had been insecure about internships for years, I realized—probably for as long as I'd been watching friends announce their life's passion and then maneuver, by whatever means necessary, to score the matching internship.

The office was located in the Borough of Islington, an NGO (and intern) ghetto of sleek little offices hidden down narrow streets. During the dampest half of a London year, I spent two days at the NGO each week, unpaid except for a basic lunch stipend and transit costs. Often barely noticed, I'd look up from my laptop, brought from home, to the rain dripping down beyond the window. My "desk" could be anywhere in the hip disarray: interns shifted spots depending on the day's configuration of regular staff. I translated material on the NGO's website from Chinese to English. When there wasn't anything left to translate, I wrote comments in the online forums, did image searches, or finished schoolwork. The interns—and there was a merry little band of us doing this—earned an honorable mention during the office Christmas party, but it backfired in humiliating fashion: no one knew who we were. The clapping of our full-time colleagues was polite and confused; they craned their necks in various directions, attempting to direct their forced smiles toward someone. Soon after, sitting around a dingy lunch counter where the measly sandwiches fit our reimbursement budget, a fellow intern said to me, "The best thing about internships is that you can spin them."

This was our typical dispirited talk—I barely noticed it at first. But the sentence stuck in my head: he had it exactly right. Internships are a world of spin. And the reason you can spin them—whether you're an intern or an employer—is that no one knows what they mean. Internships may be everywhere today, but they remain such a recent, chaotic phenomenon that there are seldom any rules of the road, any standards or codes of conduct that are honored—only vague expectations, for which no one is held accountable. Even the word *intern* is a kind of smokescreen, more brand than job description, lumping together an explosion of inter-mittent and precarious roles we might otherwise call volunteer, temp, summer job, and so on. Until just a few decades ago, the word referred almost exclusively to a particular period of hands-on apprenticeship in the medical profession.

The internship has become a new and distinctive form, located at the nexus of transformations in higher education and the workplace. Ever since the Victorian demarcation of childhood as a time for learning rather than laboring, capitalist societies have struggled over how to usher young people from the world of the classroom into the world of factories and offices. At the same time, corporate manpower needs and national policy objectives have staked claims of their own, carving out a distinctive niche for youth labor and calling for schools to produce a constant stream of skilled workers. After a century of experimentation, the internship, a late-comer to the field, has emerged victorious as the unrivaled gateway to white-collar work, now backed by government policies across the globe, employers' hiring practices, a nearly unanimous Academy, and a million auxiliary efforts. How did we get here?

Today interns famously shuttle coffee in a thousand newsrooms, Congressional offices and Hollywood studios, but they also deliver aid in

Afghanistan, write newsletters for churches, build the human genome, sell lipstick, deliver the weather report on TV, and pick up trash.[1] They are college students working part-time, recent graduates barely scraping by, thirty-somethings changing careers, and—increasingly—just about any white-collar hopeful who can be hired on a temporary basis, for cheap or for free. They're our favorite peons, loaded with little indignities and pointless errands. An intern for a New York theater company carries urine samples to her boss's doctor. A supervisor directs an intern to load his own car with leaking bags of garbage and drive around until he finds a dumpster. A public relations intern finds herself cleaning out an attic, dusting, watering all the office plants, shopping for full-time staff, and doing heavy lifting that leaves her with back pains. Required by their school to take "a social internship," two girls in the Netherlands, aged fourteen and fifteen, intern as prostitutes in the local red-light district.[2]

Even law firms specializing in employment issues have the gall to flout labor law by taking on unpaid interns and providing scant training. In the last few decades, internships have spread to virtually every industry and almost every country, while internship-related businesses and campus career offices also proliferate (hawking internships, organizing internship fairs, declaring an "internship week" on campus, and so on). Even intern alumni groups—like the Peggy Guggenheim Interns Society, an in-gathering of some of the thousands of interns who have served the Guggenheim empire over three decades—extend their tentacles in the familiar alumni network fashion.

"Celebrity interns," mostly in the fashion media industrial complex, show just how absurd and easily co-opted the word itself is—these are celebrities who do internships *after* they've become famous. Kanye West working as a fashion intern for The Gap, Philadelphia Eagles linebacker Stewart Bradley at *Elle*, and Lady Gaga seeking internhood with a famous hat designer—all surely no hardship for the millionaire participants. "Lyle the Intern," a sketch on Letterman, and "Ross the Intern" (no relation to the author) on Leno show a modicum of self-awareness, but it's reality TV that truly embraces the intern: Lauren Conrad and Whitney Port are icons of intern cool for the teenybopper set, with televised pseudo-internships among the fashion glitterati. Intern drama may even sell better than porn: Playboy now has a miniseries called "Interns." Art mirrors life in the Wes Anderson film *The Life Aquatic with Steve Zissou*, where the Team Zissou interns are bland, faceless minions in matching uniforms, tasked with theft, beleaguered by pirates, serving Campari on the rocks. When one frustrated intern threatens to leave the expedition, Captain Zissou retaliates by vowing to withhold his academic credit. In its own affectionate, distorted way, popular culture alone seems to understand the intern.

Yet comparatively little that is solid, sober, and actionable is known about the internship explosion: how many there are, in what fields, and what social and economic consequences arise from what interns do. On the one hand, the rise of internships has come at dazzling speed; on the other hand, they have been thoroughly naturalized, and young people can hardly believe in a world before internships. Researchers and policymakers have maintained a near-complete silence, despite the fact that internships were originally a creature of the academic and political spheres. A half-century boom in nonprofit work and the much-touted blossoming of "civil society" have been powered unmistakably by the internship explosion. Employers have embraced an informal, unregulated practice which they have been able to shape for their own needs—celebrated awkwardly by Jeffrey Tucker in the *Christian Science Monitor*: "The rise of the internship is the market's finding the workaround to government regulations, evidence of the tendency of liberty to grow up like grass in the cracks of sidewalks."[3]

We are reaching a period when the commanding heights of American life are already dominated, with fewer and fewer exceptions, by former interns—senators and cabinet members started political life as DC interns, Wall Street's "masters of the universe" cut their teeth during collegiate summers, cultural and intellectual elites broke in through cozy unpaid gigs, and on it goes. It comes as little surprise that these successful former interns now perpetuate the system that gave them a start and an "in"—today, working your way up from the mailroom or entering a profession directly from school are almost unheard of by comparison. "Regular jobs"—whether as a waiter, a camp counselor, or salesperson—are shrugged off as irrelevant, despite the lessons they can offer. Like the relentless push for university degrees, the mad pursuit of internships is justified as precious insurance against a bewildering and demoralizing job market. "You will not get a high-level job now in the economy without an internship"—this is the blunt assessment of Phil Gardner, head of the College Employment Research Institute at Michigan State University, who has watched the boom for thirty years.

Internships are changing the nature of work and education in America and beyond. Over the last few decades, they have become the principal point of entry for young people into the white-collar world. A significant number of these situations are unethical and even illegal under U.S. law—a form of mass exploitation hidden in plain sight. Those who can't afford to work without pay are effectively shut out, while a large group of interns from low- and middle-income backgrounds barely scrapes by. Plum internships are overwhelmingly for the wealthy and well-connected —to an extent that would be shocking if it involved regular jobs. Yet no one budges, nothing happens.

The number of students attending four-year colleges and universities in the U.S. is approximately 9.5 million—a large majority, perhaps as many as 75 percent, undertake at least one internship before they graduate. This is a striking and novel development. In 1960, the vast majority of internships were still confined to medicine; by 1970 the concept had spread to public administration, some large companies, and segments of a few other professions; even in 1980 they remained a relative rarity. Today, internships are ubiquitous among university undergraduates in the developed world—and it seems that their spread has only just begun. No firm figures for the internship boom currently exist, but it is probably a conservative estimate that between 1 and 2 million people participate in internships each year in the U.S.[4] Globally, the number is many times that. Due to their failure to pay minimum wage and overtime, tens of thousands of unpaid and low-paid internships each year—at the very least —are illegal under federal or state laws that are rarely enforced. Interns enjoy no workplace protections and no standing in courts of law, let alone benefits like healthcare. If we tracked their numbers, and recognized them as workers, interns would emerge as one of the fastest-growing categories of American worker. And most of them *do* work.

Most internships may be relatively innocuous, as mine was, but their cumulative social impact is enormous and troubling. I worked over 300 hours without pay for the NGO, but at least I had a scholarship that covered my living expenses. Others were supported by their parents or dug deep into their savings. But what about those qualified young men and women, I wondered, who couldn't depend on their families or their rainy-day funds to pay for housing and food? Would they ever be able to enter the do-gooder world of Islington NGOs? With unpaid internships virtually a prerequisite for getting hired, I had to admit that the answer was probably no.

Internships quietly embody and promote inequalities of opportunity that we have been striving diligently to reduce in courts, schools, and communities. But even for those who can afford them, focused training and mentoring are vanishingly rare, as interns soon discover: most ultimately learn the ropes on their own if at all, on the sly if necessary. Employers dictate all the terms of hiring and employment: don't expect protection from courts, unions, universities, or anyone else. Just as troubling is the devaluing of young people's labor. Once you start "spinning" your work, it's hard to stop. Once you're told that your work isn't worth anything, you stop taking pride in it, you stop giving it your best. A tacit mutual agreement sets in between supervisor and intern: I'll write the letter of reference, you make the coffee. Instead of finding dynamic, character-building, entrepreneurial opportunities, despondent interns cycle through uncompensated, impotent roles, collecting nebulous lines on their CVs.

All of us—employers, parents, schools, government agencies, and interns themselves—are complicit in the devaluing of work, the exacerbation of social inequality, and the disillusionment of young people in the workplace that are emerging as a result of the intern boom. Informal, barely studied, and little regulated, internships demand our scrutiny. We need a view of the entire sprawling system and its history, a glimpse of its curious blend of privilege and exploitation; we need to hear from interns themselves, and also from those who proffer internships, the people who sell them, the few who work to improve them, and the many who are unable to access them at all. Only then can we consider ethical, legal alternatives to a system that is broken, a practice that is often poisonous.

I began the research for this book in 2008, conducting interviews with economists, sociologists, historians, employers, career experts and, above all, a huge number of interns. Many of the findings are damning. Still, this book contains neither the dispassionate findings of a sociologist at far remove, nor the diatribes of a victim—and it doesn't contain any recommendations on how to land one of the top 666 internships in the field of direct-mail marketing, nor provide the companies' contact info. We have to be critical and satirical about a system that has gone off the rails, while admitting some of the merits of the basic concept, as well as the real good that internships can do and have done for particular individuals; we have to tackle a massive, sprawling topic that has never before received sustained attention, while remaining grounded in the lived facts of internships.

This is the first book-length analysis of internships, a first attempt to take in some of the phenomenon's incredible variety, including the good, the bad, and the ugly; the paid and the unpaid; the ostensibly academic and the completely untethered; part-time internships lasting a few weeks and full-time ones lasting a year. The interns described may be in their teens or in their fifties, and the organizations where they intern may be of any size or description. Most of our focus will be on the U.S., ground zero of the internship explosion, and on internships undertaken during and just after college, as these still represent far and away the most common scenario. A strict definition of "internship," whether promulgated by colleges, employers, or politicians, may well be desirable from a public policy point of view—it would allow us at least to know how many there are, for instance—but our first responsibility, before all else, is to gauge the spirit of the internship phenomenon, to take stock of where things stand.

The structure of the book is as follows: a look at one of the world's largest internship programs, which keeps Disney World running, followed by a general introduction to the internship explosion of the past few decades and its important precursor, apprenticeship, which survives today in a little-known but impressive and humane form. We will then examine the questionable legality of working for free, and how interns are effectively barred from asserting any rights in the workplace. Following chapters will cover the decisive role in promoting and enabling internships, the world of unpaid labor in the political and nonprofit sectors, the economics of internships, a booming internship industry, and the fundamental social inequalities that internships exploit and intensify. Finally, we'll cover the spread of internships around the globe, along with some of the strong responses that it has evoked, and examine the possibilities for reform.

As this book goes to press, illegal internships are flourishing as never before thanks to the Great Recession. In a time of chronic high unemployment, internships are replacing untold numbers of full-time jobs: anecdotal evidence abounds of managers eliminating staff and using unpaid interns instead, and of organizations replacing paid internships with unpaid ones. There is reason to believe that the relatively enlightened, decently paid internship is becoming an endangered species, going the way of the old entry-level job. Employers are making an increasingly brutal calculus concerning interns, but no one has been holding up a mirror to their actions.

More and more college graduates unable to find work are taking on internships, feeling they have no other choice. Perhaps they're right. As a result, the internship is fast becoming a significant post-graduation phenomenon as well. Ignoring the system's flaws, universities are increasingly making internships a requirement for graduation, and now even governments are hatching national internship schemes, providing firms with hundreds of thousands of free workers at public expense from the U.K. to South Korea. In the U.S., internships are also rapidly gaining a foothold in high schools, while at the other end of the spectrum, many more middle-aged people and even retirees are also entering the internship ranks.[5] For the young and the less experienced, and perhaps soon for everyone else, what's left of the ordered world of training, hard work, and fair compensation is in danger of disappearing, in large part because of internships.

Yet the beginnings of a backlash are also apparent. In the spring of 2010, a *New York Times* report by Steven Greenhouse stirred up a discussion that has worked its way through almost every major media outlet in the U.S. However gradually, a few employers are questioning and even changing some of their practices; students, parents, and teachers are learning about the legal and social problems with many internships. In the wake of the *Times* article, the Department of Labor publicly reiterated the definition of a legal internship—the result of a 1947 Supreme Court decision—and confirmed that a broader effort to enforce existing labor law was under way at the agency. Political sides were quickly drawn up:

much of the Left hypocritically feigned shock over internship abuses, while the Right foamed at the mouth that "Obama's war on internships" would hurt small businesses and violate the free market. Yet for now the politics remain purely on the surface, and any attempts at reform embryonic—interns continue to be used and abused by employers of all political persuasions in Washington and elsewhere, in organizations of every conceivable stripe. This book is meant as a step towards sanity and towards justice.

CHAPTER ONE

The Happiest Interns
in the World

Disneyland is presented as imaginary in order to make us believe that the rest [of America] is real ...

—Jean Baudrillard[1]

The curtain rises on Disney World: interns are everywhere. The bell-boy carrying luggage up to your room, the monorail "pilot" steering a Mark VI train at forty miles per hour, the smiling young woman scanning tickets at the gate. Others corral visitors into the endless line for Space Mountain, dust sugar over funnel cake, sell mouse ears, sweep up candy wrappers in the wake of bewitched four-year-olds. Even Mickey, Donald, Pluto and the gang—they may well be interns, boiling in their fur costumes, close to fainting in the Florida heat.

Visiting the Magic Kingdom recently, I tried to count them, scanning for the names of colleges on the blue and white name tags that all "cast members" wear. I met interns from Kent State in Ohio, from Lock Haven University in Pennsylvania, Lehman College in the Bronx, Miami-Dade College, Kean College in New Jersey, and the University of Nebraska. They came from public schools and private ones, little-known community colleges and world-famous research universities, from both coasts and everywhere in between. International interns, hailing from at least nineteen different countries, were also out in force. A sophomore from Shanghai, still bright-eyed a week into her internship, greeted customers at the Emporium on Main Street, U.S.A. She was one of hundreds of Chinese interns, she told me, and she was looking forward to "earning her ears."

These were just a few foot soldiers out of Disney's intern legions. Beyond the Magic Kingdom stretch three more theme parks, two water parks, twenty-four on-site themed hotels, an entire "downtown," countless restaurants and stores, a full-blown transportation system, and a host of other miscellaneous "entertainment and recreational venues." The world of Disney sprawls untrammeled over forty square miles, almost all of it thick with interns. Further hordes waited "off-stage" and out of sight —in warehouses, in kitchens, or underground in "the utilidors": a nine-acre tunnel system of warehouses, hallways, and offices, home to the computer system that programs parades, cues fireworks, and runs a vast surveillance network. Then there are the four gated residential complexes, some miles off, where Disney requires these low-paid thousands to live.

Disney runs one of the world's largest internship programs. Each year, between 7,000 and 8,000 college students and recent graduates work full-time, minimum-wage, menial internships at Disney World. Typical stints last four to five months, but the "advantage programs" may go on for up to seven months. These programs all overlap with the academic year. Rather than offer traditional summer internships, Disney's schedule is determined by the company's manpower needs, requiring students to temporarily suspend their schooling or continue it on Disney property and on Disney terms. The interns work entirely at the company's will, subject to a raft of draconian policies, without sick days or time off, without grievance procedures, without guarantees of workers' compensation or protection against harassment or unfair treatment. Twelve-hour shifts are typical, many of them beginning at 6 a.m. or stretching past midnight. Interns sign up without knowing what jobs they'll do or the salaries they'll be paid (though it typically hovers right near minimum wage).

"Do any of these guests know that if not for these students their vacations would not exist?" asks former intern Wesley Jones in his book *Mousecatraz.*[2] Although sometimes more inclined to rumors than to rigorous research, *Mousecatraz* is the one suggestive, in-depth look at the Disney program, written by someone who clearly knows it well and has talked to hundreds of other Disney alumni.

Disney labor is meant to have an almost invisible quality. Except for the name tags, nothing obvious distinguishes interns for the casual visitor —and now, in certain parts of the park, at certain times of day, they are simply the norm, comprising over 50 percent of staff. The work they perform is identical to what permanent employees do, and there's no added supervision, training, or mentoring on the job. The educational component is meant to come from a three- or four-hour class each week, offering some of the easiest college credits in the land. Students are also encouraged to obtain credit through networking, distance-learning, and "individualized learning opportunities." In any case, many interns do nothing educational at all, in the traditional sense of the word, given that Disney doesn't require it and that twelve-hour shifts are exhausting enough already.

Like other employers across the country, Disney has figured out how to rebrand ordinary jobs in the internship mold, framing them as part of a structured program—comprehensible to educators and parents, and tapping into student reserves of careerism and altruism. "We're not there to flip burgers or to give people food," a fast food intern told the *Associated Press*. "We're there to create magic."[3] Should the magic fail, the program at least seems to promise professional development and the prestige of the Disney name, said to stand out on a résumé regardless of the actual work performed. Yet training and education are clearly after-thoughts: the kids are brought in to work. Having traveled thousands of miles and barely breaking even financially, they find themselves cleaning hotel rooms, performing custodial work, and parking cars. The housing provided is hardly given out of generosity, but rather a calculated move to scale the program to massive proportions, where the real savings of not employing full-timers kick in. Communal housing may be part of what makes the experience fun and memorable, just like college, but day-to-day life at its worst looks suspiciously like a term of indenture: living on company property, eating company food, and working when the company says so.

In its scale and daring, the Disney Program is unusual, if not unique— a "total institution" in the spirit of Erving Goffman.[4] Although technically legal, the program has grown up over thirty years with support from all sides and almost zero scrutiny to become an eerie model, a microcosm of an internship explosion gone haywire. An infinitesimally small number of College Program "graduates" are ultimately offered full-time positions at Disney. A harvest of minimum-wage labor masquerades as an academic exercise, with the nodding approval of collegiate functionaries. A temporary, inexperienced workforce gradually replaces well-trained, decently compensated full-timers, flouting unions and hurting the local economy. The word "internship" has many meanings, but at Disney World it signifies cheap, flexible labor for one of the world's largest and best-known companies—magical, educational burger-flipping in the Happiest Place on Earth.

L ike many a corporate titan, Disney likes to give the impression it's in the education business. Disney University, born in 1955 as the company's training division, beat McDonald's Hamburger University, Motorola University, and others to the punch, prefiguring what Andrew Ross has called "the quasi-convergence of the academy and the knowledge corporation." Since 1996, the Disney Institute has charged "millions of attendees representing virtually every sector of business from every corner of the globe" for the privilege of learning about Disney's "brand of business excellence."[5] The Disney Career Start Program attracts high school drop-outs and graduates, promising a custom-designed "learning curriculum." The Disney Dreamers Academy targets 100 high school students each year. Interns are not the only ones on the receiving end of a dubious Disney degree. The company has every demographic, every part of the life cycle, covered.

The very name Disney World honors the universal intentions of a single individual. But there is also a much more prosaic title for these 25,000 acres of former swampland: the Reedy Creek Improvement District (RCID). An administrative fiction signed into law by Florida Governor Claude Kirk, Jr., in May 1967, RCID effectively granted the Walt Disney Corporation free rein over a sizable chunk of central Florida.[6] Yielding an unprecedented fiefdom to the imagineers of Burbank, the move enthusiastically welcomed a fait accompli—for the previous three years, Disney had been covertly amassing tens of thousands of acres in Orange and Osceola counties for a nebulous and grandiose "Florida Project." Keeping its intentions secret from local communities, partly in order to prevent a land rush, Disney deployed willing proxies, shell companies, and other false fronts: the Compass East Corporation; Tomahawk Properties, Inc.; Ayefour Corporation; and the Latin-American Development and Management Corporation, among others.

RCID continues to be the Walt Disney Corporation in all but name, allowing the company a quasi-governmental authority, including the extraordinary power to pay certain taxes to itself and to make land use decisions virtually without obstruction. The unique arrangement has been one of the principal factors in the remarkable expansion of Disney World attractions over the past two decades—another has been a compliant, scalable workforce of young people, employed at the company's whim and under educational pretenses.

With some 63,000 people now working on the property, Disney World is the largest single-site employer in the U.S. With the 1978 announcement of the building of EPCOT (Experimental Prototype Community of Tomorrow), Duncan Dickson and his fellow managers in Disney's Casting Department (read: Human Resources) conducted a manpower forecast to gauge their readiness for the coming build-up. Dickson says the prospects of finding enough workers in the Greater Orlando region looked bleak. At the time, the big question was "Where were we going to get these five to six thousand people?"

Dickson and his colleague John Brownley thought of Harry Purchase, head of the Hotel Management Department at Paul Smith's College in upstate New York. Through connections on the Disney staff, Purchase had been bringing his students to the Magic Kingdom every summer since 1972 to work in the Food and Beverage division and take classes with him off-site. Then in 1978 came a year-round arrangement with the much larger Johnson and Wales College in Rhode Island, which wanted to increase its enrollment of culinary students without building more kitchen space on campus. As Dickson remembers, the school proposed that "they would send an instructor down, they would have classes off-site … and the students would work." Disney readily agreed.

Could these minor applied learning initiatives be magnified into something significant, wondered Dickson and Brownley, big enough to make a serious dent in Disney's hiring needs? In early 1980, they hosted a three-day meeting in Orlando with a few dozen educators—"department heads of various programs and directors of cooperative education from different universities"—with the goal of setting out "a blueprint for the College Program." The educators were strongly supportive of the concept, stressing only that Disney should handle housing and provide some sort of classroom experience. The senior Disney executive in charge of all the theme parks gave his enthusiastic approval—after all, Disney parks had always employed some number of college students and young people, like many service providers. The idea of the College Program was simply to institutionalize and legitimize this on a massive scale, tapping colleges as key sources of recruitment and closely controlling the entire process. "To build it to any size, we had to have the academic piece," says Dickson. Besides scale, "the other impetus was to provide a flexible labor force that can adjust to [seasonal] operating fluctuations."

The Magic Kingdom College Program launched in the summer of 1980, restricted at first to some 200 students from three universities in the southeastern U.S. The immediate plan was to ramp the intake up to 400 interns in spring and summer (then the busiest times in the park) and drop to 200 in the fall. Until 1988, interns lived in the Snow White Village Campground, a mobile home park set amidst the strip malls and discount motels in the nearby town of Kissimmee. The units there usually accommodated eight people in four bedrooms, sharing two bathrooms and a kitchen. Then as now, housing was required for interns and the cost was deducted directly from their paychecks, in part for sheerly economic reasons. According to Dickson: "The company has to go out and secure the housing, so then to have students say, 'I don't want to live there,' [leaves the company with] the financial obligation, so that creates an issue."

Renamed twice to capture its widening scope (first to other parks inside Disney World and recently to California), the College Program has employed more than 50,000 interns over the thirty years of its existence. Its expansion has been exponential and opportunistic. The program has spawned imitations at the Disney theme parks in Hong Kong and Paris. From the late 1980s through the 1990s, more than 10,000 new hotel rooms were built at Disney World. Interns were promptly rushed in to fill a large number of the new positions, although hotel work had not originally been part of the program. The earlier focus on students majoring in hospitality, theme park management, or culinary arts disappeared as Disney ceased to require or seek out students studying particular majors: now you're more likely to find history majors dunking fries in hot oil and psychology majors working as lifeguard-interns. The loosening of immigration regulations in the late 1990s prompted the massive recruitment of ICP's (International College Program interns), more than 1,000 of whom now come to work at Disney World each year, under dubious interpretations of the J-1 "cultural exchange" and H2B "seasonal work" visas.

If Disney's motives are transparent and readily grasped, more surprising is the passionate support of Disney's dozens of cheerleaders at colleges and universities. Dickson himself, who ran the program until 1995, is now an Assistant Professor of Hospitality Management at Rosen College, down the road from Disney: a symbol of the easy traffic between academic departments and industry in "experiential" fields. In another example, Kent Phillips, Educator Relations and New Market Development Specialist for the internship program, recently received a major award for his good offices from the Cooperative Education and Internship Association.

In a promotional video aimed at students, over a dozen internship coordinators, career counselors, and professors of experiential education intone one after the other:

> "Disney is not just a place to work—it's an experience, and it's an experience you can't get anywhere else."

> "We tell students that the Disney College Program is for students of all majors, from engineers to business to students in the liberal arts."

> "The best thing … is what it does for the students' self-esteem."

> "They've learned people skills, they've learned accountability, they've learned how to be creative decision makers."

> "By far the best intern program I've seen in the nation."

Do the colleges understand that Disney sees their students as "a market" to "develop"? Why are twenty-two educators—including college provosts and the Executive Director of the National Association of Colleges and Employers (a major voice on internships)—willing to sit on an advisory board for the program, while many others serve as "faculty representatives" for Disney at their respective colleges?[7] Uncompensated "campus representatives"—former interns who want to keep their free passes to Disney parks—spread the message on hundreds of campuses across the country, assisting a staff of full-time Disney College Program recruiters during countless presentations each year. Educators and campus career development professionals are patently thrilled to have been consulted by Disney and to feel that they can offer their students a way in to a major name-brand company.

More troubling than this is the imprimatur of academic credit that these colleges lend to laboring for Disney: a summer job with a thin veneer of education, virtually unleavened by substantive academic content. After all, the thousands of students who do receive academic credit are paying their schools per credit for the privilege—a considerable financial windfall for schools, considering the minimal cost of providing these credits. If an institution refuses credit, Disney helps its interns look elsewhere, to more accommodating colleges and universities that are happy for the revenue stream, no matter where the students are from or what they do. Among those which have made arrangements with Disney are Purdue, the University of North Carolina, Tulane, and Central Michigan University (which charges up to $2,630 in any given semester). In order for its legions of international interns to secure their J-1 visas, Disney has also concocted relationships between willing American schools and foreign counterparts, such that—to take a single example—Montclair State University can charge thousands of dollars of tuition for a student from Beijing to work for Disney at minimum wage.

It would be unfair to assume that the educators involved are prompted solely by mercenary motives. Bud Miles, a professor at the University of North Carolina at Greensboro, which has sent hundreds of students to the program, told a reporter that "when the students come back here, I have local employers ask me if they can have some of the students who were in the Disney program ... because Disney has such a reputation in the area of customer service." Educators acknowledge that Disney's name recognition alone can help break the ice during a job interview. But many also subscribe to an educational philosophy wherein Disney World, or perhaps any workplace, is "a learning laboratory," as Disneyspeak would have it, and for these experts, the distinction between work and education has become almost nonexistent. According to Dickson, the approving educators have been "absolutely" aware from the beginning that the majority of interns work in fast food and sit-down restaurants, park cars, clean up after guests, and perform other routine maintenance tasks—indistinguishable by all accounts from the work performed by regular employees. Jerry Montgomery, another member of Disney's HR team involved in managing the program early on, defends it as helping to manage students' career expectations. Not everyone in life gets to be "the CFO's assistant," says Montgomery, and young people trying to get ahead often need a reality check, someone to "slap them upside the head"—something Disney presumably accomplishes by giving its interns mundane, real-world roles. Dickson points to "guest contact," along with showing up on time and being neatly attired, as key educational components. Yet many intern roles are now entirely "backstage," and even so, should service industry experience count as formal education just because you deal with customers?

Having secured its new cheap labor source, Disney could afford to let the program's academic facade crumble a bit—apparently less than half of all interns now seek or receive credit, far fewer than was initially the case. One Disney recruiter reassured his audience of intern hopefuls that it is "a networking program"—"a lot of students don't take classes: do networking instead." A former intern confirmed this emphasis: "Despite taking Disney courses, there was absolutely no connection between my [internship] experience and my academic progress … Folks that just wanted to learn were disappointed." But those who wanted to network "loved" it.

During peak periods, classes may be canceled so students can put in longer hours. When they are running, standard offerings include "Corporate Communication," "Experiential Learning," and "Marketing You" (all about developing "a marketing plan for yourself, including CV, cover letter, and networking strategy"). The "professors" have traditionally been Disney managers, but there is now a dedicated staff of instructors, some with Master's degrees and even one with a Ph.D. in Applied Ethics.

Disney boasts that eight of the courses are recommended for credit by the American Council on Education, and that fourteen small study rooms, branded as Disney Learning Centers, are scattered across the property.

In *Mousecatraz,* another former intern had this to say of the Disney Practicum, the core course for credit-seeking interns: "All we heard about in the class was how wonderful Lee Cockerell, the Vice-President of Walt Disney World Operations, was. It was Lee this, and Lee that and then more Lee. Perhaps Lee should have taught the course because most of the students walked away with the impression that it was all about Lee." Interns commonly complain about feeling brainwashed (or "Mouse-washed") by the courses, and report an emphasis on personal appearance over course content (though many are happy to have few tests, papers, or grades). Those who complete a course earn their "Ducktorate," those who complete other "Disney learning activities" (read: networking events) earn their "Mousters." Graduation caps are in the shape of mouse ears.

The Rolling Stones' "Start Me Up" is the ringtone on Ed Chambers' cell phone; he answers it with a friendly growl: "Big Ed." His desk is weighed down by a massive Rolodex, which he isn't afraid to use. He wears a sports jersey to work, but he's just been in Washington D.C., deftly lobbying Florida congressmen to pass healthcare reform. Over the past few decades, Chambers has brought a savvy, aggressive brand of "Yankee politics" to union-building in redneck Florida—but Disney has him on the defensive.

"I'm an organizer—that's what I do," says Chambers. "I was the orga-nizer who organized Disney World." He quickly adds that he wasn't alone in that. Now head of the United Food & Commercial Workers Union (UFCW), Local 1625, Chambers represents 6,000 full-time employees at Disney World—one of the six major union presidents in the Service Trades Council, whose contracts cover the majority of workers at Disney World (but not interns, of course). For union members, the debate about Disney's massive College Program is about more than issues of academic worthiness: it's about their livelihood. As one worker said to me of the interns, "We're trying to make a living, and they're here to play."

Ironically enough, unions came to central Florida in part thanks to Disney. When Walt was planning the future Disney World in the 1960s, says Chambers, "the building trades came down [from California] and pressured him, so it became union—[Disney World] was built with union construction. They chased him," he adds with a smile. "Walt sat down and said, 'Fine, you can be union.' " Four decades later, the orange groves and the open Ku Klux Klan membership drives at local supermarkets have largely disappeared. The area covered by Local 1625 now has the highest concentration of union members in Florida. In 1997, Chambers' union won a battle to organize at the Lakeland Regional Medical Center, setting off a domino effect: "Then we won the LPN's [licensed practical nurses] and the lab techs, then the police went union and the firefighters went union, then the sergeants of the police went union. Then we started picking off nursing homes around here, and the electric company just went union."

The success stories of UFCW Local 1625 represent a rare reversal for American organized labor in a bleak era. But handling a massive influx of intern labor at Disney has proven to be an unusual challenge. "Unfortunately, Walt would probably be rolling in his grave with some of the things they do," says Chambers, who refers to Disney's interns as "indentured." The unions initially made a handshake agreement over the tiny pilot program in 1980, understanding that it would relieve full-timers during the year's busiest periods. But they have been powerless to stop the program's massive, year-round expansion. "They just went ahead and did it," says Eric Clinton, a former Disney worker who is now president of UNITE HERE Local 362, another of the six major unions. "This is totally and purely about labor costs ... The College Program is almost as good as subcontracting. They've found a way to 'insource'," given that Disney World itself can't be moved offshore.

Disney would not respond to these charges or comment on anything else for this book, despite repeated requests. With the help of Chambers and Clinton, among others, I spoke to a number of former and current employees there, all of whom were understandably reluctant to be named. Indeed, the array of flexible, contingent labor at Disney World is stunning —interns are just the most visible and closely monitored group. The nomenclature is baffling to outsiders, but second nature to workers at Disney: CMs (full-time "Cast Members"), CPs (College Program interns), ICPs (International College Program interns), CRs ("casual regulars," i.e. part-timers), CTs ("casual temporaries" i.e. seasonal employees), and a sizable, separate group of management interns. Over the last decade or so, Disney has also started subcontracting out whatever support jobs they can: from food preparation to hotel cleaning and custodial work. Some of the subcontracted work differs little in substance from what the interns do for similar compensation (minimum wage, no benefits, no workplace protections), but many of the contract workers are undocumented immigrants, according to Clinton, who has assisted some of them in their conflicts with Disney and the subcontracting firm.

According to reports which Disney submits to the unions, "total casual employee utilization" hovers above 25 percent—meaning that one in four hours at Disney World is worked by a casual employee, whether CP, ICP, CR, or CT. The company's contract with the Service Trades Council allows for that number to go as high as 35 percent, and Disney has tried at different points to push it to 40 percent. "Hell will freeze over first," says Chambers, who sees it as a strike issue. "We will never, ever give that up." Disney World has never seen a strike before. But union membership has climbed to over 60 percent of the workforce, in response to company attacks on wages and benefits, and this in a "right-to-work" state, where nonmembers are covered by the union contract without having to pay dues. Still, says Clinton, "There's a lot of internal organizing that has to go on. Disney will only take us seriously when we have 75 percent membership."

This magic proportion—determining that 35 percent of all hours can be worked by casual employees—covers virtually the whole of Disney World, including what are necessarily bastions of full-time employment where interns are not permitted. For instance, bus drivers must meet certain of professional standards, due to Department of Transportation regulations (though these don't apply, curiously enough, to a monorail system that carries more riders than public transit in many cities). Usually given free rein, Disney pays little heed to maintaining a healthy balance of full-timers and interns at any given workplace or on any given shift. At the shops in Downtown Disney, for instance, it's common to find many more interns than full-timers at all hours of the day, but especially during the manic closing shift (6 p.m. to midnight).

"The percentage is out of control," says one veteran full-timer. His shop currently has fourteen full-time employees, twenty-one interns, twenty-one "casual regulars," and forty-three "casual temporaries" (who work very few hours and tend to cycle through quickly). By far, the largest share of hours is taken by interns, though he says that "really the full-timers run the shop" because of their experience. There is little to no time to provide training to the hordes of interns. "There's no continuity to anything," he says of the shop, "and the interns get blamed for anything. They work the worst hours. This place is a zoo." When the shop first opened, it was staffed almost entirely by full-timers.

The story is similar at the attractions, where the most coveted internships are. According to one long-time employee, the Animal Kingdom's "Asia" attraction had approximately sixty-five full-time employees and just under thirty interns before the most recent recession. Since then, with a virtual hiring freeze on full-timers, the number of interns has shot up to almost equal the number of full-timers. "It's a revolving door," he commented, and both the visitors' experience and the running of the theme park suffer as result. For Disney, he says, "It's all about the numbers." In a single hour running at full throttle, the full-time staff can put some 2,000 visitors through a major ride like the Mount Everest Rollercoaster, but "when you get a whole bunch of new folks, those numbers plummet, and the managers ride us, saying we've got to work on our OHRC, our Operational Hourly Ride Capacity ... Collective lack of experience on the ride systems is kind of scary." If this hasn't actually put visitors in danger yet, it has certainly translated into much longer waiting times for rides.

Chambers and Clinton both agree, as do many other Disney-watchers, that the company changed in the decades after Michael Eisner became CEO in 1984. "It's more about profits," says Chambers. Free family healthcare disappeared, along with the defined benefit pension plan for new employees. The pension plan for older employees may soon be gone as well, replaced by nonmatching 401K plans to which few of these low-paid hourly employees can afford to contribute. The unions were also powerless to stop the imposition of a new two-tier wage system, which has meant much lower pay raises for all new workers. (Starting salaries are barely above the federal minimum wage of $7.25 and climb 4 percent each year.) After five years at Disney World, a typical worker would now be lucky to make $9 an hour, and even twenty-year veterans are likely to have their salaries "top out" below $13 an hour.

According to a report by economists Bruce Nissen, Eric Schutz, and Yue Zhang, Disney's move to a two-tier wage structure saved the company close to $20 million in 2006 alone. The economists estimated that, as a result, $23.4 million was lost in goods and services in Orange and Osceola counties in that one year, bringing about further ripple effects: job losses, depressed wages, lower tax receipts for local governments.[8] Between wage squeezes, benefit cuts, and the broad casualization of the Disney World workforce, the company has clearly saved itself hundreds of millions of dollars over the years, if not more. With Disney the largest employer in the region, these changes do significant damage to the local economy.

In the beginning, Dickson and his HR team had to convince executives that the internship program would bring serious savings in labor costs: "We fought that battle all the way up to the Chief Financial Officer." No one questions it any longer. In Dickson's words, anyone who "looked at having to replace the College Program employees with full-time employees" would realize that the savings from having interns instead are "substantial." Who could doubt that this perpetual minimum wage machine would bring big returns? Besides having no benefits and being a captive audience for Disney paraphernalia, Disney rent, and Disney food, the interns never get genuine raises. Any changes in salary have closely followed adjustments in the minimum wage. In the meantime, the price of admission to Disney World has risen over 100 percent since 1990, around when the College Program started to take off.

Back in 1980, Dickson and the Disney HR team might have been partially justified in looking beyond Orlando to grow their workforce, but the excuse has long worn thin. One long-time employee told me that his manager had gone to Shanghai for a three-week recruiting trip in the midst of the recession hiring freeze: "He said he was interviewing 600 Chinese a day. It's nothing to do with cultural exchange—it's about money." Unemployment in Greater Orlando has been in the double digits recently, and the foreclosure rate on homes among the highest in the nation. Says the same Disney worker: "My sister was unemployed and she couldn't get a job at Disney, because they're recruiting kids from

Shanghai." Workers brought in from hundreds or thousands of miles away are always easier to control, even more so if the legality of their presence depends entirely on the employer. And needless to say, the international interns pay their own way to Disney, like everyone else.

"The company is misusing these temporary work visas," says Eric Clinton, careful to state that he does not mean those working in cultural-themed jobs at EPCOT and Animal Kingdom, who are typically union members with workplace protections. The Code of Federal Regulations, which covers implementation of the J-1 visa, forbids unskilled labor by these visa-holders and does not permit them to replace American workers "under any circumstances." Yet apparently following Disney's example, another major employer in Florida, the Publix supermarket chain, has launched a dubious international internship program of its own, also based on the J-1 Exchange Visitor Program. Disney is also starting to sponsor three-month H2B visas as yet another way to bring in flexible labor from overseas, though persons on these visas are also not supposed to displace U.S. workers. "If one of them gets fired, they're immediately deported," says Clinton of the international interns, who in some cases have been escorted directly from Disney housing to the airport within twenty-four hours by a friendly delegation from ICE (Immigration & Customs Enforcement).

A common complaint is that international interns speak halting English, directly affecting the experience of visitors—though this is far less of an issue at internationally themed attractions, where foreign accents are meant to add a certain authenticity. "We're responsible for tremendous amounts of knowledge to operate these rides safely," says one full-timer who believes poor spoken English combined with a lack of experience has created a spike in safety issues. In one incident, a maintenance worker was inadvertently locked in a control tower for a frightening period of time. A Chinese intern, in a safety-critical position, should have been responsible for releasing the worker but, according to the full-time employee, was "'afraid' to answer the radio or even answer the phone due to her language barrier," and she failed to help the trapped worker.

Because the requirement to live in Disney housing is galling to locals, even the American interns are usually from well beyond the Orlando region. "They're not committed to the community, they don't have the same investment in central Florida as people who've been here a long time," says Eric Clinton. "These jobs could be an incredible thing for central Florida." Although they use local services, the interns pay no local taxes, and Disney deliberately isolates them from the surrounding communities. With interns guaranteed at least thirty hours per week, and many working closer to forty, it is universally acknowledged that the interns are taking what would otherwise be full-time jobs. Departing or fired full-timers are often replaced with one or more interns, according to many people I interviewed. Thus one custodial worksite has gone from having close to 120 full-time employees (with no interns) to eighty full-timers, sixteen interns, and twenty subcontracted jobs. "They've done it through attrition," says Clinton of the way interns have entered the custodial group. A small recruiting project, supposedly intended to relieve workers during peak periods, has turned into a monster.

One overcast night I slipped into Vista Way, home to a thousand interns. I didn't have to scale fences or dart past the intimidating security gate, where interns are required to show their name tags every time they enter. As I approached, a caravan of American Coach buses was discharging a slew of exhausted interns with a mechanical yawn; following an intern's friendly nod, I quickly made my way inside. The buses are an endless source of grief for the interns, I learned later. When there aren't enough of them, a five- or ten-mile commute to work becomes an hour-long nightmare. The buses stop running at a certain hour, often stranding those with the earliest or latest shifts. The small number of interns who bring their own cars become gods among men.

All guests, including family members, must be signed out and off Vista Way property by 1 a.m. Interns violating any of a long list of rules can be forced to leave the property with twenty-four hours' notice. Regular searches of cars and rooms are conducted, with a policy of collective responsibility often applying: it's common for a whole group of interns to be "terminated" for the infraction of a single roommate (there is no court of appeals, needless to say). Those under twenty-one are placed in "Wellness Apartments," where a can of beer must not darken anyone's doorstep. One of the largest communities of interns living together anywhere in the world, Vista Way looks a lot like a college where both hedonism and surveillance are on steroids.

Somewhere in the undifferentiated sprawl of the Reedy Creek Improvement District, there is a pitiless intersection where you make the turn for Vista Way. Within walking distance there's only a Wendy's, a Chevron, 7-11, and a Walgreen's (with a conveniently massive liquor store annex). The "Vista Lay" mythology is all play and no work, toga parties and top rankings from Playboy as the home of the world's sexiest internships—but the reality on any given night is just a gated stretch of company housing, devoid of glamor. Interns were doing laundry, sharing cigarettes, shooting hoops, recovering from one shift and getting ready for the next one.

The grounds are filled with nondescript stucco apartment buildings in white and red. Most interns live four or six to an apartment, two to a bedroom, all sharing a kitchen. Directly behind the complex roars the endless traffic of I-4. There's a "clubhouse" used for College Program events, with a massive painted image of mouse ears emblazoned at the front entrance. The apartment blocks surround tired-looking lawns, a basketball court, large sumps filled with brackish water. Any bustle in the complex is around a blindingly fluorescent fitness center and a notorious hot tub.

Who are the interns and how did they get here? "I had the [Disney College Program] on my radar since I was about ten years old," said one intern, whom I'll refer to by the pseudonym Kyle. "I even went to a recruiting presentation at a nearby college while in middle school." Others said they'd been "Disney kids" as long as they could remember: just being able to inhale a little of the pixie dust was enough for them, they explained. Many simply heard about the program on their college campus, dropped by a recruiting presentation, and decided to give it a shot. In a world of competitive, often unpaid internship programs, Disney's is easy to get—and at least it's paid.

"Candidates rarely inquire about the dirty details such as the long hours, low pay, and tight living conditions," writes Wesley Jones in *Mousecatraz*. Kevin Yee, a fifteen-year Disney employee who wrote the critical memoir *Mouse Trap*, has known many of the interns over the years: "These are kids lured to the promise of working Pirates of the Caribbean but ultimately cleaning toilets, or serving hamburgers," although a few do end up working the attractions. "They are often lured with the idea of 'internship' or management, and in reality, they do grunt work."

On the other hand, Disney isn't hiding anything. Detailed and basically accurate information about the program, the different internship roles, approximate pay, and hours is clearly discernible beneath the program's avalanche of colorful propaganda about the intangible magic of it all. A recent recruiting event that I attended featured no fewer than three slideshows buzzing with upbeat orchestral jingles, inspiring testimony, and clean-cut, attractive young people. The ordinary white conference room (inside a campus career center) was opalescent with a million tiny bits of glitter strewn everywhere, along with Mickey Mouse stickers and photo-heavy brochures. The preternaturally cheery recruiter ("I represent the Disney College Program, but not only do I represent it—I'm an alumni!") cajoled a distracted student audience into his call and response shtick: "Help me help—" "You!" In one of the promotional videos, we hear from Stephanie (the perky blonde with a nauseating smile) and Tenoccus (the sensitive, soft-spoken African-American male): "We're here to tell you about what we think is the coolest paid internship in the entertainment business." Disney is "the place where dreams come true" and "every morning is a magical morning." Before leaving, the recruiter scolded the students good-naturedly: "Don't underestimate the power of that name. Disney is the third most-recognized brand in the world." (Global branding consultancy Interbrand put Disney in ninth position in its 2010 rankings.)

When they apply, would-be interns list their top-three overall work preferences (Operations or Merchandising, for instance), but the ultimate assignments are entirely at Disney's disposal. And even within an area like Operations, the different "lines of business" vary tremendously, from valet parking to crowd control to the delivering of memorized spiels—the actual roles are given only after the intern has arrived, based on up-to-the-minute labor needs. (For the same reason, interns don't know their exact hourly salary until they're on site.) As one intern wrote on a message board: "You have virtually no say in your hours or work location." An intern from the mid-90s, "Christine" told me that she and her fellow interns felt harried as they "rotated from job to job and area to area." Interns often have no regular schedule that would allow them to do anything more than party or decompress outside work—they are expected to take whatever shifts are left over and to work at multiple locations. During his internship, the author of *Mousecatraz* reported to five different supervisors. With very few exceptions, there is no pretense that the work students will be given will match their areas of study.

Tales of financial hardship while interning are common. At Disneyland in California (where there are typically *only* 150 of them), many interns begin the program by writing Disney a $736 check (deposit plus the first month of rent). In the Orlando area, where housing is cheap, Disney charges anywhere from $82 to $108 per week, depending on the complex and the apartment size, as well as a one-time $100 "Program Assessment and Activities" fee. In an online FAQ section, Disney reassures parents that the costs "are relative to what's typical in Central Florida, and Walt Disney World Co. actually subsidizes a portion of the overall housing cost." Employees from the area cry foul. When students are living four or six to an apartment, the rent charged by Disney (or its proxy, a residential management company) appears to be well above market rate for the town of Lake Buena Vista, sometimes as much as double. Just across from Vista Way, for example, is the similar-looking Sabal Palm apartment complex, where comparable three-bedroom apartments rent for around $1,000 per month. On Disney property, the six interns in such an apartment are paying a combined $2,000 per month, at the very least.

Bureaucratic snafus, overbooking, and health problems can all prevent interns from getting their guaranteed thirty hours of work per week, making it easy to end up behind the financial eight-ball. Says one full-timer who manages interns, "I've seen negative checks for them, especially the first couple of weeks." A shop steward sees interns struggling to make ends meet all the time and provides free food to tide them over. "She didn't work her thirty hours because they switched her schedule," the steward said of a new merchandising intern. "She's pushed into three different jobs. For one of them they had hired too many people, so they had to transfer thirteen people out ... So on this paycheck she got $2, after they took out the rent." The shop steward has seen a number of interns leave the program early because "they're not making any money, they can't make their bills," and schedulers avoid giving them overtime. Unless you consistently work long shifts for a number of months, many interns told me, almost all of your earnings will go towards rent and basic expenses. Parental support is common—"I needed my parents to wire me money just to make it through the first two months," said one former intern.

If interns are sick or need time off, they lose the hours and have to find someone to substitute—someone not already on overtime. On the exhaustive message boards of the website College Confidential, the mother of one Disney intern wrote of how her daughter "was injured on the job down there and it was a nightmare," as Disney "wouldn't let her leave to go to the hospital, and did not accommodate her injury when she returned. They repeatedly penalized her for missing hours or days that she needed for medical care." The intern left the program early to get medical attention at home. (Apparently the pixie dust is still potent, however: "She was brought up as a Disney kid … She is planning on going there on her honeymoon.")

Like workers without rights everywhere, the interns vote with their feet. There are no official statistics on drop-out or termination rates, but they appear to be uncommonly high. "I would wager a 20–30 percent termination/dropout rate just based on my own observations," Kyle told me, adding that he had enjoyed the program. During his first internship, four of his five roommates left the program. Clearly, some of the attrition has to do with housing policies and college kids being college kids, but there are also many who hightail it back home after they see the actual work. "I didn't travel clear across the country to work in a store," said one such intern. "I was cast as a Custodial Host, but I wasn't going to spend my hot summer days cleaning up people's crap," said another. In response to questions about termination and high turnover, Disney spokeswoman Kim Prunty commented in 2005 that the company aims for every participant to complete the program and that disciplinary action is taken based on the available facts.

If few of these problems seem visible in the smiling faces of housekeeping and fast food interns, you can thank the Disney Look. A College Program recruiter calls it a "clean, classic, timeless look, [that] goes back to Walt Disney himself," where "timeless" apparently means 1950s suburban America. "Intentional body alteration or modification" (visible tattoos, piercings etc.) is out, needless to say, except for "traditional ear piercing for women." An extensive literature covers the regulations for hair (in a word: short for men, long for women; "extremes in dyeing, bleaching, or coloring" not permitted)—mustaches are permitted under certain conditions, as well as sideburns that extend to the bottom of the earlobe but no further. The frames and lenses of eyeglasses must be "neutral" in color, any make-up should be "applied in a blended manner and in colors complementary to the skin tone," and so on. "Stage presence" means no chewing gum, no smoking, no sleepiness, no moodiness, no eating or drinking. Don't point with your index finger, either: use "the Disney point," a reassuring two-fingered gesture (index plus middle finger, if you're wondering).

Along with the Disney Look—common to all Cast Members—every intern picks up at least a bit of Disneyspeak. Playing on the title "CP" (College Program), a Disney intern may be known as Corporate Prisoner, College Puke, Company Pee-On, or Closing Person (as interns usually work the dreaded closing shifts). Customers are "guests," positions are "roles," and a crowd is "an audience"—some of the best euphemisms are for vomit ("protein spill"), janitor ("custodial host"), and work in the various trinket shops ("merchantainment"). Disneyspeak elevates the work of interns and full-timers alike, and is readily adopted. Jane Kuenz, who has written about "working for the rat," comments that the parks are "a place where an entire workforce shows up each day, not in uniform, but in costume. Most have internalized this distinction; they *never* say uniform, just as they always say, 'on stage', and 'backstage'."[9]

For all those who leave the program or are "terminated," for all the false pretense of an educational "internship," and for all the negative impacts on other workers, park visitors, and local communities, the fact is that many interns love it. Free access to the parks and employee discounts are more than enough for some of these Disney kids who have grown up to be Disney interns and may yet become Disney parents. "I'm a Disney slave and I wouldn't have it any other way," tweeted one intern proudly. As Kuenz writes, even the receding horizon of a decent, full-time Disney job is still a major draw for the contingent hordes: "Almost everyone aspires to be 'permed'—Permanent Full-Time—at which point pour down the manna of Disney benefits." Still, there's no pretense that Disney interns will ever be able to work for the company, or even in the hospitality industry more generally, given the gulf between menial theme-park work and well-paid jobs in management.

More recently, the company has realized that it can do even better than five or even seven months of cheap labor per intern. Interns are now encouraged to re-up and stay as long as a year at a time—and some keep coming back. To take just one example, a student active in the College Program blogosphere has done the program four times, served as a campus representative, and intends to go back for more. The ability to do an internship during the summer (the most convenient time for students) is now a privilege allowed only to "alumni" interns who have worked a previous semester. All this is not even to mention the white-collar management internships (formerly called "advanced" internships), which predate the College Program's founding in 1980 and are much closer in spirit to typical internships in the rest of the world. In the elaborate hierarchy of intern labor, a College Program internship is now a prerequisite for the management internship.

Walt Disney's original vision for EPCOT was a modernist utopia in the Florida swamps, half-Le Corbusier and half-Fordlandia, "a planned, controlled community, a showcase for American industry and research, schools, cultural and educational opportunities": yet the built reality is just another theme park, wheeling out empty slogans about progress and tired national stereotypes for profit. Wesley Jones jokes in *Mousecatraz* that the Disney College Program might justifiably be called "the Experimental Prototype 'College' of Tomorrow." One of the world's largest internship programs—touted as a massive and wondrous experiment in experiential education—is a minimum-wage, corporate paradise, endorsed by schools and accepted by students, as much a mirage as the original EPCOT.

CHAPTER TWO

The Explosion

Flexibility and willingness to work under pressure in a chaotic news environment with ever-changing responsibilities and deadlines a MUST.

Must be available at least 80 hours a week and able to work most weekends and all major holidays.

This is a non-paying internship.

Great opportunity to get your foot in the door and gain news experience.

A minimum of ten years' experience.

—McSweeney's Internet Tendency, "A Great Job Opportunity"

What is an intern anyway? A burger-flipper at Disney World or a rising star shaping policy in the White House? Does the word mean anything at all if it can include undergraduates and retirees, the unpaid and the well compensated, rigorous training programs and "virtual" positions without any oversight or mentoring?

The very significance of the word *intern* lies in its ambiguity. It represents a broader concept, and sends out a more targeted social signal, than "temp" or "freelancer" ever has. Of more importance than any definition is the rhetoric that flavors the internship discourse: "a foot in the door" for young people and a way of "paying your dues," internships are also "a great way to get experience," "build your résumé," and "make contacts." A "win-win" for employers and "go-getter" interns alike, "you get out what you put in." We understand from these hopeful, endlessly echoed sentiments that the burden of creating something meaningful falls squarely on the shoulders of the intern, new to the workforce and desperate to squeeze in, tasked with making an impression at any cost and learning on the fly. The image of the cheerful, obsequious intern is not a hollow caricature. While freelancers may often be characterized by a certain proud independence, temps and part-timers by detachment and even alienation, and volunteers by a supposed selflessness, interns perform as affective labor what others would call menial. They work, after all, for their own good name, so that someone, some day, will vouch for their fitness to do "real" work.

"You can get more out of the person because they're your *intern*," a congressional candidate (and former serial intern) said to me, explaining his "understanding of the internship culture." "What I did in my campaign is I advertised a bunch of internship positions—like 'You can be the New Media intern, you can be Communications intern'—so I got these people to come more on a regular basis." Other employers described switching from advertising "summer jobs" to offering "internships" as a way to boost interest among young people; many confessed that "internship" was simply a buzzword they latched on to, looking for free, temporary help around the office. The fact that no definition of internship is in common use is particularly convenient in such scenarios—some people assume that they are unpaid by definition, while others think the exact opposite. Those closer to university campuses (and especially in career services offices) tend to claim an educational component, or assume academic involvement, despite the vast number of internships with no educational content whatsoever.

"For my work, I say an internship is 'any experience of the world of work from which a student can learn about a career'," says Natalie Lundsteen, an Oxford doctoral student who is undertaking some of the first academic research on the topic. Previously, she worked as an internship advisor at Stanford for five years. "The example I usually give is: simply making coffee as a barista is a summer job, but having the opportunity to meet management, learn about logistics, marketing, advertising, sales, etc. makes it an internship!" The association between internships and university students learning management skills remains strong—but the reality is that nowadays there are barista internships too.

Michael True, another internship professional from an academic career advising background, has recently proposed a paragraph-long definition of academic internships, heavily referencing experiential education and singling out "structured and deliberate reflection contained within learning agendas or objectives"—yet the definition remains agnostic as to pay, hours, or any actual work conditions.[1] On the other hand, employers are most likely to recognize internships as flexible, temporary work arrangements for young people, where there is at least some vague idea of getting ahead, although interns are commonly understood to be at the bottom of the office hierarchy. Whether or not there is a dedicated learning or training component depends on perceived legal requirements, the initiative and status of the intern herself, and any requirements set by her school. As Lundsteen says, "Employers don't care about the development of their interns—why should they? The bottom line for employers is usually productivity, not personal development."

Interns themselves seem to grasp the inadequacy of any particular definition—an internship is understood more in terms of its cultural and professional function than in terms of actual responsibilities: a box that has to be checked, a rite of passage, a prerequisite for future ambitions. One former intern told me that even before she entered high school she "understood that an internship was a thing you did to make yourself look better"—that was all. Despite the Disney College Program, an internship is still usually perceived as being different from flipping burgers or waiting tables. It is "relevant" to one's career, a step up the ladder, however tentative and lowly: analogous to the inevitable but temporary shame of being a college freshman or rushing a fraternity. The sixteen definitions of intern in the collective unconscious of Urban Dictionary invoke this discomfort, but with stark, overdramatized images of exploitation: interns are "company bitches" who provide "slave labor," and objects of sexual attention for the regular staff. Yet it is also the most transient of work identities—only as prestigious as the name of the employer you intern for—and a status hopefully vaulted over as rapidly as possible. Only poor Monica Lewinsky remains ever and always an intern.

Unlike apprenticeships, which continue to have a fairly concrete meaning in the workplace (as we shall see in the following chapter), what defines an internship depends largely on who's doing the defining. At the same time, internships are part of a nebulous cluster of job titles that have characterized the surge in nonstandard or "contingent" labor over the past forty years. "We've just bastardized all the language across the landscape," says Phil Gardner of the College Employment Research Institute. "Nobody knows what anything means anymore." It's true that temps, part-timers, freelancers, permalancers, permatemps, externs, trainees, and certain volunteers all share a family resemblance; operationally and in terms of the worker demographics and industries involved, however, they tend to be quite distinct. Even just in the realm of different experiments at bridging the school-to-work gap, internships jostle with "job shadowing," formalized "mentoring," cooperative education, "school-sponsored enterprise," and "tech prep." Yet of all the different terms and titles, internship covers the broadest range of industries and work arrangements and resonates with the most prestige and possibility.

Solid statistics about the internship phenomenon have remained as elusive as a proper definition. A notable exception is the recent studies produced by the research and consulting firm Intern Bridge, working in conjunction with Gardner. "There hasn't been anybody that's really monitored it," says Gardner of the internship explosion. "Right now the research capacity in this area is dismal. Most schools don't even know how many of their students actually have internships, period." Only now are reports such as *The Debate Over Unpaid College Internships,* published by Intern Bridge, finally beginning to shed light on the shape and scale of the internship explosion. Based on his survey work, Gardner estimates that 70 to 75 percent of students at four-year schools undertake at least one internship. This is in the same neighborhood as the impressionistic figures provided by individual schools and by companies such as Vault and Quintessential Careers, two career information websites. Gardner sees this figure as being at least double what it was in the early 1980s, and studies by the National Society for Experiential Education and the National Association of Colleges and Employers (NACE), undertaken over the same time period, have similarly registered exponential gains in the percentage of college students who graduate with an internship.

According to *The Debate Over Unpaid College Internships,* nonprofits, government offices, and small for-profit companies emerge as the worst offenders, but nearly 20 percent of large for-profit companies (over 5,000 employees) also have unpaid internships. "Women were significantly more likely to be engaged in an unpaid internship (77 percent)," states the report. This explosive new finding alone demands further study, and it dovetails closely with my own anecdotal research: internship injustice is closely linked to gender issues, both because of the fields that women gravitate toward and possibly also because female students have been more accepting of unpaid, unjust situations. Class differences in the internship world are no less stark, as we'll see in Chapter 9: according to *The Debate Over Unpaid College Internships*, most unpaid interns are from low- and middle-income families, except in the "glamor" fields of finance, entertainment, and the arts, while "[h]igh income students through their preferences, social networks, and status, enjoy more opportunities at the largest companies, are more likely to be paid, and have access to a limited number of opportunities in organizations their peers compete fiercely to enter." A student's academic major is another key factor: as many as 87 percent of engineering and computer science majors reported having paid positions while 70 percent of business students and approximately two-thirds of science and agriculture students had them. On the other end of the spectrum are students majoring in education (34 percent paid), social sciences (35 percent paid), health sciences (39 percent paid), communications (41 percent paid), and the arts and humanities (43 percent paid).

The conservative estimate of 1 to 2 million internships annually in the United States, mentioned earlier, does not begin to account for internships taken by community college students, graduate students, recent graduates, and others—all major growth areas. Nearly a million registered members of LinkedIn, a professional social networking site, list themselves as former or current interns. *The National Longitudinal Survey of Youth 1997* (*NLSY97*), a major representative study of 9,000 young people, found that approximately 4 percent of *high school* students take an internship or "apprenticeship"—also unaccounted for in my estimate. A list of the largest intern employers compiled by CollegeGrad .com is indicative, although it misses the massive Disney program, among others: the top ten firms were planning to hire a combined 26,000-plus interns in 2009: the industries represented include general merchandising

(Walgreen's, primarily in the pharmacies), insurance (New York Life), consulting (Deloitte & Touche), aerospace and defense (Lockheed Martin), and automotive rental (Enterprise). That's 26,000 interns for 10 employers—and internships have a very, very long tail.

The best current estimate is that as many as 50 percent of all internships in the U.S. may be unpaid or paid below minimum wage. (Recent research in the U.K., undertaken by a major professional association for Human Resources, found that 37 percent of all internships were unpaid; in Germany, a survey found 51 percent.) In *The Debate Over Unpaid College Internships*, based on a broad sample of student responses, Intern Bridge found that 57 percent of nonprofit internships, 47 percent of government internships, and 34 percent of for-profit internships were unpaid—not to mention those that were underpaid. And the ranks of the unpaid are swelling, while paid positions disappear. Studies across the board, including a recent one conducted by Internships.com, have found that unpaid internships continue to grow at the expense of paid opportunities.[2]

Vernon Stone, a professor of journalism at the University of Missouri, documented early on how "[u]npaid internships, once rolling, tended to crowd the paid ones off the road." Stone found that, in 1976, 57 percent of TV and 81 percent of radio interns received some pay; by 1991, those numbers had sunk to 21 percent and 32 percent respectively. "Seven times as many [unpaid interns] were in TV newsrooms in 1991 as in 1976," wrote Stone. "Radio's increase was fivefold." A similar pattern has been noted for a variety of industries—and according to Intern Bridge, compensated internships in some industries are in danger of disappearing altogether: only 11 percent of interns in the field of game design are now paid, and under 16 percent of interns in law enforcement and security.[3]

Unsurprisingly, organizations and businesses in the internship space boast that employers regularly list internship experience as a top hiring criterion—50 percent of new college graduate hires came out of internship programs at the same firm, according to a Michigan State University study, while an *additional* 40 percent had interned at other firms.[4] Among employers surveyed by NACE, who are more likely to care about internships and university recruiting in the first place, 76.3 percent reported that relevant work experience was the critical factor in making hires.[5] There is no denying this crucial signal that internships send in the post-college job market.

At the same time, there is a largely unexplored distinction between employers who use internships as an efficient and far-sighted recruiting tool, where there is a real possibility of being hired, and those that use internships as a simple money-saving device. At many of the latter firms, there may be no hires at all from a pool of dozens of interns, and there are never positions reserved even for the best-performing interns. Sociologist Mark Granovetter notes that, even when converting an internship to a full-time position is unlikely, an unrealistic sense of hopefulness can persist: "There may be just enough cases around that people know about to give people encouragement, but not enough to really make it likely that that's going to happen for any particular person."

No rigorous studies have yet analyzed the importance of internships over the course of a career or their contribution to lifetime earnings, or even the details of how much interns really learn from their positions. Crude measures of intern satisfaction do exist for individual internship programs and segments of a few industries, showing predictable variation, but in general the experiences of interns remain little understood. In two telling findings from Intern Bridge, some 65 percent of former interns said that the programs they participated in needed improvement; and, when asked whether their work had benefited their employers, rated their contributions on average over 4.2 on a 5-point scale. The statistics that exist don't yet paint a full picture, or even include the experiences of noncollegiate interns, but they do illuminate the overall contours of the internship explosion. If many key questions remain unanswered, and economists, sociologists, and policy-makers continue to look the other way, this is at least in part because the Bureau of Labor Statistics, the Census Bureau, and other large-scale research initiatives have left internships in the shadows.

As with all efforts to integrate young people into the workplace, we should ask who bears the burden and who stands to gain: internships in this regard are a dream solution for employers, allowing them to "test-drive" young workers for little or no cost. Just as the federal government has increasingly shifted the financial burden of a college education onto students and their families, companies have effected a similar stratagem by transitioning from training programs and entry-level jobs to internships. In the breathless rhetoric of the age, the intern is an "entrepreneur" and a "free agent" from Day One (read: an at-will employee, often without pay or protections), "learning on the job" (since savvy firms do not invest in dedicated training—and an ever-changing, intangible economy would supposedly make it irrelevant anyway) and building up a "personal brand." With internships, this message now penetrates almost every institution of higher education in the developed world.

The first interns were medical students. Until World War II, the term "internship" was associated exclusively with hospitals, where aspiring doctors were interned (in the sense of confined) within an institution's four walls, enduring a year or two of purgatory before entering the profession. The practice of apprenticing boys to physicians and apothecaries stretched back centuries, but only in the final decades of the nineteenth century—with the establishment of major medical schools and an upsurge in the number of hospitals—did formal internships come into being. One of the earliest mentions appears in the second annual report to the trustees of the Boston City Hospital in 1865. American hospitals of this period, according to historian Rosemary Stevens, began to use the term "interne," apparently a borrowing from French, to describe house surgeons, house physicians, and assistant house physicians—junior medical men busy anesthetizing, bloodletting, vaccinating and the like, not yet qualified to be resident physicians.[6]

In 1904, in the midst of momentous changes in the medical profession, the American Medical Association (AMA) created a Council on Medical Education to reform and standardize a wildly uneven landscape of practices. A year later, the Council recommended internships as a postgraduate year for medical students, who would have just completed four years of study. A decade later, the AMA set standards for the approval of internships. In theory, writes Stevens, "as part of medical education, the internship should have been under the guidance of medical schools; but it was not." The hospitals were in charge. The internship was soon pervasive, virtually mandatory: by 1914, a U.S. commissioner of education estimated that 75–80 percent of medical graduates were taking an internship; in 1932, the Commission on Medical Education put the figure near 95 percent.

Much of this supposed training was "virtually unsupervised," according to Stevens; critics were soon accusing hospitals (as many still do today) of squeezing exhausting, cheap labor from young medical graduates. The alliance of hospitals and medical schools would "make it more difficult for outsiders, including minority groups, to enter the system at any level," and internships were frequently secured through personal connections. William Mayo, one of the founders of the famous Mayo Clinic, wrote that medical interns "seem to spend their days in permanent yessir-ing, in being flunkies for the permanent staff." His answer was to establish a three-year training program for "fellows." In a similar vein, the medical school at Johns Hopkins, drawing on the German practice of "assistantship," introduced the term "resident" in the 1880s to mean an advanced trainee level beyond the internship. In the 1920s and '30s, the notion of residency began to take hold—and "internship" has since come to denote only the first year of clinical training and practice undertaken after medical school. In 1975, just as the internship boom was getting started in other fields, ironically enough, the Accreditation Council for Graduate Medical Education officially dropped the term altogether.

Today, there are approximately 200,000 medical residents in the U.S.; a significant fraction of them are still known as interns while in their first year. The exclusive association between internships and medicine has long disappeared. The disconnect seems all the greater given that medical interns tend to be significantly older and more experienced than office interns; they are paid; and they are highly likely to become medical professionals. They have a fifty-year-old union, the Committee of Interns and Residents, which boasts 13,000 members from coast to coast and affiliation with the mighty Service Employees International Union. On the other hand, medical interns work famously long hours, performing difficult and serious hospital tasks for little pay and an often empty promise of supervision and training—the internship condition taken to the nth degree. The Committee of Interns and Residents has had to fight tooth and nail just to win an eighty-hour work week.

There is evidence from as early as the 1920s that other professions were interested in following medicine in the establishment and formalization of internships. Dr. A. I. Gates of the Teachers College at Columbia University delivered a speech advocating "a more gradual transition from school to work" and the completion of a "social internship" emphasizing civic responsibilities. A professional journal for accountants ran an item in 1928, airing the idea of "a probationary period comparable to the internship in medicine." In 1937, the *Journal of Marketing* wrote, in the context of business school education, that "a sort of internship is highly desirable so that students may perform activities involving various applications of the principles of retail store management." Although none of these proposals was directly acted upon, as far as I know, their tenor is clear: internships were conceived as part of "the progressive rationalization of management," linked to the professionalization of training and the growing standardization of higher education.[7]

The first real application of the internship concept beyond medicine came in the political realm. The model established here would in many ways set the tone for the coming internship explosion. Some of the earliest efforts were at the state and municipal levels, including programs launched in the 1930s by city governments in Los Angeles, Detroit, and New York City, and by the state of California. Drawing on and enhancing these models, the long-forgotten National Institute of Public Affairs— once a prominent nonpartisan organization, dedicated to promoting public service—developed an early influential model that put internships on a national stage. Otis Theodore Wingo, executive secretary of the National Institute, described the program's launch in February 1935 as a "hopeful experiment," bringing thirty "carefully chosen" recent college graduates to Washington D.C. for broad training in public administration.[8]

Compared to other forms of civil service training, the distinctive feature of the National Institute's program was that it aimed to provide young people of promise, not currently government employees, with *general* training in public administration. The interns worked without pay for an entire year, but the range of training compares favorably even with some of the best-organized programs today. Fifty years later, Herbert Kaufman, an alumnus who became a professor of public administration, remembered that the program "opened the way to placements in the federal administrative establishment to which I could not otherwise have aspired realistically even if I had known about them." After a few weeks of orientation on issues like budgeting, congressional appropriations, government accounting and auditing, and so on, Kaufman found himself in the Administrative Management Division of the Bureau of the Budget, where he did "a variety of simple clerical chores in return for the privilege of sitting in on the conferences." When the work "began to pall after a while," Kaufman was able to intern for a while on the research staff of President Truman's Committee on Civil Rights. Wingo emphasized that, although "interns in the current program of the Institute are uniformly performing work of considerable responsibility," they "[i]n no event ... replace paid government personnel, and their assignments are to work that would not be carried on by regular personnel in the due course of government business."

Even after the National Institute itself had disappeared from the scene, the internship program was carried on under the auspices of the Civil Service Commission—it remained a high-profile model for decades. The Legislative Reorganization Act of 1946 equipped lawmakers and congressional committees with large staffs of experts for the first time, vastly expanding the world of Capitol Hill, where interns would soon be pervasive. The massive growth of Washington D.C. itself from the 1940s and 1950s onward—enabled to some extent by the spread of air conditioning, as Nelson Polsby has argued more broadly for the American South—was both a cause and effect of the internship boom.

Municipal- and state-level internships proliferated as well. A survey of public administration internship programs, conducted by the National Civil Service League in 1956, turned up forty-two different internship programs across the country, a testament to steady post-war growth. Fifteen cities, thirteen states, and four county or county-city systems had embraced the model, from Philadelphia to Phoenix, from the Massachusetts Department of Health to the Minnesota highway authorities, often working in concert with local schools. Many of the positions were paid, but some were not: for example, over 100 interns employed by California's Department of Mental Hygiene were receiving only "maintenance" as opposed to a regular salary. The report lauded such programs for giving undergraduate and graduate students "a front-seat view of government in operation" and noted significant variations in terms of how long internships lasted, the degree of collaboration with schools, and the legal status of the interns, who were considered "exempt" in Florida and Massachusetts; "provisional" in Wyoming; "probationers" in Illinois and New York; and so on. In one jurisdiction, a host of future problems was tellingly prefigured by the report, which bemoaned a "tendency of departments to use interns as temporary employees rather than trainees, insufficient length of the internship period, insufficient coordination between academic instruction and work assignments, and difficulty of fitting interns into the permanent civil service." Legislative internships in both Congress and various state assemblies were also launched during the 1950s.

In the 1960s, a new impetus developed for the growth of public-spirited internships, this time from schools and students caught up in the social and political ferment of the time. According to Eugene Alpert, a past president of the National Society for Experiential Education, "Many schools felt that they wanted to have their curriculum become more relevant and more socially-oriented—and more students were interested in donating their time, but they wanted credit for it for the first time." Internships in teaching, social work, psychology, criminal justice, and journalism began to proliferate. In Washington, a further upsurge came with the Congressional Reorganization Act of 1974, which created the current sprawl of sub-committees. "That meant there were multiple access points," says Alpert, "and that brought in all the nonprofits and the lobbyists to town," who in turn actively sought young, free labor. In this period, internships became an entrenched feature of the Washington scene in something like their current form, although they were still little known elsewhere. "Back in the 1970s I was a Washington intern," political commentator Jonathan Alter has written. "In those days, identifying oneself as such in your home state sometimes met with a puzzled stare, as if you were a medical student."

The adoption of internships in other industries followed fast and furious, decisively picking up steam in the 1980s and 1990s, the period when they became standard operating procedure, with some firms formalizing and expanding what had been smaller-scale, informal arrangements based on connections. The genealogies of influence are almost impossible to trace, but it appears that a wide range of industries began experimenting around the same time, drawing on the models from medicine and public service. Management training programs at large firms gave way to summer internship programs.

A few highlights may suffice to illuminate the broader picture. In some cases, earlier models have come to be seen and described as internships, such as the legendary "guest editor" contests at the fashion magazine *Mademoiselle*, which continued for years. In June of 1953, the poet Sylvia Plath was one of these twenty female college students, selected from an enormously competitive field for a brief stint at the magazine. Paid only a modest $150 stipend, the guest editors were wined and dined around New York: the high-society social functions attended by the young women made great fodder for *Mademoiselle*, and one of Plath's biographers has described the program as "another marketing scheme on the part of the magazine to increase sales and advertising." Other fashion magazines launched similar efforts—in 1951, then a senior at George Washington University, Jackie Bouvier (later Kennedy) won a year-long editorial internship (half in New York, half in Paris) in the Prix du Paris contest hosted by *Vogue*.

In 1967, less glamorously, the Northwestern Mutual Life Insurance Company of Milwaukee began a program that has become one of the nation's largest, ballooning to include 2,500 interns each year—interns work on commission selling insurance as "fully licensed financial professionals." By 1979, a national survey of undergraduate sociology departments found that more than half supported internship programs, described as "field-work placements ... under the auspices of cooperating agencies, such as a city planning department." Many banking and financial internships, among the best-paid and most prestigious of all internships today, began over twenty years ago, according to Natalie Lundsteen. In a 2000 survey, 92 percent of business schools and programs reported having internship programs, and one-third claimed that more than half of their students take on internships.

It is particularly telling that new companies, industries, and academic degree programs, especially those emerging in the 1990s and 2000s, have unquestioningly given internships pride of place almost from the very beginning. A 2001 report on degree programs in sports management, for instance, found that 76 percent of responding programs required students to complete an internship. With each new wave of tech start-ups, Silicon Valley becomes more and more awash in interns—the latest batch are "Twinterns," interns tasked with promoting their employers via Twitter (even Pizza Hut has one). "I saw first-hand how interest in internships began growing in the late nineties," says Lundsteen, who set up the first corporate headquarters internship for Gap, Inc. during this period, when internships made a perfect fit with the go-go rhetoric of the dotcom bubble and the New Economy. Programs continue to sprout and take on massive proportions virtually overnight. The retailer Target, for example, went from having no internship program at all before 2006 to taking more than 1,000 just a few years later.

The internship explosion, like any major shift in how people work and shape their careers, could not have occurred in isolation. Changing attitudes among lawmakers, educators, parents, and young people have all played a critical role, as we'll see in the following chapters. For the moment, though, there are two other shifts in the workforce that need examining, both of which have propelled the rise of internships—and help to explain it.

Post-industrial, networked capitalism has provided the ideal petri dish for the growth of internships, which are only one of many forms of nonstandard or contingent labor that have mushroomed since the 1970s. The term "contingent labor" was first used in 1985 by economist Audrey Freedman, in reference to "conditional and transitory employment relationships as initiated by a need for labor—usually, because a company has an increased demand for a particular service or product or technology, at a particular place, at a specific time." Included are part-time, temporary, seasonal, casual, contract, on-call, and leased employees, among others—what Andrew Ross calls "an explosion of atypical work arrangements far removed from the world of social welfare systems, union contracts, and long-term tenure with a single employer."[9] The Bureau of Labor Statistics estimated in 2005, using what they called "the broadest measure of contingency," that about 4 percent of the total work-force in the U.S. fits the description, approximately 5.7 million workers. These contingent millions were twice as likely as noncontingent workers to be under twenty-five years old, and a clear majority said they would prefer full-time employment. If you include regular part-time workers and the self-employed, who often work under contingent circumstances, figures from a Government Accountability Office (GAO) report in 2000 paint a much starker picture: nearly 30 percent of the American workforce, comprising almost 40 million individuals, is involved in contingent, nonstandard employment arrangements.

Ross and others have pointed out that the Keynesian decades of "standard" employment may in fact have been "a brief exception to the more general, historically enduring rule of contingency." Nonetheless, as law professor Mark Grunewald writes, "traditional, full-time, long-term employment" rapidly assumed a wider importance in the mid-twentieth century: "It has been the core for the development of collective bargaining. It has been the institutional base for the assurance of health care. It has bankrolled the private pension system. In short, it has marked most of the important differences between staked members of our society and the economically vulnerable and insecure."

As many authors have documented—including Luc Boltanski and Eve Chiapello, for the French case—the push for flexibility emerged at least in part from a "revolt against work" in the 1970s, initiated by workers themselves. Another driving force behind contingency, as economist Greg Kaplan points out, "has been an increase in female labor force participation—*the* big thing in the last fifty years." Many workers, interns among them, have undoubtedly welcomed the more positive aspects of their contingency—the ability to plan their own schedules, work from home, or spend more time with family, for instance—and the youth labor market usually tends to center more on short-term, flexible contracts anyway. There's also evidence that what Gina Neff calls an "increasing spirit of entrepreneurial behavior" has been effectively hammered into many young people: "It's a move from the company man to 'I am the CEO of me' ... to Daniel Pink's notion of the Free Agent Nation," says Neff. According to Andrew Ross, "the flexibility [which free agency] delivers is a response to an authentic demand for a life not dictated by the cruel grind of excessively managed work," despite the uncertainties it brings.

If the revolt against work began on assembly lines and in the alienating offices of large bureaucratic firms, management soon learned to reap the benefits and actively promote the "casualization" of the workforce. Ross writes of "the steady advance of contingency into the lower and middle levels of the professional and high-wage service industries" after companies began to realize "lavish returns from low-end casualization—subcontracting, outsourcing, and other modes of flexploitation." According to the GAO report, "regular part-time" work increased from 14.5 percent to over 18 percent of the total workforce over the course of the 1970s and 1980s, with the largest increase in the late 1970s and early 1980s, due to changes in business cycles—such as the recession in 1983.

Most prominent and explosive of all has been the growth of the temporary help industry (from 0.5 percent of the total workforce in 1982 to over 2 percent in 1998) and of independent contracting. Indeed, much of this supposed boom in independent contracting—with its positive associations of being one's own boss—has been revealed as a massive tax dodge by corporations. A recent federal study found that employers were illegally passing off 3.4 million regular employees as independent contractors, and the Labor Department has identified up to 30 percent of companies as engaging in such misclassification. In other words, many workers are still performing the same work they always have, only under increasingly precarious, contingent conditions, at the behest of employers. Microsoft's "permatemps"—thousands of employees deliberately misclassified as independent contractors, though they worked for years alongside full-timers, often performing identical work—achieved a rare victory in 2000 in reclaiming their status as regular employees. Seen in this light, many interns could be considered workers who have been purposely misclassified as students and trainees.

The independent contractor tax dodge may be one indication that a shift in employer practices, and a lack of legislation and enforcement, are more responsible for the rise of contingent labor than sweeping changes in the economy. In the GAO report, employers cited the need "to accommodate workload fluctuations, fill temporary absences, meet employees' requests for part-time hours, screen workers for permanent positions, and save on wage and benefit costs"—worker advocacy groups responded that contingent hiring also allows companies to "avoid paying benefits, reduce their workers' compensation costs, prevent workers' attempts to unionize, or allow them to lay off workers more easily." All these same motives, those reported by employers and by advocacy organizations, have played into the internship explosion. In one way or another, interns have fallen into every single category of contingent labor.

"The general attitude in the labor movement about contingent workers across the board is they're more of a pain in the ass to organize than it's worth," says Jim Grossfeld, who has written on the disconnect between contingent youth workers and organized labor. He adds that unions have failed to understand the appeal of flexible working conditions and the dynamics of organizing contingent workers. Small wonder then that interns, substantially but not entirely in nonunion, office environments, have been submerged in the larger rise of contingent work and attracted little attention from organized labor. "People think of internships as part of their strategy for becoming autonomous," says Grossfeld —and go-it-alone autonomy is pitched as the way to survive a brutal economy. As Andrew Ross writes, "self-direction morphs into self-exploitation, and voluntary mobility is a fast path to disposability."

A second massive shift in the post–World War II workplace, contributing in equal measure to the internship boom, has been the rising field of Human Resources. At least at the mid-size and larger organizations that have led the way, internship programs are typically the responsibility of HR departments, which continue to have a strong interest in both initiating and institutionalizing them. "They've realized it comes to bite them in the butt when they don't," one HR executive told me, explaining that the original impetus to bring in interns may come from executives or other employees, but that HR professionals can ultimately be held accountable for the safety and legal issues that sometimes result.

Companies are usually looking for immediate benefits from their interns, and the creation of such roles is often a response to the most local of concerns, like returning a favor or handling overflow work. Given such informal beginnings, many internship arrangements fly under the radar for years, even at larger firms. It's still common for "Hey, let's get an intern" to be the impetus, leading to a casual post on Craigslist or the company website with little thought given to setting up a professional, sensible program. "Economic rationality would say that of course they would have all this worked out," says sociologist Mark Granovetter of organizations, "and that they would only invest up to the point where the marginal return equaled the marginal cost, but it's so hard to gauge that. And you have to figure out what the likelihood is of the employee staying with you, and what the training is worth, and no one really knows those things." Not to mention that sometimes the motive is as simple as wanting to copy other firms in one's industry. "One of the things that sociologists find about a lot of HR practices is that there's a high level of what is called mimetic isomorphism," adds Granovetter, "which basically means that whatever everyone is doing you do, because otherwise you look like you're not a modern firm."

Indeed, even the establishment of HR departments, beginning particular in the 1920s and accelerating during and immediately after World War II, fits the copycat pattern. In 1946, the number of Americans employed in labor relations and what was then called "personnel" was under 30,000, increasing markedly to 53,000 in 1950 and 93,000 in 1960—a growth pattern far in excess of other professions and the broader workforce during the same period. From a relatively rarity before World War II, personnel departments rapidly became a virtual requirement for modern firms, represented in 63 percent of surveyed companies by 1946 and 79 percent by 1953.

If many of these departments were first established to thwart or parley with labor unions, they have taken on a raft of much broader functions over the years. Finding a cost-effective method of recruiting new employees and replacing departing ones came to be considered one of their core responsibilities. To the extent that it drew on corporate initiative and interest, the later rise of internships was predicated on and shaped by the human resources profession. By now, almost all sizable employers have more or less formal internship programs of one kind or another—in many cases, an outgrowth of college recruitment efforts for which the company has dedicated HR personnel. "'Efficiency imperatives' became less imperative as modern personnel administration became standard operating procedure," write Baron, Dobbin, and Jennings in their analysis of the rise of HR. Pamela Tolbert and Lynne Zucker, looking at the spread of "best practices" touted by and shared between many HR departments, echo this view: "As an increasing number of organizations adopt a program or policy, it becomes progressively institutionalized, or widely understood to be a necessary component of rationalized organizational structure."[10]

"Back then, Human Resources was—not entirely, but almost entirely —transactional," says Howard Curtis, a long-time human resources executive, of the profession's early decades. "Certainly leaders understood that there was a cost to hiring, a cost to turnover, a cost to leaving a job vacant" and a cost to strikes, but not much more than that. As late as the 1970s and 80s, the profession was dominated by perspectives from psychology, counseling, and labor relations—the traditional subjects in which many HR managers received their degrees; more recently a marked business orientation set in. The constant push, evident in countless books and conferences, has been to promote HR as a "strategic function" with "a seat at the table" on big decisions. At bigger firms, internships can be seen as part of the HR repertoire, one tool among others for advancing and justifying the HR profession on a wider stage. Internships have become part of an unstoppable, unimpeachable standard operating procedure.

CHAPTER THREE

Learning From Apprenticeships

An investment in knowledge pays the best interest.

—Benjamin Franklin

Melanie Johnson is changing careers. In her mid-thirties, a single mother of four in central Texas, she left her job at a manufacturer of automated mannequins (used in medical training) and went looking for stable, skilled work that's in strong demand. Now her goal is to become a highly skilled laboratory animal technician, responsible for handling and caring for the animals used in medical research. She splits her time between the lab and the classroom, both supporting a family and working her way up.

Michael Baldwin blogs about life as a budding twenty-four-year-old electrician in the Washington D.C. metro area. To learn the ropes of the whole profession, he rotates around different job sites picking up a wide range of skills—most recently, he's been learning how to replace fire alarm systems. The fire alarm crews are "more reserved" than the construction teams he was working with before, he says: "I do miss being surrounded by nothing but concrete and guys you might not find in an office building." On a good day he's "running pipe" with his "trusty pipe bending textbook"; on a bad day, he's the newbie setting off a false alarm down the street, mixing up circuits and battling reverse polarities.

Beth Szillagi, tired of leafing through the classifieds every Sunday morning and working at a bank for "starvation wages," became a sheet metal worker almost on impulse. One of three women surrounded by 200 men, Beth faced down active hostility from a macho union local and got herself "an education and a half." "I've worked on everything from air handling units that push tons of air and will literally knock you off your feet, down to the smallest bathroom exhaust fan," she tells Molly Martin in *Hard Hatted Women*, a powerful series of oral histories from "women in the trades."

Melanie, Mike, and Beth: three snapshots of modern apprenticeship, a large-scale, humane model for training and beginning a career.[1] Unlike interns, they work with healthcare, pension plans, and worker's compensation behind them. Their paychecks are substantial enough to support a family, dwarfing those of all but the best-paid finance and engineering interns. Their training is structured and long-term, a combination of serious classroom time and learning on the job. Apprentices may be college graduates or prison inmates, single mothers or third-generation construction workers: unlike interns, they don't have to pay their way in, struggle to survive, cut their teeth on photocopying and learn sheerly by osmosis.

"You want the people erecting the next nuclear power plant in this country to know what they're doing," says John Ladd, the federal administrator in charge of the Office of Apprenticeship (OA) at the Department of Labor. An apprenticeship, says Ladd, is "an integral transfer of knowledge," traditionally used in "trades where you learn with your hands and learn by doing," but there are no practical or theoretical limits to how the apprenticeship concept can be applied. To many people who've done apprenticeships or seen the apprentice system in action, he says, internships are "apprenticeship lite" by comparison, with "no consistency or standard"—brief in duration, often unstructured and barely supervised, precarious and unsustainable for interns and employers alike. Ladd likes to call apprenticeships "the gold standard in training" and "the other four-year degree" (as opposed to a Bachelor's). "If you're serious about having a skilled workforce," he says, "you have to have a standard."

The contrasts are stark—apprentices and interns seem to inhabit different universes. At this moment, there are nearly half a million active apprentices across the U.S. Nearly 200,000 people of all ages enter some

28,000 registered apprenticeship programs each year, learning a dizzying variety of over 1,000 skilled trades. Yet white-collar America imagines apprenticeships in medieval or Victorian caricature—blacksmiths and carpenters keeping young ruffians in line—and misses the modern picture entirely. Are internships white-collar apprenticeships? The answer is yes and no: on the one hand, internships are clearly presented in the same spirit, as a way to launch young people into their careers; on the other hand, internships fall far short of the modern apprenticeship model in nearly every respect, despite the wealth and sophistication of white-collar firms and industries. Dan Jacoby, a historian of apprenticeship, sees internships by comparison as "a chance to look at an environment rather than as a chance to learn the job."

Here's the typical scenario of how a modern apprenticeship comes into being: an individual employer, employer association, or labor-management organization (in unionized industries) decides to take on apprentices, devises a training program, and registers it with a state or federal apprenticeship office, whose staff often lend their own expertise in setting up the program. Often, a community college or vocational school provides apprentices with the required minimum of 144 classroom hours each year, typically held in the evening—sometimes a dedicated training center fills this role. A contract between sponsor and apprentice lays out the obligations and expectations of each. Most programs are small-scale and highly personal; some have been around for decades. Although apprenticeships in construction trades usually comprise more than half the total number, the model has become important in fields as disparate as aerospace manufacturing, seafaring, cosmetology, and law enforcement, to name just a few. Major growth areas include green energy and social services such as childcare.

The motivations for setting up and maintaining such programs differ widely. In an Urban Institute survey of apprenticeship sponsors (mostly employers), harmony in the workplace, increased minority recruitment, and the desire to mentor young workers were all mentioned as reasons to support apprenticeships; one respondent added that the program "provides a living wage for a human being and an opportunity to pursue dreams." More pragmatically, Ladd admits, an obvious benefit for employers is that they are able to pay apprentices "less than the prevailing wage."

Nonetheless, the average starting wage in these programs—across all regions and industries—is almost $13 an hour, an amount which rises rapidly with time and increased skill level.

From the perspective of labor unions (often, but not always, involved), the registered apprenticeship system represents an extension of hard-won benefits and humane working conditions down to the next generation of up-and-coming workers. Apprenticeships also enable unions to play an active role in recruiting and managing the local labor supply for a given industry. That's why there aren't too many unpaid sheet metal or ironworker internships, yet.

For apprentices themselves, what clinches the deal is the ability to "earn while you learn" and to enter stable, highly skilled trades that can support a solidly middle-class lifestyle. Program graduates earn an average of $45,000 per year and maintain benefits long lost to many white-collar workers. According to one study in Washington State involving thousands of former apprentices, "During the course of working life to age sixty-five, the average apprentice will gain about $229,800 in net earnings … and $41,200 in employee benefits" when compared with similar workers who never apprenticed.[2] Lucky ex-interns may earn much more, of course, if they ultimately climb the corporate ladder with success—if.

Historians of apprenticeship pride themselves on the antiquity of their subject matter, trundling out the Code of Hammurabi, with its stern Babylonian injunction that master craftsmen pass on their trade. Some even assume or argue for the universal nature of apprenticeship, though this could only hold water in the broadest possible sense, as skills transfer varies greatly by culture and time period. For us, the quintessential image of the apprentice is a medieval one, with particular archetypes also stemming from Colonial America and Victorian England. The institution of apprenticeship grew out of the guild system of Gothic Europe—despite radical changes in socio-economic organization and the nature of work, the basic outlines of a continuous apprenticeship tradition endured down to the nineteenth century and arguably are still with us today.

In the intervening centuries, apprenticeship became a central metaphor and model for education more broadly. A widespread medieval term for guild was *universitas*, and some scholars assert that the first universities—

early gatherings of scholars at Bologna, Paris, Oxford, and elsewhere—fancied themselves *guilds* of scholars, and that everything from set terms of student enrollment (inspired by indentures) to the concept of the dissertation (the "masterpiece" of a scholarly apprenticeship) drew on the model of guild apprenticeships. Apprenticeship as metaphor still seems modern and useful to most of us, but the actual practice is considered antiquated; we talk more of journeyman power forwards in the NBA than of journeyman craftsmen (who traveled to ply their trade, gathering funds to set up shop after completing their apprenticeship); the origins of the masterpiece (once the culmination of an apprentice's labors) are largely forgotten.

The basic structure of English apprenticeship, an import from the European continent, is already discernible in the limited records of the thirteenth and fourteenth centuries, although the actual content of most apprentices' training remains unknown. A typical term lasted seven years; the (mostly male) apprentices usually took up their indentures, with a nudge or a shove from their family, when they were around fourteen years old, the common-law "age of discretion." These indentures spelled out mutual obligations, more or less formally—the apprentice would work for such and such a period, at tasks relevant to the craft (there were sometimes specific prohibitions against an apprentice performing grunt work considered the preserve of servants). In return the master was obligated to teach the apprentice his trade, while also providing housing, meals, clothing, and so on. Numerous other kinds of stipulations also commonly bound both parties—that the apprentice should not marry during his term, for instance, or that the master should provide bedding or clothing of a certain quality.

It is striking that so much of our evidence for apprenticeships, in every period, is gleaned from legal records. By contrast, the meteoric half-century rise of internships has left barely a trace in official records. A possible explanation is that apprenticeships emerged and flourished in a mercantilist world and were cemented with contracts, both written and unwritten, between master and apprentice (or sometimes the apprentice's parents). Another impetus came from the guilds, which struggled both to ensure quality outcomes and to avoid a glut of entrants into their professions. Indeed, the main purpose of these early regulations was often to control the number of apprentices a master could take on at any given time (usually one or two). Other legal provisions focused on runaway apprentices, the bane of masters from the very beginning and still a challenge for modern programs—the considerable length of apprenticeship terms means that completion rates have often hovered around 50 percent, historically and down to the present day. For many medieval apprentices, the most compelling reason to stick around was "the freedom of the city" gained upon completing one's indentures—a kind of urban citizenship that ensured entry to a professional guild, the ability to set up shop and trade freely, and the right to participate in local politics and to take on apprentices oneself.

In England, the local statutes emerged gradually from guild regulations, and apprenticeship became somewhat more uniform across professions, although geographic variation remained considerable. A signal moment came in 1563, with the Elizabethan Statute of Artificers. This law "codified and systematized at the national level preexisting customary and statutory practices," fixing the character of apprenticeship until 1814, when the statute was finally repealed. Seven years or more was now fixed as the standard term of indenture, ending at age twenty-four or older. The sheer profusion of apprenticeship opportunities in mid-seventeenth-century London is worth remembering too. The very names of these trades peel back the surface of a vanished world: linendraper, mercer, merchant-tailor, silkman, woollendraper, salter, hosier, skinner, silkthrower, trunkmaker, buttonseller, hotpresser, girdler, sempster—all had apprentices.

Equally exotic now is the nature of master-apprentice ties, to which modern society has no real equivalent. (Of course, in certain cases the master actually *was* a relation of the apprentice, sometimes even his father, or else a friend of the apprentice's family.) From the records of Bristol apprenticeships in the early seventeenth century, historian Ilana Krausman Ben-Amos concludes that these involved "young men probably able to rely on some parental help to establish themselves," largely the offspring of a nascent middle class of yeoman and other craftsmen. As a result, "apprentices expected to live to the same degree of comfort as their new household," writes historian Bernard Elbaum. Historian Margaret Pelling has described in detail, for early modern London, the degree to which masters were held responsible for the health and wellbeing of their apprentices—and might be accountable to both law and custom if anything went wrong. Pelling traced the decline of this strong in loco parentis tradition over time, as capitalist market relations set in and masters decided that it was easier to pay a wage and let apprentices manage their own expenses.[3]

Enforcement and monitoring of the system was entrusted to the guilds, though apprenticeships ran substantially on trust. In small towns and in the countryside, wrote Adam Smith a few decades before the statute's repeal, the Statute of Artificers was little heeded anyway, given the desperate demand for skilled labor, from whatever source. Over time, the range of professions covered by the Statute remained of a basically Elizabethan cast—newer craftsmen (watchmakers, for instance) embraced neither guilds nor the apprenticeship system to the same degree. As some of the older professions fell from favor or relevance, the Statute's influence receded.

By the eighteenth century, broader economic changes opened apprenticeship up to criticism. Most famously, Smith roundly abused the English system established under the Statute of Artificers, pillorying it in *The Wealth of Nations* as "a manifest encroachment upon the just liberty, both of the workman, and of those who might be disposed to employ him." Payment in lodging, meals, and so forth, rather than cash, Smith averred, disposed the apprentice to slothfulness, since "the sweets of labour consist altogether in the recompence of labour." He criticized apprenticeships as restraining trade and holding back competition in the natural division of labor, given the continuing caps on the number of apprentices most masters could take on. In Scotland, he noted, the typical term of indenture was a much milder three years in length, and in France usually five years (though five more as a journeyman followed). (Smith overlooked the fact that masters made back their investment on early training by keeping apprentices longer.)

Another common charge in early modern Europe was that apprentices made up a motley society of their own, a rough lot known for stirring up considerable mischief and social unrest. Poor conditions and abusive masters fed hooliganism, adolescence *avant la lettre*, and frustrated acts of rebellion. Robert Darnton resurrects this forgotten milieu in *The Great*

Cat Massacre, drawing on Nicolas Contat's detailed account of his own apprenticeship in an eighteenth-century Paris printing shop.[4] "Life as an apprentice was hard," writes Darnton. "They slept in a filthy, freezing room, rose before dawn, ran errands all day while dodging insults from the journeyman and abuse from the master, and received nothing but slops to eat. They found the food especially galling. Instead of dining at the master's table, they had to eat scraps from his plate in the kitchen. Worse still, the cook secretly sold the leftovers and gave the boys cat food—old, rotten bits of meat that they could not stomach and so passed on to the cats, who refused it." Relatively well off and self-important, the master neither worked with nor ate alongside the apprentices; this was the foreman's job. Worst of all, the apprentices foresaw little opportunity to become masters themselves one day: by this time, the number of printers in Paris was fixed by law, and the privilege tended to pass through families.

Under these circumstances, the apprentices staged a small but significant subversion, an act of what Darnton calls "ritual punning." The boys were menaced by "a profusion of alley cats who also thrived in the printing district and made [their] lives miserable." For several nights one week, they decided to imitate the horrible howling and meowing of the cats outside the master's bedroom. Driven to madness by the boys' pitch-perfect imitation, the master and his wife commanded the apprentices to purge the alley cats, which they did with delighted abandon, bludgeoning and smashing the poor animals with bars of the press, broom handles, and other printing equipment; afterwards, they "dumped sackloads of half-dead cats in the courtyard," staged a mock trial declaring the animals guilty, and hanged the cats on the gallows, all the while laughing wildly and uncontrollably, to the horror of master and mistress.

The modern reader, finding this vignette "unfunny, if not downright repulsive," thus discovers "the distance that separates us from the workers of preindustrial Europe," as Darnton wrote. The cat massacre is a window onto a world of dead-end apprenticeship—will future historians find similar accounts of tongue-in-cheek intern rebellion? The *Guardian* recently reported on an intern at the London fashion magazine *Grazia* whose symbolic practical joke may one day seem just as opaque. Regularly dispatched to buy skinny lattes for the beauty desk, the intern announced on her last day that she had been buying the staff full-fat lattes all along—distant but unmistakable echoes of a modest sedition.[5]

"Printer's devils," as printing apprentices were called, could be among the most troublesome, particularly with their ability to read and write. It was in fact a "bookish inclination" that "determined my father to make me a printer," writes Benjamin Franklin in his *Autobiography*. "I stood out some time, but at last was persuaded, and signed the indentures when I was yet but twelve years old. I was to serve as an apprentice till I was twenty-one years of age, only I was to be allowed journeyman's wages during the last year."[6] The master was none other than Ben's older brother James, who reprimanded and beat the young apprentice in spite of fraternal ties. Although Ben learned his trade well, and would later take on apprentices himself in his Philadelphia printing shop, he broke his indentures and skipped town, seizing the chance to stow away on a ship in Boston Harbor. "In three days I found myself in New York, near 300 miles from home," writes Franklin, "a boy of but 17, without the least recommendation to, or knowledge of, any person in the place, and very little money in my pocket." He did, however, know how to work a printing press.

Franklin's flight was emblematic of the rough start faced by apprenticeship in the New World. Without professional guilds (which never took hold in North America), the master-apprentice relationship often became a one-on-one struggle, with the apprentice always poised to take flight across state lines or to an expanding frontier where new opportunities beckoned. Though it never became "entrenched" as it was in Europe, writes Gillian Hamilton, apprenticeship was nonetheless the "principal means of acquiring skill in the colonial era." By and large, it followed the English model set out in the Statute of Artificers, as far as age and indentures went. The American heyday of traditional apprenticeship was the mid-to-late-eighteenth century; even today, the Office of Apprenticeship likes to remind Americans that nearly all the founding fathers started out as apprentices.

Yet it was the American Revolution, made by these ex-apprentices, which ironically spelled the institution's decline. Wars were always a notoriously difficult time to hold onto apprentices, many of whom would change their indentures for army service on a moment's notice. There is evidence that the American Revolution in particular broadened the discourse of freedom in a way that threw indentures into a bad light. From 1783 to 1799, twelve states passed apprenticeship laws that aimed at solving the runaway problem—apparently to little avail (along with Franklin, Andrew Johnson, Kit Carson, and George Westinghouse, Jr. were other famous runaway apprentices). The dawn of the industrial revolution and westward expansion across the continent added substantially to the problem. Hamilton sees rapid population growth as the larger catalyst, bringing with it "improved local market opportunities and a decline in neighborly familiarity" that mortally wounded the institution of internships.

Between 1800 and 1860 in a single Maryland county, William Rorabaugh discovered, the percentage of white males in formal apprenticeships fell from nearly 20 percent of the population to under 1 percent.[7] In Montreal, where apprenticeship records are unusually complete, Hamilton found that decline set in around 1815, due at first to "difficulties in contract enforcement"—the age-old problem of apprentices leaving their indentures early with impunity. It was rarely worth the cost or the trouble for a master to chase down an apprentice who had run off. The rise of larger workshops and firms, more likely to hire women and children for less skilled work, also put a dent in the apprenticeship market in nineteenth-century Montreal. Another telling change emerges from the Montreal records: the percentage of apprentices receiving cash wages climbed from 35 percent in the 1790s to 82 percent by the 1830s, while payment in kind (housing, clothing, etc.) plunged.

The revival and modernization of American apprenticeship would not come for another century, and the rise of compulsory public education in the meantime would impose powerful constraints. In Europe and the British Commonwealth, apprenticeship persisted much more strongly through the nineteenth century, setting the stage for its broader use down to the present day. In the British case, "customs, inherited from the guilds, that favored training certification for entry into skilled jobs" played a major role, writes Elbaum; in Germany, "government legislation has been integral to the apprenticeship system." Twenty years ago, Elbaum found that apprenticeships accounted for only 0.3 percent of civilian employment in the U.S., as opposed to 2–3 percent in Commonwealth countries, and 5–6 percent in Germany, Austria, and Switzerland—in the last-mentioned countries, he wrote, apprenticeship remains "the principal means of training for skilled manual trades" and a serious alternative to college. In 2009, a German study found that 40 percent of young people who had the opportunity to attend college free of charge nonetheless chose instead to enter apprenticeships instead.

In the U.S., the system continued to wither away—while Dickens' Pip in *Great Expectations* served as a blacksmith apprentice, Horatio Alger praised the upward mobility of newsboys, peddlers, and young shoeshiners in New York; Andrew Carnegie was getting his start as a telegraph messenger boy in Pittsburgh; and the largest cohort of all was heading west. The apprenticeships that survived were "far closer to an arm's-length market transaction," in which "apprentices generally lived at home and were paid money wages," writes Elbaum. If the wages were relatively low, barring entrance to many lower-class hopefuls, an apprenticeship nonetheless "promised earnings far superior to those of alternative working-class jobs" over the span of a career. A nail in the coffin came with the spread of schooling—"increasingly sought as the vehicle for upward social mobility," as Jacoby writes. The rise of schooling placed "the expense of and the responsibility for training upon the learner," achieved significant economies of scale, and helped companies and employer associations to keep control of the labor supply away from ever more powerful unions.[8]

American apprenticeship was an institution on the margins by the time social psychologist G. Stanley Hall coined the term "adolescence" in 1898. For Hall, this transitional phase of life could begin as early as age twelve and still apply even to the occasional twenty-five-year-old. High school, a world unto itself, became the new crucible of youth culture, making the antics of printers' devils and runaway apprentices a distant memory. Hall's concept of the adolescent had come into wide circulation by the 1930s and 1940s, writes Grace Palladino in *Teenagers: An American History*, as modern youth culture became a full-fledged reality. It was a momentous change: "When a teenage majority spent the better of their day in high school," writes Palladino, "they learned to look to one another and not to adults for advice, information, and approval."

Youth labor, if it was encouraged at all, became primarily a summertime activity, except school-year jobs taken "on the side." At the end of the nineteenth century, as the mania for fresh air and leisure time took hold, reformers challenged year-round education and labor, advocating a dose of recreation for young people. In the same period, summer camps, deliberate communities dedicated to outdoor activity and education, were "transformed from experimental institutions to mainstays of mass culture," as Leslie Paris describes in *Children's Nature: The Rise of the American Summer Camp*. As Paris writes, "summer camps have provided many American children's first experience of community beyond their immediate family and home neighborhoods ... children found the experience of attending camp revelatory and formative." Founded in 1910, the Boy Scouts were only one of a raft of new youth movements emphasizing group activities and the outdoors—laboring, implicitly, was seen as less formative. Older teens and college students, gingerly entering the working world of adulthood, earned money and forged a work ethic by gravitating to light summer jobs: scooping ice cream, working as camp counselors, lifeguarding, waiting tables, helping out with the family business.

The demise of traditional apprenticeship and the triumph of schooling had this unintended effect. The classic American summer, which internships are now finally eroding, became an escape valve, a time and space comparatively beyond the reach of authority and given over to spontaneous, sentimental, and practical education. Although never available or even desirable for all, those summers have been a space to grow in: barbecues and stickball in the streets, family visits and camping trips, romantic flings and assorted mischief. For many teens and college kids, those two- to three-month breaks represented a first shot at freedom and self-determination.

Off an anonymous white hallway—lined with quiet, orderly offices, with names like "Employees' Compensation Appeal Board" and "Division of Trade Adjustment Assistance"—John Ladd sits beneath a large framed copy of the 1937 Fitzgerald Act, the 200-plus words that finally stabilized and revived apprenticeship in the United States. Buried inside the concrete modernist honeycomb of the Department of Labor, just a stone's throw from Capitol Hill, Ladd quietly and persistently makes his case for keeping a medieval institution alive in the twenty-first century.

Unassuming, unsmiling, Ladd speaks pragmatically and to the point —in a broad Boston accent and without a whiff of politics, surrounded in his office by obscure bureaucratic trophies for competence and efficiency. To oversee nearly a half million apprenticeships, Ladd has a staff of only twenty in Washington D.C. and a further 125 people "in the field," largely in the twenty-five states without apprenticeship programs of their own. With employers and community colleges bearing many of the costs of apprentice training, the Office of Apprenticeship (OA) runs on a miniscule annual budget of some $20 million, making it about as small and unobtrusive as a federal program can be. "Compared to the systems in some other countries," write the authors of the Urban Institute report on the future of apprenticeship, "the apprenticeship system in the U.S. is far more decentralized and relies more on employers' decisions."

The Fitzgerald Act empowered the Department of Labor "to promote the furtherance of labor standards necessary to safeguard the welfare of apprentices and to cooperate with the States in the promotion of such standards." That is to say—if modern apprentices like Melanie, Mike, and Beth are paid fair wages and enjoy good working conditions, they have in large part the Fitzgerald Act and the OA to thank. If American apprenticeship today is a humane, rational system—with statistics and goals like any other public policy initiative, provisions for racial and gender diversity, and a steady supply of skilled labor coming out the other end—the credit is due not only to unions and decent employers, but also to Ladd's office.

Registering an apprenticeship program with the OA and meeting its detailed standards is voluntary—Ladd is in every way a promoter, hardly at all an enforcer. Registration creates "a portable national credential" for skilled workers, says Ladd, "akin to accreditation," setting certain standards around fair application procedures, supervision, classroom instruction (144 hours annually), on-the-job training (2,000 hours), wage increases, anti-discrimination policies, and so on. From a public policy perspective, a central aim of apprenticeship is to ensure a continuing supply of highly skilled labor to power the American economy. The higher taxes paid by well-compensated graduates of apprentice programs more than make up for the small investments made by federal and state governments. Unregistered apprenticeships, however, exist in much the same liminal space as internships, numbering in the hundreds of thousands and operating well beyond Ladd's purview. Less likely to be comprehensive, life-changing experiences, they at least tend to be decently paid, influenced by the strong gravitational pull of OA's national standards.

As so often in the U.S., federal legislation was the culmination of decades of activism and law-making at local levels. Union-backed state legislation and local industry-specific programs powered the rebirth of apprenticeship. In 1911, Wisconsin (then a nexus of progressive policy-making) made the first attempt to organize apprenticeship at the state level, putting it under the supervision of an industrial commission and mandating an educational component. With guarantees of fair pay and decent treatment, young people flocked back to apprenticeship and employers snapped them up: in Wisconsin, the number of recorded apprenticeships grew from five in 1912 to 821 in 1925. During this period, the number of apprentices nationwide grew steadily with the overall size of the workforce, from approximately 44,000 in 1880 to 140,000 in 1920. The new apprentices were likely to be older as well, having completed some schooling. Fears of a skilled labor shortage crystallized during World War I, fueling the rise of cooperative education (see Chapter 5), the growth of vocational programs under the Smith-Hughes Act, and finally the creation of national apprenticeship standards.

The early twentieth-century revival of apprenticeship has been enduring; the Fitzgerald Act has weathered seven decades. In a recent study, 86 percent of apprentices expressed satisfaction with their classroom training, 84 percent with their on-the-job training. One large-scale survey of nearly a thousand apprenticeship sponsors found that 97 percent would recommend the program to others, and 86 percent would "strongly" recommend it. An overwhelming majority of these employers cited apprenticeships as helping them meet the demand for skilled workers, raising overall productivity, improving safety, and strengthening worker morale. The "poaching" of apprentices by other firms—a theoretical worry of economists since Gary Becker, who thus counsel against providing general training—does not emerge as a major concern in reality.

Recently, in Oakland, California, I attended a town hall meeting about proposed reforms to update the Fitzgerald Act for the twenty-first century. The youngest person in the room, I was surrounded by an audience of passionate apprenticeship supporters, mostly men in jeans and black leather jackets, many sporting the insignia of unions or apprenticeship programs. Sitting in the sun-filled conference room, I was half nodding off through the opening Powerpoint presentation until the floor was opened to comments and questions, and the floodgates burst open. Why is apprenticeship looked down on, despite all its benefits? everyone wondered aloud. Why are there still so few women and minorities in skilled labor trades, beginning with the apprenticeship years? They argued and wrung their hands, but I was fascinated—watching an open, spirited debate, aimed at realistic reforms, such as the world of internships has never produced.

Apprenticeship has been "the best-kept secret" for too long, said Don Davis, an electrician who mentors apprentices in Los Angeles—"we need to educate this country that it is a very viable means to an education and a very viable means to a career." Davis bemoaned "the lack of respect and the loss of interest" in skilled labor, such that people are "ashamed to be called an apprentice"; Jamie Robinson, a former carpentry apprentice, described the disdainful "physical reaction" when telling friends and family that she had chosen an apprenticeship over college. "The audience isn't there, the attention isn't there," averred John Bullock, a union carpenter for four decades and a member of the Carpenters Training Committee for Northern California during half of that time. "Nobody knows about it. You don't have to pay to go to school!"

A range of ideas and critiques were floated, while an OA administrator listened attentively and a court reporter tapped each word into the record. "Invest time and effort in the high schools," counseled an ironworker from San Francisco who coordinates an apprenticeship program. End the nepotism in the trades and the reign of "FBI 'families, buddies, and in-laws,'" which begins at the apprentice level, added an African American journeyman mechanic. Solve child-care issues for single-mother apprentices, said women apprentices—while still others responded with examples of programs that have made their own daycare arrangements. Imagine an internship where daycare is provided!

The analogy between internships and apprenticeships is thin enough until you consider modern apprenticeship—then it vanishes almost entirely. A better comparison in the historical record might be with someone like William Cheselden, "the well-known lithotomist, with Newton and Pope among his patients," who, according to historian Joan Lane, received 150 [pounds], 210 and 350 as premiums in the years 1712–30 for taking on apprentices.[9] Wealthy parents were often willing to pay to place their offspring in such exceptional, prestigious apprenticeships—but with internships, the practice has now reached an unprecedented scale. On the whole, modern apprenticeship in the West is the justified successor to the European tradition of craft apprenticeship, minus the cruelty, coercion, and familial arrangements and sensibly updated for the twentieth and now twenty-first centuries. Long after guilds have vanished, the endurance and adaptability of "learning by doing," in small settings and over significant lengths of time, is worth pondering. Will there still be internships eight centuries hence, in some form or other?

Without question, apprenticeships have been stymied in the white-collar world, pre-empted by the short-term, unpaid, employer-dominated internship model. The history of internships suggests an explanation: no one has been watching. Internship boosters have invoked apprenticeships without studying their history or evolution. In cubicles and offices, but *not* construction sites, the battle to protect young people on the job and to balance working and learning remains much as it was in the nineteenth century, or the thirteenth. Internships have grown up in a permissive period, ill disposed to regulation and blind to labor issues.

Jacoby offers a more sanguine view: "Apprenticeship works better in a stable technology environment, so if the skills are constantly shifting or if the jobs aren't going to be there, then the willingness to make an investment in those skills and jobs is going much more difficult." This is one of the strongest justifications for internships—that their very pliability is suited to a fast-changing, intangible economy built on networks and highly general skills. Nonetheless, says Jacoby of internships, "We don't really grapple with what you have to master to move to the next level effectively … They create the sense of an open architecture where people feel like they can move into fields where they don't have a lot of background

… but I think that's going to be more sleight-of-hand than reality." Through high school and college, everything is made to seem possible, and internships extend the fantasy, until it comes time to land a stable, comfortable, decently paid job.

CHAPTER FOUR

A Lawsuit Waiting to Happen

I've employed interns my whole career, gotten lots of "immediate advantage" out of them. They've done most of the research for my books and most of the research that won me Emmy Awards for consumer reporting. I asked my TV bosses to pay for the research help, but they laughed at me, saying, "You think we're made of money?" From then on, I got much of my best help from unpaid college students.

... Am I evil? Am I going to jail?

—John Stossel

Every year, hundreds of thousands of interns in the U.S. work without pay or for less than minimum wage. Many of these unpaid or underpaid internships are at for-profit companies and closely resemble regular work: thousands upon thousands of labor violations each year, hidden in plain sight. An Intern Bridge survey, involving 42,000 students at 400 universities, found that 18 percent of the respondents had received neither pay nor academic credit for their internships, a likely indication that these positions were illegal. In certain for-profit industries—fashion, publishing, entertainment, journalism, to name a few—demanding unpaid internships dominate, with illegal situations possibly constituting a majority of all available opportunities. This chapter focuses on the core legal issues surrounding pay and workplace rights in private-sector internships. Just as troubling, however, is the preponderance of unpaid internships in the public sector and at nonprofit organizations: a legal gray area explored in Chapter 6.

The broad outlines of a broken paradigm are clear. Unless substantial training is involved, an intern is considered to be an employee, however temporary or inexperienced, and entitled to minimum wage and other protections under the Fair Labor Standards Act (FLSA), the central piece of federal legislation that addresses the rights of American workers. It doesn't matter whether it's at a blue-chip company or a small business, whether it's full-time or one day a week, whether the goal is academic credit or a midlife career change—by law, there are very few situations where you can ask someone to do real work for free.

And there are good reasons why that's the law. Working for free is a way of radically underbidding the competition and prompting "a race to the bottom"—after all, why should an employer pay for something ever again once it can be had for free? Every time young people scramble for an unpaid position, they reinforce the flawed perception that certain kinds of work have lost all value. Whether or not any given individual is happy to make this trade-off, the decision has consequences for everyone else. For an inexact but suggestive comparison, imagine if Chinese carmakers, keen to capture market share and subsidized by Beijing, started offering their cars to American customers for free. This would be considered illegal for more or less the same reason: using an unfair advantage to drop the price to zero both distorts markets and destroys livelihoods.

Yet illegal internships are spreading openly and inexorably; they have become a social norm propagated by employers, schools, parents, and interns themselves. The publisher of a storied California newspaper attempts to replace his reporting staff with full-time, unpaid interns, recruited from top journalism schools.[1] Wall Street firms, hedge funds, and asset management companies, sensing students' desperation in tough economic times, offer unpaid brokerage internships, involving financial analysis and investment research as well as secretarial work. Start-ups pencil interns into their business plans as a cost-saving measure, with empty promises of a distant salary or a stock option bonanza. Nearly every day, in every major city, employers post ads for illegal internships on Craigslist, Monster.com, and countless college job boards, describing serious work roles for qualified individuals, promising no pay and little or no training.

The cheerful, little-noticed manipulation of twenty-somethings constitutes a serious violation of law and basic ethics. Having inured ourselves to their informal, banal character, we make excuses for the unregulated and irrepressible spread of internships, to the erosion of the concept of work. The mutual consent of employer and intern should not be mistaken for proof that all is well or legal. After all, most sweatshop workers also consent to their toil, for lack of a better option. We tend to assume, reasonably, that something so widespread, so openly touted by respectable institutions, must be legitimate. Entire industries rely unabashedly on this source of free or cheap labor; an increasing number of placement firms are building multimillion-dollar businesses around selling such internships; thousands of educational institutions lend them credibility and resources. Why is no one blowing the whistle on illegal internships?

Michael Tracy, an employment lawyer who has written about internship law, succinctly states the issue: "The law is not widely known." For a long time, this was true of students and parents, university personnel and employers alike—but there was nothing accidental about this blind spot. A quick internet search reveals the basic criteria that make an internship legal or illegal, information that media outlets and bloggers have now published thousands of times. Still, virtually no one mentions the law in conversation or takes it very seriously. Employers, schools, and professional associations benefit from the current system; parents and students largely accept it and bear the costs.

Interns themselves *do* communicate, sometimes feverishly and effectively, about which internships are revelatory or useless, fun or mind-numbing—now increasingly through dedicated internship rating websites—but there's very little discussion of whether many internships are legitimate in the first place. According to Tracy, "The problem is that there are 'willing victims.'" Yesterday's interns need their former employers as references or contacts, and today's interns trade their half-understood rights for a résumé boost. Some parents, raised in an era when work entailed pay, try to impart this old-fashioned idea to their teenagers and twenty-somethings, but many also encourage and badger their progeny into getting a leg-up on the competition, no matter what. Indeed, parents are often the ones indulgently but misguidedly underwriting illegal internships, in effect subsidizing the companies that reap free labor.

And it's not just about minimum wage. A host of other, related rights are at stake with illegal internships, from overtime to sick days to basic workplace rights. With their rights under the FLSA ignored and unenforced, interns face a second, equally cruel injustice: those working without pay are also left without legal standing and effectively "in legal limbo"—unable to bring lawsuits against employers, internship programs, or colleges. Our youngest workers, least likely to be wise in the ways of the workplace, effectively have no legal voice; they are considered no different from bystanders who just happen to be holding down a cubicle. Those subject to sexual harassment or racial discrimination have no legal recourse. No fair hiring practices pertain. In the world of internships, anything goes—inhumane employment practices, right out of the nineteenth century, are resurfacing in twenty-first-century office parks and skyscrapers.

Hugo Black had the kind of outsized, self-contradictory American life that hardly seems possible anymore. A charismatic senator from Alabama and later a Supreme Court justice, Black's most enduring contribution may prove to be his authorship of the bill that became the Fair Labor Standards Act. Yet the tangle of his ideological convictions seems impossible to unravel: he launched his political career as a member of the Ku Klux Klan, and later become an outspoken New Dealer. He saw no contradiction between his literalist reading of the Constitution and professed veneration for the Bill of Rights, and the majority opinion he wrote in the 1944 case of *Korematsu v. United States*, which sanctioned the internment of Japanese Americans.

In June 1938, as the country's economy stalled in the second trough of the Great Depression, Congress enacted Hugo Black's bill, establishing a federal minimum wage, guaranteeing extra pay for overtime work, and ending the national disgrace of child labor. It was a moment of dizzying triumph for unions and progressives—the culmination of a half-century's struggle to protect America's new legions of industrial laborers. When he signed it into law, FDR proudly called the FLSA "the most far-reaching, far-sighted program for the benefit of workers ever adopted in this or any other country."

Much of the law has weathered the last seven decades remarkably well. With little fanfare, its basic architecture has become a bedrock consensus. Aside from a libertarian fringe, few people would openly advocate the return of young children to factories, or a total scrapping of the minimum wage. The law's stated aim—the "elimination of labor conditions detrimental to the maintenance of the minimum standards of living necessary for health, efficiency and well being of workers"—still sounds vital. Yet within a decade, the Supreme Court—yes, under Hugo Black—had opened up an important loophole in the law. Sixty years later, many interns are still caught in that loophole.

Initially, the FLSA declared only well-salaried, white-collar workers to be exempt from the law's provisions: the familiar distinction between exempt and nonexempt employees. In the 1947 case *Walling v. Portland Terminal Co.*, the Supreme Court held that a further group could be treated as exempt from FLSA protections: trainees. This second exempted group was not at all like the first, comprised of valued professional employees whose salaries, typically far in excess of minimum wage, are calculated on an annual basis. An exemption for trainees, on the other hand, meant that they would receive at most a "training wage" below the federal minimum, or possibly no salary at all—it was at the employer's discretion. *Walling v. Portland Terminal Co.* involved a seven- or eight-day training course for brakemen in a railway yard. After watching regular employees complete a task, the trainees were allowed to do it themselves under close supervision, even if this slowed down the railyard's operations. In such a context, creating an FLSA exemption for trainees must have seemed like a reasonable proposition: a way of encouraging firms to provide vocational training for future employees without having to pay them like regular employees.

For interns, the crux of the matter is whether they fall into this trainee exemption. Such is the novelty of the internship phenomenon and the effective freeze on new labor legislation in recent decades that the internship phenomenon has never been directly addressed by federal regulations: instead there are older terms such as *employee, trainee, volunteer,* and *apprentice,* which jurists and regulators still struggle to define, let alone graft onto internship situations. Circuit court precedents since *Portland Terminal* have been murky and contradictory, but day-to-day enforcement of the FLSA and its trainee exemption rests in the hands of the Wage and Hour Division (WHD), an office at the Department of Labor established specifically to enforce and interpret these fundamental labor laws.

As distilled by WHD, the Supreme Court's decision identified six relevant criteria for determining an exempt trainee, all of which must be met (see Appendix B):

1. The training, even though it includes actual operation of the facilities of the employer, is similar to that which would be given in a vocational school;
2. The training is for the benefit of the trainee;
3. The trainees do not displace regular employees, but work under close observation;
4. The employer that provides the training derives no immediate advantage from the activities of the trainees and on occasion the employer's operations may actually be impeded;
5. The trainees are not necessarily entitled to a job at the completion of the training period; and
6. The employer and the trainee understand that the trainees are not entitled to wages for the time spent in training.

This test—buried in the Department of Labor's Field Operations Handbook (section 10b11, if you're curious) and a series of administrative letters—is clearly concerned with both protecting workers *and* encouraging employers to provide training. If an internship meets all six criteria, that makes it a traineeship for which wages are not required, but if even *one* of the six criteria is not met, the internship is legally considered a job, bringing the benefits of the minimum wage, overtime pay, and associated rights.

It's into this little-known exemption that employers have tried to squeeze unpaid internships. The *Portland Terminal* scenario is a far cry from most of today's internships, which typically last anywhere from a few months to a year and tend to involve real tasks, whether menial, administrative, or more substantive. Dedicated training is rare, and there is hardly more supervision than would be accorded to a regular employee, and sometimes less. Criteria 1, 3, and 4 are violated day in and day out, by design, in most internships. David Yamada, a law professor who has written on illegal internships, analyzed major internships at MTV and Sotheby's as being in clear violation of these three. Indeed, only a small minority of real job-shadowing or trainee situations, which might happen to be marketed as internships, can pass the six-point test with flying colors.[2]

In particular, the criterion that an employer derive "no immediate advantage from the activities of the trainees" stirs up the most rancor. As part of the supposed win-win of internships, employers believe that they should benefit from day one: the idea that investing in an intern's future might impede business activities is now anathema. In a nod to these employer concerns, some court decisions—and a recent move by California's Division of Labor Standards Enforcement—have sought to weaken the "immediate advantage" criterion. The method is to take a "totality of circumstances" approach to the six criteria, rather than strictly requiring the fulfillment of all six, as the Wage and Hour Division does. "The difference in results can be a potentially significant one," writes Yamada, who has warned that the "totality of circumstances" approach may involve an "extensive, drawn-out factor analysis that, by necessity, requires a great deal of subjective judgment … [and] virtually ensures inconsistent results."

There's a more philosophical question lurking in the legal legerdemain as well: How clearly can the law differentiate between training and work, especially in an ever-more intangible service economy? Under the "totality of the circumstances" approach, the legality of an internship would rest on whether the benefit an intern received from his or her training *outweighed* the benefits that the employer derived from the intern's free labor. Can you balance out thirty hours of data entry with thirty minutes of database training or a brief powwow with executives? Is it vocational training to learn by osmosis, from being cc'd on emails or by sitting in on staff meetings? The judgment may vary in each case, but the spirit of the law is still clear: even if an internship is hands-on enough to produce real benefits for the employer, clearly identifiable training must remain the larger motive. Employers just out for cheap labor need not apply.

In March 1995, fifty-four unpaid interns got justice. By order of the Department of Labor, A. Brown-Olmstead Associates, a prominent Atlanta public relations firm, paid its former interns $31,520 in back wages—after having had the gall to bill its clients explicitly for the hours worked by unpaid interns.[3] The pattern of abuse had occurred over a period of two years; among the interns affected, only two were still in school when they worked at Brown-Olmstead, while the other fifty-two already had college degrees, and a few even had previous PR experience. Few companies are brazen enough to put interns on a client's bill, but overall Brown-Olmstead's actions were barely distinguishable from thousands of other firms: they just got caught.

In April 2010, Steven Greenhouse of the *New York Times* reported that officials charged with labor enforcement in California, Oregon, and New York had recently handled cases involving illegal internships. Although few in number, and initiated by the interns, the cases gave prominent publicity—for the first time since the Brown-Olmstead case fifteen years earlier—to the fact that unpaid interns can fight for employee status and win backpay under the FLSA. In the interim, illegal internships have only become more, not less, embedded in the world of work. A tremendous outpouring of illegal internship accounts followed the publication of Greenhouse's story: on personal blogs, on message boards, in the comment sections of articles, and into my personal email inbox. In most of these accounts, either intern or employer came anonymized—and it remained far from clear whether the interns would ever file formal complaints or lawsuits. Calling out abusive employers seemed to bring relief to the victims, but fear and uncertainty still hung in the air.

The employers indicted in these accounts run the gamut. The *Times* article described an NYU student who took an unpaid animation internship at Little Airplane, a children's film company. She soon found herself working for the facilities department and wiping down door handles to prevent a swine flu outbreak. (Tone Thyne, a senior producer at Little Airplane, told the *Times* that the company's internships are usually highly educational and often lead to good jobs.)

This anecdote alone unleashed a chorus of accusations from the throngs of young animators who have tried to break into the field with the requisite unpaid internships. Corporate giants such as Nickelodeon and the Cartoon Network were quickly accused of similarly using unpaid interns under false pretenses, as were many smaller studios. On the website Cartoon Brew, one recent graduate from a 3D animation school wrote of his experience: "I was unable to gain employment in the field so jumped on the chance to work in a small start-up company with a whole team of recent grads for free. Somehow, the employer was able to string us all along for six months ... claiming that he was in midst of talks for a movie deal in which he would hire all of us for and he constantly pushed back the date he claimed work would start." The intern only departed, he said, after the employer "sexually harassed one of the female interns (judging from email evidence and her personal accounts)." Other anima-tors pointed out that Little Airplane had once made its unpaid interns dance in gorilla costumes to amuse a staff member on his birthday, that another animation studio made its interns "mostly responsible for doing dishes, putting away folding chairs, and emptying trash," while at a third firm "interns have worked as many as three seasons without seeing a paycheck."

A magazine intern interviewed for the *Times* piece spent much of her unpaid summer "packaging and shipping 20 or 40 apparel samples a day back to fashion houses that had provided them for photo shoots." At a company that books musical talent, an unpaid intern toiled at photo-copying, filing, and emailing for her boss. In the midst of the bailouts, famous banks were revealed to have approached NYU to advertise new unpaid internship positions on campus. A law firm that had promised "an educational $10-an-hour internship" was accused of not paying their intern and "requiring him to make coffee and sweep out bathrooms." The recent cases of intern abuse in Oregon involved a solar panel company, an organic farm, a food-cart operation, and an interior design firm. Bob Avakian, Oregon's Labor Commissioner, commented that these formal complaints are probably not even "reflective of all the situations out there where you might have people working for free or sub-minimum wage that should be entitled to more."[4]

On the website One Day, One Internship, which profiles internship opportunities for college students, a former unpaid intern for Merrill Lynch defended his role regardless of legal questions: "I would say it was an even trade. I have a top company on my résumé and they got some free labor." Another poster described "an unpaid, telecommuting internship where … I'm basically developing tours to help launch a tour division of a company"—she and her two fellow interns are designing a total of ten tours with meaningful profit potential for the company. A blogger who goes by the name "Maggie Stewart" works for an entertainment PR firm, "hoping to break the cycle of needing entertainment experience to break into the industry." As she describes the situation, "I work for nothing, yet I diligently sit on the floor of my employer's apartment organizing his CDs. I work for nothing, and get papers thrown at me without a please or thank you. I work for nothing, and I have yet to get the one thing I was promised in return for working for free. Experience."

All these are enraging, but garden-variety illegal internships, where employers skimp on wages while pretending to offer a valuable experience, willing to break the law and take advantage of young workers to save a few thousand dollars here and there. Other kinds of schemes abound in the internship underworld. One Day, One Internship, among others, has documented the internships advertised by pyramid marketing schemes like the Landers Group, which advertised itself as a prominent sports marketing firm in Southern California. After an "informational interview" full of fast talk and obfuscation, intern hopefuls were required to participate in full-day "interviews" where they were in fact thrust into doing the company's real work: selling possibly fraudulent coupons door to door in poor neighborhoods. "You'll essentially spend the day working for free," writes Willy Franzen of One Day, One Internship, citing numerous accounts he has heard. "If you're lucky, you'll just end up having wasted a day. If you're not, you may end up stranded many miles from home or having a gun pointed at you and with mud all over your only suit." A host of other fly-by-night entities are doing something similar, pushing "multi-level marketing" (also called pyramid selling) on internship- and job-seekers—Granton Marketing, DS Max, After Five Marketing Group, and Innovage, and so on.

Other variations on the illegal internship include unpaid trial periods, when an employer claims to be testing out a potential employee, and multiplying schemes to hire interns as independent contractors. Campus Career centers receive these proposals from employers all the time. "Our college has noticed an increase in elaborate payment schemes employers are concocting to try to get around the laws," wrote one career counselor recently, referring to an interactive marketing internship in which the intern would be paid as an "independent contractor" $500 for three months of work. She also described "a large and well-respected media chain" that wanted to provide a paid internship, equivalent in hours and job description to an entry-level position, by giving a "scholarship" to the university in question, which would then channel the funds to the student. The stated aim was "to keep FTEs [full-time employees] off the books."

One could go on with countless examples—the reality is that very few interns employed in illegal situations have ever sought or received justice. As David Yamada writes, "Unpaid internships rapidly have become so ingrained in the culture of collegiate credentialing that the lack of compensation is considered a short-term sacrifice in return for a potentially larger payoff in the future." It simply falls under the heading of "that's life." Many interns are afraid or unwilling to burn bridges with employers, even if they know the law. The few cases that have been exposed or resolved have yet to make a real impression on the public imagination. And other pressures remain too strong.

One of the most serious effects of the internship boom has been the displacement of regular employees, directly in contravention of the six-point test, but this too has largely gone unnoticed or unchallenged, and is sometimes difficult to prove conclusively. Economist Jean-Marie Chevalier has estimated that at least 60,000 of the internships in France at any given time should be regular, full-time jobs.[5] No comparable estimate exists for the U.S., where many more internships exist, but anecdotal evidence abounds that one or more interns are often used to avoid a new hire, to replace a departing worker, to handle busier work periods or cover vital administrative work. Thus the corrosive effects of the internship boom spread, leading to the layoff of hundreds of thousands of full-time, regular employees who may well remain on the unemployment rolls because of labor performed by unpaid interns. Few of the industries where interns are having the biggest impact are significantly unionized—but even in areas like film and journalism, the union presence seems to have made little difference.

Still the most important factor by far in the rise of illegal internships is the failure of the Wage and Hour Division to enforce the law. Like any piece of legislation, however well intentioned, the FLSA is only as durable and effective as the enforcement mechanisms behind it. In the decades following *Portland Terminal*, companies loosened the definition of a trainee beyond all recognition, importing the title "intern" from the prestigious medical field and using the "trainee" exemption to wriggle out of minimum wage obligations. In the 1970s, the WHD started hearing from employers planning new internship programs: Could their interns be considered trainees under the law? The letters in response, always polite and scrupulous, rarely hand down definitive rulings one way or another, let alone follow up afterwards, all of which sends the message that employers can act with impunity: the Department of Labor acts as little more than a passive, invisible arbiter of last resort, never actively seeking out companies to prosecute, barely keeping up with shifting social norms around internships.[6]

Interns are not alone, however. Violations of the FLSA are rampant and pervasive, as enforcement by the Wage and House Division has sunk to dangerously low levels. Although most of the Division's work is devoted to FLSA enforcement, its funding has been slashed considerably and its resulting ineffectiveness documented and savaged in a series of reports by the Government Accountability Office (GAO). A national survey involving thousands of low-wage workers in New York, Los Angeles, and Chicago recently revealed that 26 percent had been paid under minimum wage and fully 75 percent had not been paid for deserved overtime during the previous week—losses for those workers of $56.4 million per week, not to mention the damage to communities and to government revenues. Under WHD's watch, the FLSA has descended into irrelevance.

"It's very enforceable," says Catherine Ruckelshaus, legal codirector at the National Employment Law Project (NELP) and an expert on FLSA enforcement. What's needed, she adds, is simply "to get agencies engaged and beef up retaliation protections so workers aren't afraid to complain." The stagnation and decline of the Wage and Hour Division has been stark—from 1975 to 2004, a period when the number of workplaces in its purview increased by 112 percent, the number of staff investigators fell by 14 percent, reaching a nadir of 732 by 2007. That year, those investigators were able to pursue only 22,374 workers' complaints (a decline of more than a third from 1998) and initiate only 7,210 claims of their own (a drop of over 50 percent from 1998). The trend has been reversed under the Obama administration, with 250 new investigators being hired for Wage and Hour alone and promises of a return to vigorous enforcement. But the results remain to be seen.

The most common FLSA violations overall, according to Ruckelshaus, are "failure to pay, requiring workers to work 'off-the-clock,' requiring workers to work through required meal or rest breaks." The vast majority of such cases are resolved administratively with straightforward, efficient justice and reasonable financial remedies (often "double damages," two times the amount of backpay owed, plus any legal expenses). The vast majority of complaints are filed by older, more experienced workers, cognizant of their rights—some also choose to file complaints at the state level, if there are relevant state employment laws, or to sue their employer directly. Many more interns could protect themselves if they knew about these tools—and WHD could make it easier for them by taking a proactive stance when illegal internships are offered so openly. "The WHD cannot rely on worker complaints to drive its enforcement programs," according to an NELP report. "It has important capacity to engage in affirmative efforts to target high-violation industries and to protect the more vulnerable workers who may not come forward."

In the meantime, without new legislation, individual internships remain subject to the six-point test—if the federal or state labor departments drag their heels, interns may need to take to the courts. Michael Tracy, the employment lawyer, says that his firm gets "thousands of potential clients inquiring about various labor code violations each year," out of which "maybe one or two will be an intern." As a result, his office has handled "hundreds of actual lawsuits of wage and hour violations," yet "never filed a lawsuit brought by an unpaid intern."

Michael Walsh, a specialist on minimum wage law, blogged that an "intern came to us recently and asked if her internship, which was unpaid, complied with the wage and hour laws. It did not; she had a handsome claim for unpaid wages … If you do work, other than pure practice, or work on dummy files, you are probably entitled to get paid, and your claim can go back four years."[7] Walsh's home state of California's has an $8 minimum wage—and intern employees are always entitled to the legal minimum or living wage wherever they work if it is higher than the federal floor. Just four weeks of unpaid work would add up to $1,280 in back wages. "Often, the claims of a few or all of the affected employees can be brought in a single case," adds Walsh. As in the Brown-Olmstead complaint, forming a class can be the most efficient step, certainly for unpaid interns at a single firm and possibly even across an industry, if there are consistent patterns of abuse.

"I think most labor and employment attorneys would take these cases if presented with the opportunity," says Michael Tracy. "I think the chance of success would be very high." Willy Franzen, familiar with numerous illegal internships from his work at One Day, One Internship, thinks that when lawsuits begin there may be no holding back the tide: "I think it's going to come. It's just going to blow up."

Even when properly enforced, the law has gaps—it may not protect people like "Henry," who is still smarting years later from an exploitative internship during his senior year in college. Caught up in a bizarre project that can only be called an internship Ponzi scheme, Henry worked hundreds of hours for a husband-wife team, yet was able to learn almost nothing about the actual business. The Fair Labor Standards Act, like most pieces of employment legislation, only applies to organizations of a certain size—in this case, there must be two employees and at least $500,000 in annual sales. Absurdly, the question of whether Henry's internship was technically illegal or not hinges on details he has no way of knowing—but the ethics are nonetheless crystal-clear: Henry was used.

Inadvertently, Henry had plunged into one of the sketchiest corners of the Intern Economy: home offices. After posting his résumé on a recruiting website run jointly by Columbia University and Monster.com, he received an email from someone at Universal HyperAnalysis Inc. (a pseudonym), which calls itself "a stealth-mode start-up" even today, five years after Henry worked there. To go with its grand-sounding name, Universal HyperAnalysis describes itself in lofty terms as offering tools to catalyze innovation and growth, and advancing scientific knowledge in biotechnology, research settings, government, and private industry. Internships are pitched at valedictorians and original thinkers attending top universities; serious prospects for personal and professional growth, with a company on the rise, are said to be on offer.

As for Henry, the pressure to add an internship to his CV had finally caught up with him: "Everybody I knew was getting internships every year. I hadn't had one. I refused ... Nobody enjoyed it, nobody learned, and I just didn't understand the point." Starting to search for a post-graduation job, he wised up—every "entry-level" job seemed to require two or three years of experience. "How does that work? Where are you supposed to get it?" Henry thought to himself. "So that's what these internship people were talking about."

Behind all the vague and fashionable buzzwords was "just this guy [the founder and president] on the Upper West Side [of Manhattan] who had turned his apartment into an office with six or seven computers." Aside from the founder (a charming ex-investment banker) and his wife, everyone else involved was an intern, as Henry soon discovered. There were three or four others who worked the same shift as Henry, two days a week for about four hours each day—but he understood that there were numerous others in at different times. All he knew was that the founder "was supposedly constructing a massive resource base about various kinds of technologies": there was no business to get to know, not even a hint of training, and no clarity about what was going on.

"I definitely didn't think it was what it was," Henry told me. Under the impression that he would be conducting research using his foreign language skills, Henry was instead tasked with "recruiting and interviewing interns in France, Brazil, Italy, Germany, having conversations on Instant Messenger in all these languages, recruiting interns and interviewing them ... and talking to institutions, asking them to recruit." Henry slowly came to understand that Universal HyperAnalysis "was amassing an international army of interns around the world" for the purpose, mostly, of recruiting still more interns and promoting ad nauseam the career of Universal HyperAnalysis's founder.

Only a tiny stipend was on offer: Henry ultimately received $500 for nearly 200 hours of work. Despite his misgivings, Henry found the work easy enough and reasoned that he was at least getting some kind of experience under his belt. The opening of a dedicated office, the founder constantly promised, was just around the corner, and he told Henry that by next year Universal HyperAnalysis would even have an international office and offer him a dream job there. (Universal HyperAnalysis still appears to be run from the founder's home.) Based on these hopes, Henry thought he might stay on for the summer after graduation, with Universal HyperAnalysis promising to pay him $3,000 for the summer, enough to survive on, if he moved to full-time.

Just as he was about to sign on the dotted line, the founder mentioned that the $3,000 stipend would come only at the end of the summer—directly contrary to what Henry remembered him saying before. Henry realized that he would have no way to support himself: "I said, 'Wait a second. How am I supposed to live and pay rent?' That didn't make any sense to me ... but basically [his] answer was, 'You just need to convince your parents to support you and then you'll pay them back. And if you need any help with that, I can help you figure out how to convince them.'"

"That was the moment when I felt that he was taking advantage of me," Henry told me, "because he thought that I was a little rich kid with rich parents." I've heard this many times from former interns: a moment comes when the scales fall from your eyes. It might be nothing more than a boss's turn of phrase or a shift in tone. You realize that you've been had—that you're cheap labor and nothing more, a schnook, a kid entitled to favors but not rights.

Henry wanted nothing to do with Universal HyperAnalysis after that, but he still hadn't even received the $500 stipend for his work during the school year—it wouldn't arrive until two more months had passed, with Henry putting pressure on all the way. And there was more: "[The founder] sends me this seven-page email, seven pages printed out ... berating me, telling me how awful I was, what a horrible job I did, how when I came in I was tired, I was not motivated, I took too many breaks, my lunches were too long—everything you could think of to criticize. And not one bit of praise. But for seven months this guy was patting me on the back, telling me he's got my dream job, and he wants me to work the summer. There's no feedback, there's no teaching me anything, no nothing." Now even getting a good reference was out of the question.

A number of interns I interviewed were exploited in ways that resembled Henry's experience—often in home offices, often with nobody telling them to be skeptical and alert about such "opportunities"—but he was particularly radicalized by the experience. "I just realized this whole internship thing is precisely what I knew it was: bullshit. The more I was thinking about it, I realized this guy is just starting a business using only interns; he didn't employ anybody; and he wanted people's rich parents to support them until he could pay them." Henry describes himself as the kind of guy who would brave call centers to straighten out a minor mistake on a heating bill. Yet his standards for the internship were pitched so low to begin with—he hadn't complained about pay, training, office conditions, or anything else—that it was only the personal stuff that finally got to him.

The biggest irony of all, Henry told me, came later, when he landed an actual dream job overseas—no thanks to the internship at Universal HyperAnalysis, which he doesn't list on his résumé. The job came with the help of a man whose son Henry had gotten to know while working at the summer camp he'd gone to as a kid. To hear Henry tell it, *that* had been a classic American summer: he earned a respectable salary, enjoyed free room and board, and took trips into the mountains. "That's how life should be!" Henry said to me. "Do what you want, and when you're doing something that you like and you're good at, you're at your best. People will meet you and they'll like you, and they'll make suggestions to you and they'll introduce you to their contacts. It shouldn't be: 'Oh my god, I have to have this internship, no matter how much coffee I have to get.' "

At least "Linda," an international student in California, went into her illegal internship with eyes wide open. During a college summer, she worked as an unpaid intern for a major publishing company, fulfilling mind-numbing but critical mailing duties. "They should have paid me but they didn't," Linda told me. The other interns that Linda met at the Wiley & Sons office *were* paid for what Linda called "the same nonwork"—but because Linda was not legally entitled to work in the U.S., Wiley & Sons could use her for free and slap the label "internship" on it.[8]

But she and the company were using each other, Linda assured me— "it was pretty casual." They quickly decided that the whole thing would be very quiet and under the table. "Free labor" was Linda's answer when I asked her why an established company would take such a risk. The position of interns is so vague and unregulated that her supervisors at the company must have thought no one would be the wiser, and they were right. For her own part, Linda, then a sophomore, described her thought process as "Oh, shit, I need to do something over the summer that looks mildly respectable because I'm graduating in two years." The previous summer had been ideal, spent on an archaeological dig in Sicily, but she took a clear-eyed approach to this one: "I needed something a little more 'meaty' on my résumé."

Wiley & Sons famously publishes the sprawling series of For Dummies books, "the reference for the rest of us." Their triangle-headed mascot (presumably the ultimate dummy) is a clip art classic. He stares out with googly eyes from the covers of those black and yellow paperback how-to guides on every topic imaginable (including *Internships for Dummies*). "There was no training," Linda said of her first day on the job. "They walked me around the office, introduced me to everyone ... showed me where the coffee was, and then started having me do the mailings. And then at four o'clock they told me I could go home."

This pattern was repeated thirty-five hours a week for the next seven weeks. The mailings meant "putting a lot of galleys in envelopes and mailing them out to journalists for review ... a ton of grunt work." She can't remember how many books she swaddled in padded envelopes that summer, nor the endless names of the small-town newspapers massed on her spreadsheets. Linda was able to live in her year-round campus housing and support herself by squeezing in research work for a professor. (Foreign students can legally receive pay if they work at the university where they're studying.) Naturally, Linda said, her interest in the publishing industry never recovered from such a dismal routine.

Unpaid internships represent a double injustice—according to legal experts, the lack of pay also means that these interns have no standing in court as employees, even if they have worked full-time for a year in the same office. Without standing, many interns can't claim the basic legal rights of the workplace. As David Yamada writes, "Student interns now exist in a legal void, falling between the cracks of legal protections for workers and legal protections for students." Cynthia Grant Bowman and MaryBeth Lipp describe the situation as "legal limbo" because the landmark civil rights legislation prohibiting age-, gender-, and race-based discrimination in schools and workplaces simply passes over unpaid interns. In the eyes of the law, unpaid interns are neither students nor employees; they are invisible.[9]

Take the case of Bridget O'Connor. A social work major at Marymount College in New York, Bridget—like an increasing number of college students and nearly all aspiring social workers—was required to complete an internship in order to graduate. Her internship at Rockland Psychiatric Center was unpaid, but she received federal work-study funding through Marymount. Within days of starting, a psychiatrist at the center was allegedly harassing her, tossing off lewd remarks and asking her, supposedly in jest, to remove her clothes before entering his office.

As if such an introduction to the world of work would not be disturbing enough, Bridget was apparently ignored when she complained to her supervisors at Rockland. Although a part-time intern because of her class schedule, Bridget was doing the work of a junior staffer—meeting with patients one-on-one, producing reports, attending meetings. Yet it seems that her complaints could be shunted aside: she was new, she was just an intern. When Bridget left Rockland soon after and moved to a different placement, she sued Dr. Davis, the psychologist in question, and Rockland Psychiatric Center, which had allegedly tolerated his behavior, under Title VII of the Civil Rights Act.

There's no question that she would have had a strong case, *if* the courts had considered her an employee, as to all intents and purposes she was. Title VII was expressly designed to prohibit workplace discrimination in cases like Bridget's as long as there is straightforward and well-substantiated evidence. Yet two courts, at both the district and appeals levels, summarily dismissed the case, holding that Bridget didn't count as an employee, and therefore had no right even to stand in the courtroom and make her case. The judgment turned on the fact Bridget wasn't paid by Rockland, which the district court called "the essential condition to the existence of an employer-employee relationship." Of the various and vague definitions for "employee" floating around the American common law tradition, the one pertaining to workplace discrimination cases happens to privilege pay above all.

In the upside-down world of internships, a responsible organization that compensates an intern—perhaps even with a modest stipend—may be subject to a lawsuit for employment discrimination or harassment, just as with any ordinary employee. On the other hand, as David Yamada writes, "An employer that fails to pay its interns in violation of the FLSA potentially gains an additional benefit by being able to parlay that violation into an argument that the lack of compensation also disqualifies an intern from claiming employee status under employment discrimination statutes." In other words, no wages, no benefits, no vacations, no overtime or sick pay—therefore also no rights in court.

As Bridget's case shows, an intern must first prove her status as an FLSA-protected employee, as a *somebody*, before a case will even be heard. With the minimum wage requirement of the FLSA in operation, Bridget would then count as a paid employee of Rockland. Only then would she receive Title VII protection against sexual harassment. On the other hand, as a student Bridget might have been entitled at least to seek redress under Title IX from her school, which was charged with sanctioning and monitoring the internship. Yet even indirect justice along these lines is in some doubt, as Bowman and Lipp show—although they write that courts may be more likely to hold schools liable rather than employers. Law professor Craig Ortner sees the key strategy as being a legal one, convincing courts that unpaid interns are compensated in the currency of opportunities and experience and that "it would be peculiar to deny an unpaid intern Title VII's protection when her internship may provide the key to long-term economic security."[10]

This injustice is far from being limited to a few cases—the failure to recognize interns as employees goes deep. Discrimination claims by unpaid interns and volunteers have emerged in California, Oregon, and Nebraska, all denied on the basis that the claimants had no standing. In *Lipphold v. Duggal Color Projects*, a New York State court dismissed out of hand a student's claims about a supervisor who "touched her breasts and buttocks, frequently rubbed his body against hers in the darkroom ... made sexual remarks to her ... put numerous raunchy nude photos on the walls of offices where she worked ... [and] refused to sign her time sheets and evaluations on time [because she had rebuffed his advances]." In *Lowery v. Klemm*, an attempt to protect a harassed intern by a Massachusetts appellate court was overturned by the state's Supreme Judicial Court, as James LaRocca has documented.[11] Interns continue to lack the proper legal remedies for discrimination on the basis of race, color, national origin, religion, age, and disability.

In another such case in 2008, a New Jersey student, interning at the Center for Integrative Body Therapies in D.C., charged a chiropractor with making sexual advances and initiating unwanted physical contact. Notwithstanding the merits of the student's suit, a judge on D.C.'s federal court ruled predictably that the intern had no standing in court, noting that the local anti-discrimination law, the D.C. Human Rights Act (DCHRA), doesn't mention unpaid interns in its definition of an employee. Mary Cheh—a law professor at George Washington University, and now a member of Washington D.C.'s City Council—reacted with indignation. "We're the intern capital of the world," Cheh said of the city. "The recent trend of unpaid internships has become so common-place that there are hordes of our students working as unpaid interns. The idea that they're unprotected against abusive behavior is unacceptable." She introduced the Intern Anti-Discrimination Act of 2009 in the D.C. City Council, simply amending the DCHRA to include interns and thus entitling them to the same protection as other workers. Cheh added that "interns could even be seen as more vulnerable than regular employees because they're just starting out."

If Cheh's bill passes—and she thinks that it is too mild and reasonable not to—it will be a small step towards protecting interns in a city where they're crammed into offices without pay, mocked privately and not-so-privately, and swamped with menial tasks. Leaving larger questions unanswered, the bill would at least allow interns to file workplace dis-crimination suits within the single jurisdiction of the District of Columbia. For the time being, progress must be measured in tiny incre-ments like Cheh's proposal, the first of its kind. Rebecca Hamburg of the National Employment Law Association, a national network of plaintiff-side employee lawyers, says that "probably the best place to start is the local level," following Cheh's lead and quietly amending local anti-discrimination laws that may already be more complete than their federal equivalents.

This lack of protection in the workplace is particularly acute when it comes to sexual harassment—there is disturbing, but unsurprising evidence that interns are more likely to face harassment than regular employees, findings that emerged from group studies of female mass communications and medical interns. As noted earlier, more than three-quarters of all unpaid interns may be young women. Bowman and Lipp outline in detail the latter's own undergraduate internship in broadcast journalism, a depressingly common scenario in which she "provided cheap, exploitable labor" and was made to feel "vulnerable, fearful, disrespected, alone, and powerless, especially when the harassment began during my first weeks at the station."

Lipp's internship was a college requirement, and she paid for the requisite credits. "An explicit preoccupation with sex and sexuality permeated the newsroom," reports Lipp, but the many offensive comments she faced were "pale in comparison to the numerous times employees stared at my body, brushed against my breast, and 'accidentally' bumped into my body." Bowman and Lipp conclude that gender harassment may even become "a means to degrade or ostracize female student interns … to discourage women from entering male-dominated fields" and that "a student intern is in a position of immense vulnerability and powerlessness vis-à-vis her supervisors, mentors, and co-workers in an external placement." From unreported incidents to local scandals and national news reports on Monica Lewinsky, Chandra Levy, or David Letterman's intern flings, the sexual power dynamic faced by interns is a depressingly familiar consequence of the internship boom. This is the part you didn't know: when something does happen, unpaid interns are largely on their own, without protection or recourse, caught in a frightening legal limbo.

CHAPTER FIVE

Cheerleaders on Campus

This country was built by unpaid interns. And in exchange, I assume they got college credit.

—Stephen Colbert

Along with the decisive intervention of the FLSA, it was the rise of mandatory schooling and the outcry of educators that ultimately overcame exploitative child labor in the U.S. That makes it all the more surprising—and all the more disturbing—that schools are now lending their moral and intellectual authority to illegal and unethical labor arrangements involving their own students. We've already seen how dozens of schools provide a dubious academic cover for Disney's menial, minimum-wage internships, but the systematic complicity of the Academy goes much deeper. An overwhelming majority of colleges and universities, as well as some high schools, endorse and promote unpaid internships without a second thought, provide the lucrative academic credit that employers wishfully hope will indemnify their firms, and justify it all with high-minded rhetoric about "situated learning" and "experiential education." Meanwhile, the internship frenzy among students and their families resembles nothing so much as the escalating competition surrounding undergraduate and graduate admissions—for which internship credentials are often considered a valuable asset.

Somehow a convenient myth has been making the rounds that interns earning academic credit fall outside the FLSA. A significant percentage of employers using unpaid interns now hide behind this urban legend, requiring their interns to be enrolled in college and to submit proof of the credit received for an internship. "To shift liability back on to the university, if something were to happen, is ultimately their goal," one career counselor told me. Employers claiming to offer academic credit instead of pay, as if it were some generous boon to the intern, are being cynical and disingenuous. As the director of career services at UCLA told *The Chronicle of Higher Education*, "What [employers are] saying is holding the institution hostage ... It's really not their call whether their experience is creditworthy."[1] If an internship *is* properly structured, such that a faculty member would gladly serve as an advisor on the academic end, then that employer has simply met the minimum conditions necessary to not pay their interns. Nor are glowing promises of skills training and mentoring are enough—what counts in terms of legality is the day-to-day reality, not the way a position is marketed.

"A student still has the right to sue under the FLSA even if academic credit is being awarded," writes employment lawyer Donald T. O'Connor. (O'Connor and other lawyers also dismiss the myth that unpaid interns can sign away their right to payment in a contract—they cannot.)[2] Deanne Amaden, a spokeswoman for the U.S. Department of Labor, has confirmed in no uncertain terms that credit is no panacea: "Academic credit alone does not guarantee that the employer is in compliance with the six criteria of the Fair Labor Standards Act."

A 2010 fact sheet from the Wage and Hour Division clarifies how academic credit is taken into account: "In general, the more an internship program is structured around a classroom or academic experience as opposed to the employer's actual operations, the more likely the internship will be viewed as an extension of the individual's educational experience (this often occurs where a college or university exercises oversight over the internship program and provides educational credit)." In other words, credit is seen as useful evidence, among other forms of evidence, that militates in favor of an intern being considered a trainee who need not be paid—but credit is far from being the single, decisive factor. Yet many employers still buy into the myth that academic credit provides a blanket legal and ethical sanction for their all-work, no-pay internships, while the real test remains centered on the six overlooked Supreme Court criteria.

The upshot is that illegal internships have become even more unfair and burdensome, as employers require not only that their charges work for free, but that they also obtain credit, which usually means paying to work. Colleges and universities have allowed the academic credit myth to spread in part because these credits, closely linked to tuition, now form a significant revenue stream at many institutions. "It's a dirty little secret" that internships represent "a very cheap way to provide credits … cynically, a budget balance" for universities, says Gina Neff, a professor at the University of Washington who has studied communications internships. Phil Gardner at Michigan State agrees: "There's much more money coming from these internship credits than [there is] going into sustained internship programs for these people." Neff mentions the example of a small PR firm where many of her students have worked: "I read the reports of what students do at this firm and it makes me cry. Here the students are paying good money—paying for four or five credits a quarter to work for this group—and they're being told to stuff envelopes or pass out flyers on the street. It's lawbreaking—it's not what an internship's supposed to be—and unfortunately there are a lot of those out there."

For graduates and older people seeking internships, the requirement of college credit for many positions is a bitter complaint for a separate reason: arguably, it represents discrimination on the basis of one's matriculation status. "A lot of the job lists that go around are all unpaid internships and offer the college credit option," one unpaid intern told me. "Paying to work for free highlights how twisted the labor market has become, but since I'm not in college anymore, I can't even apply for most internships."

In certain cases, paying college tuition to work for free can be justified —particularly if the school plays a central role in securing the internship and makes it a serious, substantive academic experience. Providing credit certainly can cost the school in terms of supervision time and administrative work, although the costs are unlikely to match those of a classroom experience. And in the most miserable, increasingly common scenario, employers use the credits in an attempt to legitimize illegal internships while universities charge for them and provide little in return, and interns are simply stuck running after them, paying thousands of dollars for the privilege of working for free. "It's insane," says David Gregory, a law professor who has written on illegal internships, adding that the widespread abuse of academic credit has barely registered so far as an issue up in the ivory tower. Gregory has written that "schools are not merely complicit in this exploitation; they often affirmatively urge students to take the path of the unpaid internship for dubious academic credit."[3]

Take Michael Feldman, who paid NYU $1,600 to take an unpaid internship on *The Daily Show* that required academic credit. A recent graduate, Feldman made a deal with the university that, in return for his payment, they would issue the minimum credit he needed to take on the internship. Ali Wiezbowski, a communications major at the University of Pennsylvania, had to shell out $2,800 to the university for a one-credit online "Communication Internship Seminar"—a thin educational veneer required by her internship at NBC Universal. Such examples are multiplying. Employers get free labor, thinking that they can hide their practices behind a registrar's stamp, and schools earn a nice chunk of change. Everybody wins except interns and their families, and those who can't afford to play the game. And it is well established that most students pay for the credit themselves (71 percent, according to an Intern Bridge report).

Schools should at least evaluate the legality of an internship—with particular scrutiny for unpaid situations—before publicizing it to their students and thus lending it their stamp of approval. Instead, employing staff whose role is typically to boost internships at all costs, universities are falling all over themselves to outsource their students' education and lend credibility to illegal employment practices. In a survey of 713 colleges, 95 percent reported that they allow unpaid internships to be posted on college campuses and websites, though a few added that they exclude unpaid positions at for-profit companies. In the same survey, only 27.6 percent of the colleges required classroom experience in granting academic credit for an internship. Even if there is no conspiracy to boost school revenues by channeling more students into for-credit internships, the conflict of interest is straightforward: colleges seek to perpetuate and control a system that benefits them.[4]

Henry, Linda, and countless other interns have trusted their schools to connect them to legitimate, educational internships, finding their positions through their college career centers. These offices—many of them employing full-time internship advisors and claiming to offer exhaustive resources—are far too often silent on questions of legality. Career offices provide little considered counsel to students about avoiding unpaid gofer work that masquerades as a career opportunity or a learning experience. For all the breathless advice on the career services websites of colleges and universities—"Create your own internship!" "Enhance your marketability!"—the issue of pay is usually treated obliquely, the law relating to internships rarely mentioned. At best, career offices are taking an agnostic approach to illegal internships, letting students decide for themselves; at worst, they are failing to prevent and even facilitating their own students' exploitation, publicizing and supporting illegal employer bids for cheap labor.

Claiming that they lack the capacity, most career centers make no attempt to weed out illegal opportunities peddled on their websites or at their internship fairs—this reluctance seems to be particularly acute if the employer is locally or nationally respected, or maintains a cozy relationship with schools à la Disney. Yet given the statements made by the Department of Labor, how can colleges continue to post unpaid, for-profit internships without questioning them? Lately, there is a better chance that a posting for an illegal, exploitative internship will be flagged on Craiglist than on most university websites.

In fairness to Career Services personnel, many students clamor for the credits when prized internships are at stake and the bill is going straight to their parents, to whom it is often indistinguishable from tuition fees for classes. When credit is refused for whatever reason (by an individual professor or department, or because of university policy), career counselors are caught between demanding employers and interns, and they scramble to make accommodations. "We do workarounds where we help them connect with a community college to get work-study credit," one university career counselor told me. Some have recognized the cost to students of paying for regular academic credits while they work for free—and are trying to craft sensible, affordable solutions. More and more career offices now issue vague letters of support for an intern to show their employer, offer the option of an official "internship transcript notation" (for a fee, usually) or produce special "internship certificates," while still others have crafted a magical "zero-credit" option. In such cases, no actual credits representing substantive education actually change hands. Although thoughtful, and increasingly popular, these strange fixes get further and further from the point, and still don't absolve employers of their legal (not to mention ethical) responsibilities.

Of course, professors sometimes intervene with their own academic and intellectual standards—many principled economists are unwilling to vouch for a shady viral marketing internship as a form of training in economics—and very occasionally the school-based component of an internship can be as rigorous and valuable as any class. Smaller and lesser-known colleges, desperate to prove the value of their degrees, are more likely to bend academic standards to meet employer requests. Elite universities often jealously guard the value of their credit, withholding it from internships just as from other academic programs they deem unworthy.

The occasional principled stance throws common practice into even starker relief. James Hughes, an economics professor at Bates College, told the *Chronicle of Higher Education* that his department has rejected dozens of requests from students, parents, and employers to supply credits for unpaid internships, mainly in finance. "We're quite adamant about our refusal to play along," says Hughes. "Why is it that we have to evaluate this experience, just so some multibillion-dollar bank can avoid paying $7.50 an hour?"[5]

Education at its most confused and commodified, the ivory tower weighed up and sold by the pound—this is the state of academic credit at many institutions. Anya Kamenetz calls it "a unique currency that is presumed to confer culture, reason, respect ... that you can't get any other way." Yet there seems to exist little moral compass in the Academy surrounding the value of work and no healthy skepticism about the unfairness and illegality of so many of the internships into which schools are ceaselessly feeding their students. In response to a roiling debate over unpaid internships, no business lobbyists were seen trying to pre-empt normal enforcement of the law—instead it was a group of thirteen university presidents who recently wrote to the Department of Labor, complaining that protecting interns might get in the way of their brisk trade in academic credit and their cozy employer relationships. "While we share your concerns about the potential for exploitation, our institutions take great pains to ensure students are placed in secure and productive environments that further their education," the presidents wrote, failing to mention their unwillingness or inability to screen out illegal placements. "We constantly monitor and reassess placements based on student feedback. We urge great caution … and we respectfully request that the Department of Labor reconsider undertaking the regulation of internships."

F inancial motives aside, why have schools lent such uncritical, decisive support to the internship boom—sometimes going so far as to require them? With the spread of career centers and career fairs over the past few decades, students "are explicitly being told you need to do an internship in order to be marketable after graduation," says Gina Neff, "but they're not given any context of what that means." The view is echoed precisely by Gardner: "They've gotten the message that it's got to be on your résumé. It's one of the checklist things you have to do, and a lot of them do it without any understanding of what they're really supposed to get out of it."

At many schools and in many departments, the nudge has becomes a shove—students are required to take internships in order to graduate or to major in a particular field. In more applied fields and professional programs, this requirement, imposed regardless of whether or not the school helps to secure the positions, keeps the supply of available interns artificially massive. Neff did a survey of communications programs and found that "a pretty high number" now require that students complete an internship, "particularly if they're in a journalism program" (even though program graduates will usually have to begin their journalism careers with an *additional* internship). In social work, nutrition, and psychology programs, influenced by the medical model, required internships are pervasive; likewise in public policy, criminal justice, marketing, advertising, management, business, human resources, culinary studies, hospitality, film, fashion, and other majors. "People within the academy don't really think about their role in an economy of internships," says Neff.

Universities apparently relish the additional influence that has come with brokering students' future careers. If professors at elite colleges were once able to informally place many of their well-heeled students in jobs, the development of internship programs promised a more scalable and practical solution in an era of heightened competition in the job market. Anya Kamenetz, who has written on both internships and the history of higher education, links internships to the "maximalism," symbolized by Clark Kerr's concept of the "multiversity," which took hold at American colleges in the 1960s. Kamenetz points to the spread of campus fitness centers, mental health counseling services, and scads of campus cultural organizations as parallel developments in which colleges have become involved "because they're vaguely in the bailiwick of your college experience." Perhaps well-intentioned, schools now push their students towards study abroad opportunities, civic engagement, "service learning," and a whole suite of other extracurricular options that ostensibly develop character and burnish a résumé—nevertheless, says Phil Gardner, "the internship has to happen and all these other things now are going to be precursors."

Although for-credit internships in many cases are a financial win for schools, some schools have also found donors to subsidize a range of scholarships, in effect helping to underwrite the internship boom by supporting unpaid positions, especially but not only at nonprofits and in the public sector. Neff says that "the biggest way internships get subsidized is through parents," but an increasingly significant flow of subsidies is coming from colleges as well. Carolyn Wise, editor of *The Vault Guide to Top Internships*, has stated that 48 percent of colleges she has looked at offer some form of financial assistance for at least some unpaid interns. In one of the most dramatic examples, Smith College launched the Praxis program in 1998, a promise to provide every sophomore or junior with a $2,000 summer internship subsidy. Connecticut College and Amherst College (which places many students with alumni and parents) have similar, heavily used programs. Most prestigious schools at least provide financial support to a few dozen interns each year, typically through highly competitive merit-based scholarships—examples include the Brown Internship Award Program and the Director's Internships at Harvard (which also arranges the high-profile placements). Such programs are as vulnerable to declines in the endowment or drop-offs in alumni giving as any others at a university: witness the planned slashes in the internship subsidies offered by the Rockefeller Center and the Tucker Foundation at Dartmouth.

The coverage provided by a Smith, Amherst, or Connecticut college is exceptional (though the actual amounts are relatively low), and administrators and students at most schools admit that subsidy programs rarely cover a fraction of the students who take unpaid internships. Kamenetz appraises the generosity of these schools in realistic terms: "The more money you spend per student, the more prestige you have [especially in collegiate rankings, which are based largely on proxies for such spending] ... Since the more money you spend the more prestige you get, it makes sense to annex any kind of program you can think of to spend money on." With reputation and alumni futures on the line, schools can't afford to let their competitors get ahead in the internship race. It isn't hard to guess where this leaves those at less well-heeled schools, or those trying to access internship opportunities outside of a school framework.

To a certain extent, and particularly in providing funding for unpaid internships, schools are simply reacting to the demands of their students, whose own role in driving the boom cannot be downplayed. High percentages of students claim that improving their job prospects is a fundamental motivation for attending college; the pressure on schools and professors to stay relevant to both social and economic realities has continued in various forms since the 1960s. Students have internalized the message that internships are the essential complement to class work, both a default summer mode and an important sideline during the academic year. If colleges, parents, and employers are pushing young people to invest in at least one significant internship, students are the ones "just collecting things," in Phil Gardner's words, piling on internship after internship in hopes of transcending ever-steeper competition.

Yet the intense competition in the job market has spread to internships themselves—for many organizations and industries, the key moment now comes at the junior or senior year internship, not after graduation: if you can break in earlier, your chances vastly improve. Getting an internship at a firm is certainly no guarantee of a job there later on, but the thinking is that *not* getting an internship may scuttle your chances permanently: at Goldman Sachs, 90 percent of entry-level hires in 2009 were reportedly former Goldman interns (that doesn't mean, of course, that 90 percent of Goldman interns received job offers).[6] Internship coordinators, especially in the "glamor industries" or at prestigious organizations, describe an ever-increasing deluge of applications: a prominent Washington think tank recently received 300 applications for five very low-paid internship slots ($1,000 per month, full-time); an international nonprofit based in Germany, though not a household name, typically receives between 100 and 400 applications for every low-stipended internship opening it has (400 Euros, or approximately $540, per month, full-time). When the director of newsroom recruitment for a small Virginia newspaper receives 300 applications for about a dozen internships offered, it should come as little surprise that internship programs at the White House, CNN, and so on accept fewer than 1 percent out of thousands of applicants.

Partly as a reaction to such stiff competition, and partly to break into organizations that might otherwise be closed to them, young people are increasingly creating their own internships—pitching their free labor to companies or bosses who are not advertising internships or planning to offer them. Employers of all shapes and sizes report receiving a stream of unsolicited emails and résumés from young people offering to work without pay. Such offers are sometimes too tempting to resist. Willy Franzen, who has reviewed hundreds of internships on his website One Day, One Internship, sees this "a lot more on the local level than on the national level"; the former has something resembling an "underground internship market" based on personal contacts. Franzen himself ended up working two summer internships for a company that makes fishing rods, marshaling a family connection and offering himself up as an intern "for the employee discount," even though the firm had no advertised internship positions or established program.

Likewise, a Connecticut College senior pitched himself as the perfect candidate for a nonexistent unpaid internship at the Buenos Aires office of Universal Music—which took him up on the offer. A *Wall Street Journal* article admiringly described the example of Stephanie Gurtman, who requested an informational interview with a Tampa, Florida advertising agency in the summer after her freshman year. Although the firm was not advertising or planning to have an internship, they were happy to have someone assembling their press kits and conducting market research for free. The author of the *Journal* article describes her triumph: "The internship was unpaid, but she walked away with three letters of recommendation that helped her land future internships." For many employers, the only limitation in accepting such offers is desk space.[7]

It is impossible to gauge, with the present lack of information, what percentage of internships are initiated by schools, by young people, or by employers—but each group has likely been a significant force, and internship positions or programs, once initiated, seem to take on a momentum of their own. The pressure for more internships—creating them, selling them, filling them, subsidizing them, legitimating them, even ranking them—is coming from all directions: from employers by turns opportunistic, rational, and afraid of being left behind; from a bottomless supply of harried, ambitious students; and from vociferous proponents in the Academy.

Internships are generally not top of the agenda for theoretical physicists and professors of comparative literature, but at least some in the Academy, perhaps unwittingly, have helped to prepare the cocktail of ideological motivations, justifications, and half-hearted excuses behind the internship boom. From new paradigms in educational theory and the sociology of work to "human capital" thinking in economics (which we'll leave for Chapter 7), high-minded concepts are offered as vindications of the Academy's role. If students and parents see internships simply as a good career move, no matter what's actually being taught or learned, educators have been more mealy-mouthed about it, using philosophies such as "situated learning" and "experiential education" to present internships in an appropriately educational light.

"Situated learning," which takes the cultural-historical psychology of Lev Vygotsky as its point of departure, "is premised on the view that knowledge is distributed across individuals and their environments, and is generated and mobilized in a constantly changing series of social interactions," as Natalie Lundsteen puts it in her research on the educational content of internships. The environments in which Vygotsky explored learning were primarily cultural and linguistic, but psychologists and educators have since extended his approach to organizational and corporate cultures. In this view, an intern (or indeed an apprentice or co-op student) is not a vessel to be filled with training or knowledge, but an active agent embedded in a particular context, whose learning is cultural and mediated above all else.

A wide array of academics, coaches, career counselors, and even employers have come to accept the importance of informal, "situated" learning—but to such an extent that many of them seem dismissive of formal training. Education expert Paul Hager writes that "advances in educational thought" effectively debunk the "learning-as-product" view at the root of traditional apprenticeship and classroom education, which can simply be chalked up to "a mass production mindset reminiscent of the industrial era."[8] The traditional master-apprentice relationship is revealed as childish and outmoded; the mentor-protégé relationship takes its place. A young person is sent to enter a "community of practice" and experience a personal transformation, rather than learn a distinct set of skills, earn a wage, and go home for the evening. Learning can be discontinuous, complex, frequently interrupted; unlearning may be just as important. This perspective helps explain why many educators have never seen an internship they didn't like—one supposedly learns as much from terrible experiences as from good ones: George Washington University states upfront that 50 percent of their students decide to leave the entire *field* in which they've just interned, not to mention individual employers. Most profound and perhaps most disturbing of all, almost anything that brings "exposure" can now be considered a learning experience—flipping burgers for Disney, having a chat at the water cooler, spending an afternoon at the copy machine.

Dovetailing closely with the theory of situative learning is the experiential education movement, traced by many of its American proponents to the writings of philosopher John Dewey. Experiential modes are now so prevalent at all levels of education and personal development that they have become almost impossible to detect, from elementary school fieldtrips to the Outward Bound program. Although associated with a progressive social and political outlook, opposed to hierarchies and engaging the inherent creativity of students, experiential education neglects the need for dedicated training and provides a convenient rationale for inexpensive, laissez-faire replacements.

Even if we sympathize with the open-minded worldview of situated learning and experiential education, we can deplore the broad misuse of these theories—they have proven to be an invitation to cost-cutting. They stand as crucial intellectual justification not only for internships, but for a whole range of practices associated with the "new spirit of capitalism" described in detail by Boltanski and Chiapello, in which networked firms leverage their "organizational capital" to move flexibly from project to project.[9] What structured training programs were to the bureaucratic firms of the mid-twentieth century internships may well be to the new network capitalism of firms dealing in intangible goods. There certainly seems to be a close match between the types of firms and industries that have transformed themselves or grown up along these lines and those that have embraced internships. One of the most common complaints about internships—"it was totally unstructured"—is little heeded.

Just as hierarchical, stepwise education has been discredited in favor of a series of immersive "experiences," steady career progress over a lifetime is dismissed in favor of lateral movement from project to project. How does a view like this impact career advancement and social mobility? The new rhetoric of "learning on the job," "learning as you go," "jumping right in," and "being a self-starter"—prevalent in the internship world— draws on these critiques of dedicated training, and opens the way to "just being there" being good enough. "People *do* learn as they do jobs," says Dan Jacoby, an expert on the history of apprenticeship who has researched different learning strategies. But, he adds, it is doubtful "whether they learn well or effectively" when it's all "on the job." "You can't put Task B in front of Task A if Task B requires that you know Task A ... It's not all that different from what takes place in math class. If you put somebody into a class doing calculus and they haven't really understood what algebra's about, they're going to have a difficult time figuring out what's going on."

No one would deny that schools have a responsibility to ready their students for work, just as much as for citizenship. Unfortunately, internships, so weakly connected to the classroom, represent only a sad feint in this direction. Indeed, present-day educators might look for inspiration to an earlier attempt to connect Industry and the Academy: cooperative education—a strikingly pre-professional approach to higher education in which college students divide their time between the classroom and a work setting. "Co-op," as it is familiarly called, was pioneered in 1906 by Herman Schneider, then dean of engineering at the University of Cincinnati. Schneider felt that a traditional university education hardly suited the demands of new technical fields and large industrial concerns—already the animating concern behind most reforms in American higher education over the previous four decades. The major new American universities of the late nineteenth century—private foundations like Johns Hopkins and Stanford as well as the land-grant colleges centered on "such branches of learning as are related to agriculture and the mechanic arts"—were already taking their cue from the industrial revolution. For Schneider, however, the introduction of practical and applied subjects was not nearly enough; he proposed the radical step of fully integrating classroom and workshop, Academy and Industry. At well-known, "true co-op schools"—such as Cincinnati, Northeastern, and Drexel, which now bills its co-op program as "the ultimate internship"—the combination of academic work and career preparation was elevated to a high art form.

Although internships are often compared to or classed alongside co-ops, there is no mistaking the differences. The co-op movement centered on a structured, intensive, high-cost model of collaboration between colleges and firms; the co-op philosophy of deep integration between school and work—such that classroom lectures on a given topic might be followed, almost immediately, by a chance to perform related tasks in the factory or office—has been diluted almost beyond recognition with internships. Compensation for the substantive work performed by students was always the norm, whether provided by the employer, the school, or some combination of the two. Most programs ultimately settled on five years as the typical length of enrollment, reasoning that students would trade the extra year in return for enhanced skills and job prospects—as much as half of a co-op student's time might be spent working in industry. The systems of faculty supervision and evaluation developed were much more standardized and rigorous than anything that has ever been the norm for internships: faculty at co-op schools were incentivized to evaluate directly their students' efforts in the workplace rather than just glance at or rubber-stamp a boss's report.

By the 1960s, the cooperative education model had become prominent and influential enough to attract Congress's interest and benefit from an era of unprecedented expansion in higher education. Over the next few decades, a total of over $220 million flowed from the federal government into the co-op programs of colleges around the country. An account published in the *Journal of Higher Education* in 1969 recorded at least 130 schools involved in co-op education nationally and over 60,000 students, earning a gross income of $120 million annually from over 4,000 employers—by 1983, the number of such programs at schools, feeding off this generous funding supply, had ballooned to over 1,000. In certain professions—engineering, most notably—co-op had very nearly become the dominant model, responsible for launching the careers of hundreds of thousands. That year also saw the founding of what is now called the World Association for Cooperative Education (WACE), which represents universities and businesses in forty-three different countries on every continent—the capstone of years of global evangelism by American co-op champions.[10]

Yet this entire system, once fired by a sizable body of research and embraced for a wide range of fields, very nearly collapsed with the withdrawal of federal funding in the early 1990s. Today it is a shell of its former self. Politicians evidently believed they had done enough for cooperative education, a mere line item for a Congress focused on bigger issues in higher education and given to capricious funding decisions. Another reason for the co-op collapse, some say, is the "vocational" stigma that it retained in the eyes of ambitious students and parents, and within the elite echelons of higher education, where co-op never penetrated. Co-op booster Richard Walter also admits that, although federal funding led to rapid development, "unfortunately, some [co-op programs] were shams created solely to secure funds rather than as a means of providing students with the advantages gained through well-run programs."

Phil Gardner watched events unfold at close hand: "A lot of co-op programs just collapsed or were converted to internship programs ... Now co-ops have many of the same characteristics as internships." Unable or unwilling to prop up their co-op programs without outside support, many schools turned to internships as a low-cost, au courant solution that shifted the responsibility and the financial burden onto the student. Where co-op offices arranged and actively managed placements, career offices instead provide vague internship tips and administer Myers-Briggs tests. "Now you can't get the genie back in the bottle," says Gardner of the transition made by many schools from co-ops to internships, where there is little attempt "to integrate an academically oriented classroom with its application outside the classroom." Although supported by schools in several integral ways, internships remain much more at arm's length than co-ops ever were, and Gardner sees the gradual decoupling of internships from schools as a significant, worrying trend for educators, not to mention interns and their families: "Too many students just do these on their own, nobody knows what they're getting out of them. They throw it on their résumé and then when you start talking to them about their skills, they can't define them. It's not been a routinized experience that actually positions them for the jobs they want."

Today, co-op programs have remained a force at relatively few schools —the University of Waterloo in Ontario, for one, still soldiers on with the world's largest program, enrolling 11,000 co-op students who work for over 3,000 employers, while Northeastern offers a five-year Bachelor's that includes eighteen months of experience with up to three employers. Yet even these living models, directly descended from Schneider's vision, have been eroded and transformed by the withdrawal of funding and faculty. The *Journal of Cooperative Education*, which Gardner has edited since the co-op collapse, changed its name to the *Journal of Cooperative Education and Internships*, seeking, in vain, to engage a new audience. Co-op programs nonetheless provided, and continue to provide, a powerful alternative to the no-holds-barred race for internships, for which they unwittingly set the stage. Properly construed and implemented, they might still represent a humane and cutting-edge answer, incubated in the Academy, to the question of how students become workers. But instead of championing such a model, schools take the easier and cheaper road of promoting unpaid, insubstantial work off-campus—appealing to their students' idealism by describing all these opportunities, almost anywhere outside the business world, as a way of "serving the community."

CHAPTER SIX

No Fee for Service

Responding to criticisms that he lacks the experience to lead the nation, Barack Obama announced today that he has begun participating in a presidential internship program. Every Monday and Tuesday from 10 to 6, Obama has been interning with President Jose Luis Rodriguez Zapatero of Spain, learning firsthand about everything that goes into running a country.

—*The Onion*, "Obama Undertakes Presidential Internship"

Over lunch in the Senate Cafeteria, in the bowels of the Dirksen Building on Capitol Hill, a former intern explains "the hierarchy." Interning in a Congressman's office "back in the district" is the lowest of the low, he says—if you're locked out of the charmed circle of the Beltway, it's a sure sign that you're going nowhere. Next come the offices of "random House members"—"if you're working for [high-ranking House Democrats] Chris Van Hollen or Steny Hoyer, that's a different story," the intern is quick to add. Working in a Senator's office nudges you a little higher up the ladder, but beware of getting lost in the shuffle: "Senate offices are quite large, so [some] will have thirty-plus interns. From what I understand, there's not enough work to go around and most of them end up just doing nothing, straight, for the whole summer." A step higher, he continues, is an internship on a House committee—but "the apex is the Senate committees," since "the thing about committee work for interns is that it tends to be much more substantive—not that you're guaranteed to get to do it, but you can."

He gives me a significant look and adds, "And that's just a small part of a larger internship hierarchy in D.C. Look, every young ambitious person in D.C. is prestige-conscious, so people want to get the best-sounding internship. The White House is the highest." For foreign policy wonks, he tells me, there's a separate, steep hierarchy of think tank internships; for education, public health, and so on, a fearsome hierarchy of competitive NGO internships.

Now the former intern can allow himself a guilty smile. Soon after graduating from a prestigious private university on the West Coast, he flew to D.C. to try his luck: "I was interested in working on the Hill, and I was told, as soon as I got here, that I had to have a Hill internship before being able to qualify for a Hill job." In part thanks to two previous summer D.C. internships at nonprofits, he quickly scored the requisite House office slot, a respectable base for climbing further up the hierarchy—in just three weeks, he was out of purgatory, leaping over thousands of hopefuls to an unmistakably glamorous internship on a Senate committee. "I did a lot of things that I should not have done as an intern," he told me proudly of this four-month stint. "I would help draft speeches [for senators] and I would write memos that would get sent out under someone else's name, but I would have written the whole thing. I wasn't really going to quibble about credit." And how did he live while doing the nation's business? "My parents supported me, which was not pleasant."

According to an estimate by Politico and the Washington Center for Internships and Academic Seminars, 20,000 interns descend on the capital each summer, approximately 6,000 of them filling Congressional slots—which would come out to over 100 interns for every member of Congress.[1] Many thousands more intern in D.C. during the academic year, or soon after graduating from college. In the offices of many members of Congress, think tanks, and nonprofits, interns now outnumber regular staff, at least during the summer. Anyone who has been to D.C. between June and August knows these interning thousands, swamping the college housing in Georgetown and Foggy Bottom, mobbing the bars south of Capitol Hill, brandishing their intern badges on the Metro. The overwhelming majority is unpaid. At the very heart of American life and public policy—where pious watchwords like democracy, meritocracy, and transparency are the stuff of constant sound bites—the ground floor is now a vast intern culture, driven by money, power, and connections.

Do you want to make money, or do you want to serve? This is the guilt-inducing dilemma presented to young Americans in countless college commencement speeches, by no one more forcefully than the current President. The mantra of public service, embracing equally the worlds of government and nonprofit work, holds out the promise of personal satisfaction and altruism during one's career in place of corporate millions. But how has service also come to require long unpaid stints of mundane or taxing work, which all but the children of the rich struggle to obtain and afford? It's now conventional wisdom that Washington D.C. would collapse under the weight of an intern general strike—if this is usually said somewhat in jest, it's nevertheless widely acknowledged that a significant portion of administrative and frontline work in the capital now falls to a class of unpaid twenty-somethings. "The extent to which organizations [in D.C.] rely on the work of interns is striking and horrifying at the same time," the former Capitol Hill intern said to me. "Some things just don't get done if there are no interns, the administrative end, the small-scale research tasks, the Capitol tours." As for nonprofits, they "are able to have large operations because they can have a lot of free labor doing the bottom-level stuff. In a world without interns, all of these groups would be able to do quite a bit less."

Adrienne Jamieson, a political science professor who has run the internship-focused Stanford-in-Washington program since 1994, concurs: "Interns keep a lot of it going, moving the merchandise—the mail, the phones, that kind of thing ... Somebody else would have to do it or it would just build up." Another government intern echoes the same theme, saying of D.C. offices more generally: "If they had to pay all these people, they wouldn't be able to keep their staffs nearly as large ... [Having unpaid interns] allows their upper-level staff to concentrate on policies and politics instead of administrative work." "Amanda," who interned for five months in the office of a prominent Congresswoman, said that the office where she worked "would survive for a day" without interns, but "if it was something long-term, it would be very difficult for the office to function."

A few summers ago, in an office of seven permanent staff members, Amanda was one of 35 interns sprawled on all available couches, everyone working away on their own laptops, barely supervised or trained. "Over the summer it was a pretty fierce battle for work, because there were so many interns and not enough work," says Amanda, but what substantive work there was went to the interns who had arrived earliest—everyone else was stuck stuffing envelopes, writing bland and formulaic constituent letters, and giving Capitol tours to constituent visitors: the bread and butter work of Hill interns. What little guidance there was came from other, more experienced interns and an intern handbook that was little consulted. Many interns flitted in and out of the office. Amanda noticed many who "would get in two or three internships in a summer," spending just a few weeks at each so they could list them all on their résumé.

Performing all this standard, administrative work without pay was a cohort of college students from top schools around the country, most of them originally hailing from the Congresswoman's district, "all vying for the same spot as senior intern." A clear majority of the interns, herself included, relied on parental support, says Amanda—"internships enable those who already have some enabling." Staying on for the fall was Amanda's masterstroke, allowing her to claim the "senior intern" mantle and thus also, she says, "the duties of intern coordinator: I ended up distributing a lot of the work." If this wasn't dubious enough already—an intern effectively running the internship program—Amanda was then promoted again, still without pay, to be the interim staff assistant while the full-time staffer was on leave for a month. "I'm writing speeches, doing memos, not just grunt work, but work that's very substantial ... I asked [for pay], but nothing came of it. It came to a dead end. Because I was doing so much work, I was really being swamped, in some ways I thought it was unfair."

Being in the right place at the right time and stepping into real responsibilities: this is often the intern dream, but it quickly turns sour. There is rarely much reason to believe that internships in the public sector or at nonprofits will convert directly to permanent employment—they seldom do—so the best one can hope for is to make an impression, be noticed, position yourself for something down the road. In November 1995, with

Congress unable to pass a budget and the federal government shut down, the White House began using its unpaid interns "to fill in the gaps left by senior staff who were forced to go home," according to Andrew Morton, Monica Lewinsky's biographer. "It was a highly unusual—indeed extraordinary—state of affairs, whereby a junior White House employee came to be closely involved with the movers and shakers of the nation, working from early morning until very late at night."[2]

This was the backdrop, now long since forgotten, against which the Lewinsky-Clinton affair unfolded: many claim that only during this kind of government impasse could an intern, eager to please and available when the regular staff could not work, have gotten close enough to the President to initiate a romantic relationship. It is remarkable how little has changed since that scandal erupted over a decade ago. The culture of internships in Washington remains exactly as it was, including the creepy sexual dynamics, and interns remain a completely pliable, unpaid workforce at the heart of national affairs.

Despite claims that the White House internship program is relatively meritocratic—an estimated 6,000 applicants apply for a few hundred positions each year—Lewinsky came to her internship as many do in D.C.: through connections. ("In one [Senate] office that I know pretty well," a Hill intern told me, "they had like thirty interns, and twenty-five of them were 'packed,' so to speak"—the children of donors, friends, and important constituents.) Lewinsky, adrift after earning a Bachelor's in Psychology, took her mother's advice and applied for a White House internship, with the help of family friend Walter Kaye, an insurance mogul and Democratic Party heavyweight (whose grandson had previously had a White House internship), with a good word also promised by a White House staff member, Jay Footlik, who frequented her mother's shop. After she was accepted, Lewinsky was able to live for free at her mother's apartment in the Watergate building.

At first assigned to the correspondence section of the Office of the Chief of Staff, Lewinsky was encouraged by her supervisor to stay on for a second internship. Former White House staffer Matthew Bennett says that internships under the Chief of Staff, as well as those in Oval Office Operations, "are the most sought-after jobs in the world of White House internships, and like all West Wing internships, they often are assigned to interns with some connection (political or otherwise) to high-ranking West Wing staff." More than a dozen White House offices, usually located in the adjacent executive office buildings, have their own intern cohorts. As Bennett explains to prospective applicants: "What you will do is answer the phones, make copies, and write letters. You will help well-connected tourists cut the long lines at the visitors' entrance. You will seal envelopes, update birthday card lists, and get the soda for the office from the White House mess. You will, in short, join your intern colleagues throughout Washington in doing a lot of administrative work."

When they're not tapped by nepotism, these unpaid factotums are among some of the brightest young people in the nation, and it is not unusual for them to have graduate degrees. The lucky ones, adds Bennett, "research policy issues, compile voting record information on members of Congress, or even go outside the White House to help prepare presidential events"—but they're just as likely to be running the autopen, the mechanical device that puts the President's signature on the endless stream of outgoing mail. In stark contrast to the example set by the internship program, the White House Fellowship Program is a small-scale, high-powered program for young leaders, who are paid and receive benefits; there is apparently no thought of embroiling the Fellows in uncompensated administrative work.

Announcing the 134 interns selected for the summer of 2010, Obama characterized them as "answering the call to service." To some White House staff, taking such privileged internships without pay is an expected sacrifice, allowing full-timers to spend almost all of their time in meetings, on the phone, and delegating with an authoritative air. If there is recognition that the interns must somehow have to pay for rent, meals, and other expenses, it is little expressed; as so often, the excuse is that the White House staff is capped by the budget, which simply does not include interns. In a typical White House office, twelve staffers might be supported by the work of four interns, replaced every few months. Too busy to train or mentor, full-time staff count on the Office of the First Lady to run the application process and organize a smattering of speaker events, service projects, and so on. Here, as on Capitol Hill, the internship program is pitched as a kind of outreach, a magnanimous opening of the People's House to young Americans. The reality is that the interns do real work and rarely have the run of the place; they are glorified volunteers, usually from comfortable backgrounds and well-known four-year colleges, who help the White House staff punch above its weight without actually employing people. At 1600 Pennsylvania Avenue as on Capitol Hill, job creation is preached, not practiced.

If internships are unquestioned in D.C., it is simply a sign of how deep they go, how much they're now part of the system's internal wiring—almost everyone who is anyone has had one. Says Eugene Alpert of the Washington Center, who has observed D.C. internships for three decades: "There's been a generational change ... Now most people who are supervising interns have been interns." Bill Clinton—who himself spent the summer of 1967 interning for Arkansas Senator J. William Fulbright—was hardly original in his intern romancing; according to a new memoir, his hero JFK had a fling with a nineteen-year-old intern in the early sixties, when the White House internship program was still in its infancy. These days, sinister liaisons between powerful politicos and interns are almost a yawn, a cliché, an eternal verity. Probably even more common, one intern told me, are relations between staff members and their interns, raising "an ongoing ethical question about abuse of office." Veteran political analyst Andrew Sullivan has succinctly described the routine: "I know one long-time Washingtonian who even referred to each influx of interns, jokingly, as 'the flesh.' And yet however predatory this impulse, it was often sadly reciprocated. The 'flesh' were grown-ups, not innocent children, but they still seemed like victims to me ... Like everyone else their age, they were still experimenting in how to be a grown-up—only they had the extra liability of experimenting in what amounts to an anonymous entrapment zone."[3]

The prevalence of unpaid internships in the public sector and in non-profit work is jaw-dropping hypocrisy, couched in the fine words of altruism and public duty. The same legislative bodies that pass minimum wage laws create or assume exemptions for themselves—as when Congress, in a single little-noticed sentence, specifically exempted its own thousands of interns from FLSA protection in the Congressional Accountability Act of 1995. Evincing the same hypocrisy, Republican Congressman Darrell Issa, responding to the supposed possibility of a crackdown on illegal internships in the private sector, challenged the legality of the White House not paying its interns—but of course, Issa himself employs interns without pay, like virtually every other member of Congress.

In the U.K., the widespread use of unpaid interns among Members of Parliament has become an intermittent scandal, although the abuses of Westminster pale in comparison to the D.C. intern circuit. Of the interns working in MP offices, under 1 percent received the U.K. minimum wage, and nearly half were not even reimbursed for expenses, according to the general workers' union Unite. The *New Statesman* estimated there were 450 revolving interns connected to Parliament, providing some 18,000 hours of free labor per week, saving MPs an estimated £5 million ($7.3 million) per year. Many of these interns "have got horses and Aston Martins," according to a self-professed "middle-class" intern who had to quit his position after running out of money nine months into his internship. One intern worked at a call center to support himself; others had to call in sick from time to time because they didn't have the money to commute to work. Most of the interns interviewed by Unite had been working for over three months and were doing the same work as regular staff; many were on their second or third internship.[4]

In the U.S., none of this would raise an eyebrow. According to the Partnership for Public Service, there are over 200 different internship programs in the federal government alone. Federal agencies are not required to publicly advertise their internships, as they must for regular job openings—a recipe for nepotism and cronyism. "Almost all the interns are chosen because someone knows someone. That's true in most places [in D.C.]," says a former intern, and later full-time employee, of the Department of the Treasury, who ultimately employed two interns of his own, recruited from his personal network. The positions don't pay, although he let one of them crash on his couch to be able to stay afloat financially. "There's so much demand for this kind of career path and such a limited supply, so we're able to dictate how to get into the process." One internship often leads no further than another—a D.C. serial intern told me how an unpaid internship at the House Foreign Affairs Committee helped him land an unpaid internship at the State Department: "There you submit a formal application through the normal internship channels, but it's one of those things where it helps if someone writes an email or calls to pull you out of the pile." His secret? "You got better, more substantive work based on the attitude with which you approached administrative work. If you sat around and complained about having to answer the phone … you didn't get great work." Nobody likes an assertive intern.

Another former Treasury intern told me that he had gotten in as "a favor—frankly, I wasn't qualified," given that "almost all of the interns at Treasury have a Master's or are getting their Master's." One of his fellow interns was a Harvard graduate in his thirties, who also had a Master's degree from a prestigious international relations program *and* previous work experience at the Pentagon—there is a perennial glut of over-qualified interns. In the recent economic doldrums, internships have become a favored kind of purgatory, whether it's someone with a gap year before grad school cobbling together a résumé or the victim of a deferred offer or a hiring freeze treading water. "The sad reality," the former Treasury intern told me, is that he felt "penalized" for wanting to enter public service, relying on his parents so that he could work for free, instead of simply being able to "feel good about … contributing to something" and support himself. "People rarely have jobs lined up as they graduate in D.C.," says one intern. "Everyone told me you have to come to D.C. first before you find a job," and the usual place to perch is an unpaid internship.

The extent to which the American political system now runs on the free labor of young people—what an apologist might call, at best, an avalanche of calculated voluntarism—has never been quantified or understood. Besides internships, one of the few other ways to break into politics is the campaign trail, but this too usually entails hard work without pay, at least initially. The Obama campaign, touted as ushering in a new paradigm of idealistic, participatory politics, in fact resembled nothing so much as a massive unpaid internship program. Even the transition team, active in the months between Obama's electoral victory and his inauguration, was essentially "a protracted internship process for a bunch of people who wanted to work in the administration," according to one source. In just one transition department, twenty-three "team members" worked without pay, supplemented by four unpaid interns doing "logistical-type work." "If you can have an official role, even if you're not getting paid, it's worth a lot more than anything else," said the same source, who received some 200 résumés through various channels during that period, mostly from people willing to come to D.C. and work for free. Following the Obama model, the stakes seem to be going up—many political candidates offering even a shred of idealistic rhetoric are now trying to run their campaigns with a full complement of full-time volunteers and interns.

The supposed spirit of voluntarism on display in these campaigns is undermined by a spoils system, which has made volunteer work and unpaid internships major pathways to full-time work in politics, or else at least to more internships. Virtually every level of government in every state and many counties, cities, and towns has embraced internships, across the entire political spectrum. About half of government internships pay, as Intern Bridge has found, but an invidious and unspoken double standard seems to have taken hold, with engineering majors receiving pay while social science majors are generally unpaid. What could justify this? Not to mention that any kind of job security, benefits, protections, or guarantee of reasonable working conditions—all of which have come to characterize so much of public sector employment— are completely absent for interns. Indeed, internships seem to appeal precisely because they represent the polar opposite of a "good government job."

Participants in the massive, decade-old Federal Career Intern Program (FCIP), aimed at fast-tracking graduate students into civil service employment, are paid a decent wage, but are effectively "on probation for two years," says Mark Roth, general counsel for the American Federation of Government Employees, and their positions "can be terminated at will with no appeal rights." Colleen Kelley of the National Treasury Employees Union alleges that FCIP has grown in certain areas from a "special-focus hiring authority to provide structured, two-year developmental internships" into "the principal, and in some cases only, means of hiring." Those who graduate from the internship program have a serious in, being eligible for noncompetitive hiring for advanced entry-level and mid-level positions—that is, agencies can hire them directly, without publicly advertising the positions first.

Created by an executive order from President Clinton during his last months in office, FCIP was initially described as "another step in the Administration's effort to recruit the highest caliber people to the Federal Government, develop their professional abilities, and retain them in Federal departments and agencies." Individual federal agencies decide whether or not to establish programs under this broad FCIP mandate and how to implement them: there are internship programs now for Border Patrol agents, labor economists, and everything in between. Managers have considerably more discretion, and can act more quickly, when hiring from these pools of interns—this is said to explain the program's rapid growth from 411 hires in fiscal year 2000 to 26,709 interns in fiscal year 2009, meaning that the program now accounts for over 8 percent of all federal hires. Although distinct in some respects from the shorter-term internships covered in most of this book, FCIP likewise represents a powerful but precarious new channel for entering a certain workforce, with effects as yet little examined and little understood. In response to claims that the program discriminates against military veterans, however, President Obama recently announced that he will be ending the program.[5]

A different kind of in is provided by the Washington Center, an educational nonprofit that functions almost as an "internship university" in Washington D.C., charging hefty tuition to place over 1,500 students in internships each year, mostly unpaid. "The federal government essentially, in many cases, outsources their entire, or a portion of their, internship programs to us," says Jennifer Clinton, the COO and VP of Federal Relations. "Think about their staffing limitations, their ability to get out on campuses—they're facing a reality of Baby Boomers retiring in the next five years, and so they're really looking at internship programs as a human capital pipeline solution." The outsourcing of entire internship programs is "a growing model," adds Clinton, where the employers pay a set fee per student to the Washington Center and in many cases an additional stipend to the student. The Department of Transportation, for example, signed a five-year contract allowing the Washington Center to fill its summer internship program—and the departments of Defense, the Interior and the Treasury, as well as the Environmental Protection Agency and the National Archives have all outsourced at least a portion of their internship hiring.

"Internships in this city, partly because they are unpaid, were and to some extent are for an elite cohort of students," says Clinton. The Washington Center argues that its role is to make the distribution of internships more "democratic." Instead of needing personal connections, you can rely on those of the Center, for $9,000–11,000 per semester (including housing). Founded in 1975—just as the internship boom was getting underway in D.C.—today the Center boasts 43,000 alumni, many of them still in politics; over 400 affiliated colleges and universities, which steer their students towards the Center; seventy-five full-time employees in an ornate former embassy building just off Dupont Circle; and an annual budget of $18 million, much of it from government and corporate sources. Not bad for what was once a small operation called "University Year for Action," which sponsored off-campus programs for students at UMass-Amherst.

In contrast to for-profit companies selling internship services (covered in Chapter 8), the Washington Center still operates in certain ways as an academic institution, maintaining academic standards and building its college affiliations—between fifteen and twenty new schools are added each year, often with high-level buy-in from university administrators and "campus liaisons." With some exceptions, the program requires students to earn academic credit from their home institutions, hires adjunct faculty to teach an impressive range of courses (such as "International Human Rights" and "Ethics and the U.S. Congress"), and emphasizes concrete proof of learning. Internship placements, secured for students by the Center, typically involve thirty to thirty-five hours of work each week; meanwhile, students take one elective course, one night each week, and participate in a wide range of other organized activities around D.C. Leased housing is provided in northern Virginia and Maryland, and a $38 million "internship campus" near Capitol Hill has just been completed.

Some 60 percent of the students who come to the Washington Center are enrolled at public institutions; as President Michael Smith admits, internship tuition is "frequently twice as much, or almost twice as much" as what they usually pay. Remarkably, Smith and his colleagues have successfully lobbied sixteen state legislatures to pass appropriations bills, setting up scholarships for students at state schools to enroll at the Washington Center. "For instance," says Smith, "Massachusetts might appropriate $350,000 for scholarships for students from not only UMass-Amherst, Lowell, Boston, Dartmouth, but the comprehensive universities: Westfield State, Salem State … And that allows seventy-five students to get a partial scholarship [usually $2,000–5,000] to attend our program. It mitigates the extra cost of being in Washington." Thanks to public funding from states, the Center went from having three students from Florida to eighty-one in a single year, for example; in Ohio, the jump was from 37 to 102. These internships are directly funded with taxpayer dollars.

Programs such as the Washington Center—other examples include the Washington Internship Institute, the National Internship Program, the Washington Semester at American University, and the Institute on Business and Government Affairs ("a pro-business lobbying internship and academic program")—accept students from any school, and sometimes nonstudents too. As well-established middlemen on the ground, deploying their connections on behalf of program participants, they have done an immense amount to shape the D.C. internship explosion, channeling both the supply of positions and the supply of interns.

At the same time, dozens upon dozens of schools have set up their own Beltway operations in the last few decades, largely to position their students for the internship feeding frenzy. Among the most prominent are programs run by Cornell, Claremont McKenna, the University of California system, Syracuse, Boston University, Harvard Law School and Stanford, but there are many more. Between these university beachheads, the massive nonprofit internship centers, and personal connections, young people on their own stand little chance of landing a well-placed internship in D.C., if they can even afford it to begin with—given an estimated cost of living around $1,500 per month—on a responsible student's budget. Adrienne Jamieson, the director of Stanford's program, admits that relationships are crucial to landing the prestigious placements she is able to secure for the twenty-six or twenty-seven Stanford students enrolled in the program at any given time. Asked whether an ordinary person could snag these internships on their own, she replied: "In some cases, yes; in some cases, no."

"There certainly is more competition" for internship placements, says Jamieson, noting that she hears all the time from "[university] presidents, provosts, faculty members, alumni" of different schools who are interested in opening their own D.C. programs. "Maybe there will be a saturation point." Although Jamieson notes that the Stanford program's goals are "purely academic" and that the interns are more like "participant-observers" or "anthropologists" than junior employees, it's clear that many of the students view things much more pragmatically: they are actively positioning themselves for Beltway careers. Recent alumni of the program have run for Congress, served as general counsel for the Vice President, and handled House and Senate relations in the West Wing.

Jamieson freely admits that visiting all of her students' internship sites would be impractical, perhaps even inappropriate. Instead, she relies on getting to know the students individually outside of their work, in the sizable red-brick apartment building where the Stanford interns all live and eat together. At their placements (mostly full-time, unpaid), Jamieson considers it "fair for interns to do administrative stuff and organizational stuff ... as long as they get what they need to get out of it too." Those who have been able to push beyond the administrative work have drafted policy at the Health and Human Services Department, tracked down voting abuses for the Civil Rights Division, and taken a significant role at the World Bank in making cell phone–based financial services available in developing countries. They've enacted in miniature the whole point of internships: come in under the radar, on the cheap, just a bright kid, and then suddenly prove yourself, become somebody worth having.

Well beyond the citadels of power in Washington, a vast economy of unpaid interns supports nonprofit organizations of every description around the world, from United Nations offices to avant-garde theaters and Bible Belt religious groups (there is a "Book of Mormon internship"). In D.C. itself, where many congressional, White House, and federal agency internships were well established by the 1960s and 1970s, significant recent growth has been at think tanks, advocacy groups, professional organizations, employer associations and the like. In one sign of the times, author Jeff Sharlet, who has written extensively on right-wing Christian politics, interviewed a young evangelical woman, lured by the prospect of a D.C. internship, who ended up as an unpaid domestic servant for a group of conservative Christian lawmakers. Sharlet reports that the woman found herself doing things like "turning down sheets for [Senator] John Ensign," with "people like Oliver North hanging around and she was expected to be at their beck and call."[6] The site of her internship, the C Street Center, is a townhouse residence for prominent evangelical Congressmen, which has dubiously claimed tax exemption as a church; it became notorious in connection with a string of marital infidelity scandals and because of its ties to the Fellowship, a powerful and secretive force for Christian policy-making.

Especially common both inside the Beltway and at nonprofits around the country are serial interns—those who take on three or more internships within just a few years—in part because winning a high-prestige internship now often depends on having completed other internships, and in part because so few of these positions convert to paid, permanent jobs. Young people responding to the call of service also seem to spend longer, whether by choice or not, trying to find their niche in these relatively new and highly competitive fields.

Take the story of "Andy," who has interned at three nonprofits—at twenty-five, he seems seriously burnt out. Some twenty months of his life have passed in unpaid work—each time again taking the measure of his surroundings, learning all of his colleagues' names, establishing a set routine. To do all this three times, in three offices, has been exhausting. In casual conversation, he wouldn't use the word "intern" of his own accord —he was *working*. After all the small lessons that Andy learned from logging hours near the desks of professionals and stealthily observing how they do things, he's tired of getting everything by osmosis.

As it turns out, Andy's internships have mostly served to eliminate options, allowing him to contemplate possible futures up close before discarding them: nonprofit fundraiser, policy wonk, community activist. "When I think about my life at the Asia Society, I feel like I was a fake grown-up," Andy says of his full-time, seven-month internship at the prestigious New York nonprofit, for which he took a leave of absence from college. "If you just took down the details of my life, you'd think, 'Oh, this is a grown-up.' Until you got to the part that he's not being paid, and his rent is paid by his parents. Then you'd say, 'Oh, this is a kid.' It was cool initially, and then it was embarrassing." Andy cheerfully sublimated his interest in Chinese politics into a nine-to-five, entering data into spreadsheets and processing membership requests. "A job with real expectations and real tasks," however dull and administrative, is how Andy describes it, and at least at the time this sense of doing serious work made the lack of pay easier to bear.

Within six months of finishing at the Asia Society, Andy landed another internship, one of the most prestigious in its field, coveted by International Relations majors and politics junkies at elite universities everywhere: an unpaid summer at the Council on Foreign Relations, tracking foreign policy issues in the 2004 election. "The Council had this glow around it," Andy remembers. "They know that people flock to them. There's really no reason why they can't pay us minimum wage, but they just don't." At the same time, the air of entitlement and self-satisfaction was thick: "There was an understanding that you were among the few privileged people who get to work here for no pay"—"for all of us, there was a phone call that got our application read," says Andy. (The Council offers a tiny stipend, largely for travel expenses, granted upon successful completion of the internship—legally speaking, such a stipend, dependent on timing or on tasks completed, could call into question an intern's volunteer status.)

Andy hoped that the summer would feel like a dress rehearsal for a future career, deepening his understanding of American foreign policy and world affairs. Still supported by his parents, he was able to work full-time, but the other intern in his department couldn't. The Council allowed flexible schedules for those who had to work a paying job on the side, but Andy was at a distinct advantage, underlining the inequalities even within the elite world of Council interns: "What I understood very quickly was that, as an intern, if you showed up all the time and made yourself part of the office, then they accepted you as part of the office. Not long after I had a desk, I had a computer. The other intern in my department couldn't come as often, so they just put him wherever they could find space. Sometimes he was perched awkwardly on a stool in the corner."

A few years later, Andy's focus had moved towards human rights. Already soured on internships, and loath to depend on his parents yet again, he still felt that he had to offer his skills without pay—in part because he was still a student, and in part because he was not legally entitled to work in the U.K., where he was living at the time. He spent the better part of a year doing an unpaid stint at a small NGO in London focused on human rights issues, at an office where interns typically comprised at least half of the staff. "I hadn't been paid for work, so I didn't understand the power of receiving a paycheck. The fact that I never had a substantial amount of my own money really was infantilizing," says Andy. "I definitely think there would have been value to just being a working person, making my own money and supporting myself, just in terms of my own personal development." In London, it weighed on him to see his colleagues paid for the same work that he was doing for free: "I felt it was demeaning and it made me not want to work … I could have been a lot more creative when I was there," but the situation was "depressing."

Even after Andy graduated from college, prestigious internships still beckoned. During his job search, friends of his parents would say in a confidential tone, "I could help get you an internship"—not a job, it was clear, but an internship. As Andy described it, these family friends meant that a little backdoor maneuvering could easily finagle an internship—cheap for the organization, openly part of an economy of favors and favoritism—but probably not a job, where stricter standards would apply. Andy said no to these offers, and pushed ahead with his search for real employment. It would be too depressing to do another internship, he felt, to harbor the illusion of progress when you're really just running in place.

Andy now wonders whether the scattered clerical and software skills he learned, largely on his own, couldn't have been imparted in a single short course: "I didn't feel like I was being trained. I would try to find a task that had been done by somebody else that was similar, so that I could mimic it." Name-brand internships, he discovered, assume that interns are already magically equipped with training and ready to jump right in. In the end, what lingers for Andy is a certain feeling of emptiness about the intern years: "You can't just keep doing things for six, nine months a year and have some fundamental understanding about what they're like. Maybe the real answers come from staying with things. Mostly what stands out about the enormous amount of time I spent working for no money is that I can barely remember anything I did."

The National Center for Charitable Statistics (NCCS) reports that there are over 1.5 million nonprofit organizations in the U.S. alone, a majority of them registered with the IRS as 501(c)(3)s and the rest as public charities (primarily religious institutions). The total number of such organizations jumped 27 percent between 1995 and 2005, according to political scientist Rob Reich, and 50,000 new 501(c)(3)s are now approved each year.[7] According to a recent NCCS report, the nonprofit sector had revenues of $1.86 trillion and assets of $4.24 trillion—a mixture of payments for services rendered (the biggest chunk), government support (the second biggest), and in addition the $300 billion which Americans donate to charity each year.

Less obvious and less noticed than these statistics is the massive donation of free labor that now propels these organizations, an overwhelming response to "the call to service." With over 80 percent of nonprofits utilizing volunteers, about 6.5 percent of the entire U.S. population (15 million people) was volunteering on an average day in 2006—hours that would otherwise require the equivalent of 7.6 million full-time employees and $66 billion in wages at the absolute least (using the 2006 federal minimum wage). Of course, some of this work would simply not get done without volunteers, because of a lack of funding. Nonetheless, the call to service is far too often a convenient excuse for displacing regular employees—many of whom have fought hard to win a decent wage and reasonable working conditions in their chosen professions—with young people willing to work on more precarious terms, fired by idealistic talk. For all that its bright-eyed volunteers contribute, and all the fine-sounding rhetoric surrounding the program, AmeriCorps stands out as a notable example of this: the call to service now involves the taxpayer-funded displacement of full-time workers.

AmeriCorps positions, 70,000 of which are filled annually, pay a modest stipend of around $1,000 per month and offer some benefits, as well as an educational award up to $5,325—helping participants with tuition or student loan debt. Short in duration (typically less than a year) and aimed at young people, these positions may seem reasonable enough in and of themselves, especially given the wider social benefits; it is clear, however, that AmeriCorps resembles a relatively enlightened internship program more than an engine of the kind of sustainable, decent employment that it in fact often threatens. With AmeriCorps and similar programs, nonprofits of all sizes and descriptions have a strong financial incentive not to hire employees, or indeed to replace them, and instead rely on AmeriCorps volunteers. Despite some token language that AmeriCorps positions should not have such an effect, the program and its champions apparently have little interest in preserving regular, full-time jobs.

Take a major international NGO such as The Nature Conservancy (TNC), with nearly $6 billion in assets and a president who earns over $350,000 annually, which now fills numerous entry-level positions in this way. In 2008, Greg Vranizan, a career conservation fieldworker, found that TNC was advertising a "land steward" position in Oregon's Willamette Valley as an AmeriCorps-only role. Vranizan had applied for this very same position the previous year, when it was a regular job paid at a competitive hourly rate. "In my view," says Vranizan, "just as with unpaid student internships in business, this effectively excludes people who can't afford to give away their time and work for token wages."

Some nonprofits seem to have grown up as parasites thriving on the AmeriCorps ecosystem, their competitiveness stemming from cheap AmeriCorps labor. Vranizan says that "these organizations will partner with the U.S. Forest Service to use crews of low-paid AmeriCorps interns to do work such as trail maintenance, tree thinning and fuels-reduction projects—work that in the past was contracted out to be done by an existing workforce, at a living wage. I know, because I myself did this sort of work for many years full-time; it was my profession and my living." Making matters worse, AmeriCorps and many of its partner organizations are exempt from prevailing-wage stipulations that might apply to a government stimulus package or infrastructure project, for example. In one representative case involving the insulating and weatherizing of homes, the result was that stimulus funds went to hire near-minimum-wage volunteers from the Energy Corps, an AmeriCorps partner in Washington State, instead of regular workers. Grand plans for an upsurge in living-wage "green jobs" are particularly threatened by such unlimited volunteer subcontracting. And in fields where there has long been a mix of paid professionals and volunteers, efforts like AmeriCorps risk tipping the balance and undermining how many people make a living in the name of service and good will.

An organization's nonprofit status, often little more than a tax distinction, is thought by many to guarantee the right to bring on anyone, in any capacity, as a volunteer—this is a myth. Nonprofit organizations that take on interns, give them the same work as regular employees, and fail to pay them may be as guilty of illegal employment practices as the for-profit companies discussed in the last chapter. A surprising number of groups believe that their tax status somehow means that an intern is automatically considered a volunteer under the law, whether or not they have signed a volunteer agreement and regardless of other circumstances—if they consider these issues at all before loading up on interns, that is. Most media reports have tended to reinforce this assumption; the myth is also widespread among professors and career services personnel on college campuses.

Would we wish the same for the approximately 13 million regular employees at nonprofits across the U.S.—that we could simply call them volunteers and strip them of pay, benefits, and all workplace rights, or replace them with the revolving door of AmeriCorps volunteers? Purposefully misconstruing voluntarism, a powerful and enduring force in American life, runs the risk not only of threatening people's livelihoods, but of poisoning the idea of voluntary work. "To the extent that they are an employer," says Rebecca Hamburg of NELA about nonprofits, "they're considered like any other employers when you're dealing with the law—there's no special law for nonprofits." It is true, generally speaking, that for-profit employers *cannot* take on volunteers, even if both parties agree to the arrangement: it would be far too easy for employers in these situations to pressure desperate people into volunteering their services. In other words, when a company with 11,000 employees like Turner Broadcasting System, part of Time Warner, describes its unpaid internship program as "designed to provide on-the-job experience to student volunteers," with positions ranging from interactive marketing to web design to news gathering, they are treading on dangerous ground.

On the other hand, nonprofits *are* able to create situations for volunteers, who provide "services for civic, charitable, or humanitarian reasons without expectation of compensation," as employment lawyers Karen Gieselman and Wendy Smith write, adding: "Since the motivation for an internship is ordinarily to learn and be exposed to information that may further the intern's education or career, it is unlikely most interns will qualify as volunteers."[8]

In practice, most of us recognize a clear distinction between volunteers —contributing out of good will, often able to dictate their own schedule, and possessing other means of economic support—and interns, usually young people trying to get ahead (and still a much smaller group than volunteers overall). This is a distinction that it would be dishonest for most nonprofits not to acknowledge, although in a few offices volunteers and interns may in fact be difficult to distinguish (especially if "intern" is more marketing term than job title, attempting to attract the voluntarism of young people). Not wanting to penalize volunteers unduly, courts have ruled that that there can be "expected compensation" in the form of expense reimbursements, reasonable benefits, and "a nominal fee," set at 20 percent of what a public agency would usually pay for those same services. Yet it is ironic, again, that giving an unpaid intern a halfway decent stipend or providing him with a meaningful benefit (such as housing) might actually land the nonprofit employer in trouble. Legally speaking, complete exploitation is a more sound way to go—the position of the courts has apparently nipped in the bud the more generous impulses of some employers, hitting interns hard as a result. Still, what constitutes volunteering is far from clear in many situations—with the labor that intern volunteers perform, and the compensation they receive in various guises (including, potentially, "a clear pathway to employment"), many would surely be considered employees in the eyes of the law and entitled to employee protections.

The more profound arguments here are not legal ones, however; they have to do with just how integral interns have become to the nonprofit world, and the negative effects on struggling charities and civil society at large that could result from having to pay these young workers or go without them. A marked hypocrisy is on display here. On the one hand, interns are mocked for their incompetence and dismissed as being of less importance than employees; on the other hand, the right to use their unpaid labor is vigorously defended. At nonprofits, interns are also particularly sheepish about compensation, "believing that the profession that they're entering has something good to contribute to the world," as Anya Kamenetz says. "And to ask for money for what you're doing seems totally to fly in the face of that ... when people are being conditioned: 'This is about saving the whales.'" Over-extended and strapped for cash, nonprofits are even less likely than government offices or corporations to offer dedicated skills training that would meet the six-point test for a trainee exemption. What is to be done? Would nonprofits suffer so much if they actually treated their interns more like the volunteers they claim them to be, honestly advertising positions and allowing greater flexibility in terms of hours and projects? If financial contributions to charity are tax-deductible, should there be a benefit for labor contributions too?

The other alternative, of course, is simply to recognize the contributions of interns and reward them with a living wage—the chances of retaining them and getting productive work from them will be all the greater. Objections that there's no money in the budget for intern wages ring hollow when the directors of mid-size and large nonprofits regularly make six-figure salaries. The message from many of these groups, that they contribute to society and reduce inequalities, seems absurd when they refuse to pay for labor, or else argue that their interns come from well-off families and can afford the sacrifice. The American Cancer Society offers scores of unpaid internships, plus some with below-minimum-wage stipends, while paying its chief executive a salary of $1.2 million. The Metropolitan Museum, with an executive who makes nearly $1.4 million, offers many unpaid positions, but at least some above minimum wage. Such spreads are common now in the nonprofit world, reflecting the adoption of a "star system" and echoing the frightening salary divides on Wall Street. The very real imperative to attract and retain top-notch talent should be somewhat tempered by the idealistic ethos at such organizations—*and* by the far-sighted realization that young talent is also worth attracting and retaining.

The major international NGO where "Eva" works is fairly typical, wrapping itself in idealistic rhetoric, but compensating the director of a country office at thirty-five times the rate of an average intern ($225,000 versus $6,000 annually). "Believe me, they can find the money if they want to," says Eva. "It's not a priority. They've got free labor! People aren't pinching pennies at the top." At the organization's European headquarters, internships typically last six months, fifty-plus hours per week, with "up to 95 percent administrative work," according to Eva. In an office with 100 paid staff, there are usually more than twenty interns, most with Master's degrees—"we would fall apart if we didn't have these interns," says Eva. On a typical day in the office, "all you'll see is interns because the other staff are off traveling or in meetings. It's interns who hold down the fort."

Like approximately a third of the full-time staff, Eva began as an intern in the office ("When it came to signing my contract, I had next to nothing in my bank account"), and she often finds little difference between the work she did as an intern and what she does now as an assistant. "The way the field works now," says Eva, "is you can go on any job site—Idealist, Charity Jobs, Relief Web—and you'll see there's never entry-level positions advertised, because there are no entry-level positions. They're getting interns to do them," although occasionally such a role will be advertised internally. "Getting into an NGO so you can be exposed to these internal applications is the biggest thing," says Eva. "We actually have advertised for internships—this is incredible—saying candidates with a Ph.D. and work experience are preferred."

The fact that so many in the nonprofit field began as interns, and should understand the system's flaws, might be expected to bring about reform—but in fact it's just the opposite, the practice has become fully naturalized. It proves, to them at least, that internships *are* the way in, never mind those who get left behind or can't afford the race in the first place. "Interns get jobs and six months later they have their own intern," says Eva. "How is that good for an intern to be managed by someone who was in their position six months ago?" Despite priding itself on how diverse and representative it is, the leadership at Eva's NGO has demonstrated "not one bit" of conscience. "They think they're doing people a favor by hooking them up. We're preaching one thing and we're doing another," says Eva. "We're saying it's wrong for businesses to cut corners —it's so hypocritical because we're doing the same thing."

CHAPTER SEVEN

The Economics of Internships

Given we were light years from this being a self-sustaining business, and that with the economy in the shitter we didn't have excess financial resources to subsidize this effort, I decided to use unpaid interns. One silver lining of a "great recession" that we are now in is that there are a lot of incredibly talented people without jobs, or who have lost their jobs.

—Mark Cuban, billionaire

What counts as work? What kinds of work should we pay for and be paid to perform? When is work worth dollars and cents, versus payment in kind, or something more abstract like good will or inner satisfaction? The more I spoke to interns and their employers, the more I had to grapple with questions such as these. This chapter will examine the concrete financial calculus surrounding internships for both young people and their employers, exploring plausible economic explanations and touching on issues such as the nature of youth labor markets, supply and demand, and the economics of minimum wage.

The official line in a monetized, avowedly capitalist society is that work and financial compensation are closely linked—and the more your work is in demand, the more you'll be able to earn. But think of the things we've all done for free—without even expecting compensation—that would have been paying jobs under other circumstances. We know that there is a significant cultural dimension to what we consider "jobs," and that certain essential goods and services can't be bought and sold. Feminists have long pointed out the massive amounts of work performed by mothers and homemakers without direct compensation, and thus invisible to economists. Within the inner circle of the family, in particular, but also in networks of friends and acquaintances, the idea of directly paying for work or favors is often taboo—parents don't pay grandparents for an evening of babysitting and you don't pay a friend for cooking you dinner. "Gift economies," with their own logic of reciprocation, make possible the "real" economy of the stock exchange and the minimum wage, yet they remain almost impossible to gauge from a traditional economic perspective.

Today, we often pay strangers for services that were once free inside the family unit (and sometimes still are): we pay for clothes, for haircuts, for babysitting. Every act may be outsourced to a specialist and commodified in the process, consummated with a swipe of plastic. At the same time, there are tendencies of our service-based, intangible economy that are working in the opposite direction—complex gift economies, barter transactions, and credit schemes are making deeper inroads into the real economy than ever before. Working for free, or even paying to work—a hallmark of many internships—is held to be an innovation of precisely this type: an act of selflessness that also aids a career, a form of barter (labor in exchange for training, contacts, experience, etc.), or a brilliant investment in the future.

The broader economic impact of all this free labor is beyond calculation. Looking at internships alone, Anya Kamenetz estimated "a nearly $124 million yearly contribution to the welfare of corporate America," using the 2006 federal minimum wage and the exceedingly low figure of 50,000 unpaid interns nationwide, working forty hours per week over a twelve-week summer.[1] Using up-to-date, but still conservative figures (500,000 unpaid interns at the 2010 federal minimum wage), the money that organizations save through internships approaches $2 billion annually. Companies that benefit, concentrated in particular industries and cities, range in size from General Electric (through the scads of unpaid interns hired by its subsidiary NBC, for example) to tiny start-ups, able to keep costs down and launch new products with the help of workers.

If any generation was ever primed to offer up its labor for free, it's the one that came of age during the internship explosion of the 1980s and 1990s. In a small but significant survey, Northwestern University's career office found that 24 percent of the graduating class in 1996 was willing to work for free on a temporary basis. And this was during an economic upturn—before the internet made *free* a buzzword and a pervasive business model; before many dotcoms had thought to support their free-for-all business plans with unpaid interns; before Chris Anderson's manifesto, *Free: The Future of a Radical Price*, proclaimed that "Generation Free" (those under thirty) expected more, and was willing to do much more, for the magic price of zero.[2] (A small-scale survey in the U.K., conducted in 2010, found that a whopping 86 percent of recent graduates and soon-to-be graduates were willing to work for free, despite considering it exploitative.)

As the cost of copying and disseminating (but not creating) content has plunged towards zero, no one is quite sure what to charge for in the digital world. The position of interns is not unlike that of many young journalists, musicians, and filmmakers who are now expected to do online work for no pay as a way to boost their portfolios. Indeed the internet, more than any other model, is touted as the reason behind the generational sea change in mentality: almost no one worked for free in the offices of mid-century America. A decade ago, Anderson guessed that 40 percent of online labor (creating the content behind the trillion-plus unique URLs that constitute the internet) had been performed for free—the equivalent of 13 million people working full-time for fifteen years, constituting "a country-sized economy." Traditional companies have felt impelled to create and manage a web presence, whether or not they can make money from it. And for every website designed by a paid professional, there are hundreds or even thousands of MySpace pages, Wikipedia entries, blogs, and free content sites, created for a variety of altruistic and self-promotional purposes. The Internet behemoths, which position themselves as offering free services, stimulate and appropriate this content as a critical resource, against which they can raise money and sell ads. Until recently at least, most content creators—virtually all of us, that is, and young people in particular—have either ignored the value of what they create or been happy to trade it for convenient services or the satisfactions of virtual community.

Like the New Economy rhetoric around entrepreneurship, risk-taking, and personal branding, the ideology of *free* has flowed directly into the internship boom. If getting attention and building a reputation online are often seen as more valuable than immediate "monetization," the same theory is being propounded for internships in the analog world —with exposure, contacts, and references advanced as the prerequisite, or even a plausible alternative, to making money. "Giving away what you do will not make you rich by itself," Anderson admits, adding coyly that "every project will require a different answer to that challenge, and sometimes it won't work at all." As difficult as it is to get a consumer to pay for what they assume should be free, moving from unpaid intern to paid employee without alienating the boss is an even more subtle art, involving a major shift in how you're perceived and what you're contributing.

In his recent book, *Predictably Irrational: The Hidden Forces That Shape Our Decisions*, behavioral economist Dan Ariely relates a study about people's willingness to perform certain tasks for different levels of payment. When offered a decent wage, most people in the study were happy to help out with the unskilled tasks in question; as one might expect, this willingness dried up when the wage was lowered. Yet when people were asked to do these tasks for nothing at all, they became enthusiastic again, energized by voluntarism—a striking insight into the mentality of interns. ("I almost felt like we used them up and spit them out ... In the beginning they'd be really enthusiastic," one boss told me of her two blogging interns. "Then after a while they'd get to a point where they were like, 'Well, I don't really have to write this post. I'm not getting paid for it, who cares?' By the same token, I couldn't really force them to do anything.")

Indeed, "voluntarist" eagerness is usually temporary, according to psychologists, who note the ways in which we devalue that which is freely offered, including our own labor. The power of offering something for free—that it breaks down barriers to entry, reaches a much wider audience, and evades formal strictures such as budgets—is counterbalanced by a host of negative psychological baggage. If they're handing it out on the streets, it can't really be worth anything, can it? In a society hooked on cost-benefit analyses, *free* is not part of the accounting; *free* isn't taken seriously.

"We haven't been treated with a lot of respect when it comes to money," says Anya Kamenetz of "Generation Debt," her name for the cohorts of young people who now graduate with mountains of student debt, offer their labor for free, and are encouraged to double down on loans and max out credit cards to stay afloat. "People ask for money, because money is respect," adds Kamenetz—this is the belated realization among young people that is driving much of the backlash against the free mentality.

Free is all well and good, as long as *someone* is paying, somewhere down the line. As discussed earlier, letting people work for free—as orthodox libertarians advocate—dramatically undercuts those who need to make a living, simply by pushing the cost of labor elsewhere when, by all rights, it should be on those who benefit most directly from that labor. In the case of unpaid internships, families and interns themselves bear the immediate burden, burning through their savings or taking out loans. Governments collect no taxes on uncompensated labor, although they still provide services for interns, and the happy multiplier effect of wages —whereby decently paid workers purchase goods and services, leading to more jobs in turn and supporting those unable to work—barely takes hold, if at all.

If employers have been seduced by the prospect of getting something for free, and interns have been reconciled to *free* as part of a brave new economy of intense competition and altered expectations, economists see a deeper logic at work. In 1964, the young economist Gary Becker, already a rising star of the Chicago School, set out "to estimate the money rate of return to college and high-school education in the United States." He ended up producing a highly influential attempt to "treat the process of investing in people from a general viewpoint" and popularizing the new notion of "human capital."[3] At the very moment when the federal government was making an unprecedented push for government-supported, universal higher education, conceived as a human right regardless of social class, Becker's notion provided an explosive alternative, particularly appealing to conservatives: education and training were *investments* that individuals should make themselves, for rational economic reasons. With this "investment approach to human resources," Becker even went so far as to condone, in effect, indentured servitude, practiced in colonial America and elsewhere: these servants were simply using themselves as collateral to tap the credit markets and develop their own human capital.

Becker initially focused on human capital "returns" that came in the form of higher wages, earned by college graduates from their tuition "investment" (only several hundred dollars per year at the time) and the types of training that employers offered to their workers. Today the human capital rubric extends to a tremendous range of "inter-temporal activities," explains labor economist John Pencavel—that is to say, any situation in which an earlier investment sets the stage for later benefits, such as taking care of one's health or migrating to another country in order to reap rewards down the line. Becker's "seminal study," says Pencavel, promoted "a standard way of computing the returns, the benefits, and the costs" of such investments—by the 1980s, human capital talk flavored the speeches of Ronald Reagan and justified disinvestment by governments and companies in education and training, since individuals would rationally take up the burden themselves. And indeed, if they have no other choice, many people do take up that burden.

Some interns have unknowingly embraced the language of human capital theory, asking others to invest in them when they have nowhere else to turn. Having finished her Master's degree and struggling with student loan debt, "Stephanie" asked her extended network of friends and family to support her through an unpaid eight-month internship at the UN High Commission for Refugees in Ghana. "It was very awkward," Stephanie told me. "I was thinking there's no other way I can get this experience and do this, I don't have any other option … I wrote up a letter saying what I was hoping to accomplish and why it was important, and that I couldn't do it without help." To her amazement, "People really opened their hearts and their wallets"—Stephanie received contributions totaling over $8,000 from forty-five different people, enabling her to take the internship.

"The human capital internship story is a very easy one to see," says economist Greg Kaplan. "You get paid what you're worth, and when you start out you're not worth very much. You've got to invest in human capital. People are willing to work for nothing because they're going to get some huge payoffs in the future." As Becker predicted in his original study, human capital accounting by firms, with training costs deducted from wages, "could make the reported 'incomes' of trainees unusually low and perhaps negative, even though their long-run or lifetime incomes were well above average." This assumes of course that the employer is providing valuable training, although the notion of training, as we have seen in Chapter 5, has been significantly hollowed out by the doctrines of "situative learning," "experiential education," and "on-the-job" training, all of which cost employers very little.

Nor is it always certain that huge payoffs will result—if human capital thinking turns us all into investors in our own futures, we stand exposed to market risks just as with any other investment. A world where people have "these very steep earnings profiles" over the course of their lives, says Kaplan, is one in which young people work for free or for cheap, and borrow or beg early on, "to smooth out consumption" over the course of a lifetime—after all, "they don't want to be poor when they're young and rich when they're old." Should you run up credit card debt when you're young to make up the difference? "Economic theory says it's completely optimal to do that," says Kaplan. In the past, a firm might have effectively played the role of a bank, bolstering wages for workers or trainees early on to bring them on board and build loyalty. Today, as economist Edward Lazear, among others, has demonstrated it's precisely the opposite scenario: with the biggest payoffs coming as late as possible, so that firms can string along talented employees. In economic terms, doting parents and loose credit markets—in the form of banks, lenders, and credit card companies looking for high returns—now take the place of firms, which can pay exactly what they want to pay, or even less. *They* should pay *us*, some bosses say, infatuated with their own mentoring genius.

Applying human capital theory to internships at least allows for a guarded optimism: students and their families may feel compelled to invest heavily in education and skills-building, but they are rewarded in the end—hard work still wins out. As proof, proponents of higher education have touted the resilience of college graduate employment during economic downturns and the significant earnings gap between high school graduates and college graduates (once estimated to be more than $1 million over a lifetime, but revised downward to 30 or 40 percent of that). Economists assume that this "college bonus" (and any "internship bonus" that might exist) accurately reflects the results of human capital investment: better work and greater productivity, which employers are quick to reward. In a widget factory, the assumption makes sense and is easily tested: a worker who once produced ten widgets per hour receives training and learns how to make fifteen an hour. Productivity, or at least the number of widgets produced per worker, is measured easily enough, but the contributions of individual white-collar, service-industry workers tend to be much harder to measure. Does a BA make someone a better sales rep or a more productive project manager? We assume so, but no one really knows. A college bonus or internship bonus does not necessarily reward workers for real skills that they've actually acquired—often a higher salary is offered simply because a BA looks good on a résumé, or is required for a particular field, or is thought to indicate a certain type of social background and shared values.[4]

The way job markets actually work, argue some economists, is that graduating from college or completing an internship, regardless of the skills learned, sends a signal to employers, most of whom have little ability to gauge the human capital of a prospective hire. "We have an information problem in the society and the problem of allocating the right people to the right jobs," writes economist Michael Spence, whose early work on "signaling" has been as influential in its own way as Becker's theory of human capital. At first, employers may have to guess whether any given signal—a high GPA, for instance—will make for a useful predictor of future success, but Spence posits "a feedback loop" in which employer expectations are revised over time, as the productivity of different types of workers reveals itself. Thus if employees with high college GPAs consistently do a poor job in the office, employers should eventually discard or refine their use of the "GPA signal." In addition, if every job applicant is sending the same signal to employers (e.g. all applicants have high GPAs), the signal will quickly lose all meaning, even if considerable investment was involved on the students' part. What Spence called "systematic over-investment" in generating a particular signal can easily occur, even if "everyone is reacting rationally to the market situation."[5]

As a hiring criterion, internships have rapidly become a crucial signal for employers. Piled high on a résumé, internships at other offices, even if their exact content often remains murky, signal a go-getter applicant, already fluent in office culture (and possibly in industry culture), able to take on a new role immediately with less time and investment from the firm. In-house internships, on the other hand, allow firms to withhold permanent status, benefits, and a better wage until they've learned more about the value of a prospective employee. In a white-collar world, where every office can seem an identical sea of desks and computers, internships are a "test-drive" for both the intern and the employer, "a way to alleviate the information asymmetries between firms and workers," says Kaplan, putting the point in economics-speak. Signals play a smaller role in blue-collar contexts, where employers may be willing to pay sooner for skills—since they may be more objective and more readily demonstrated—and prospective employees can quickly gauge what they're getting into.

With the demise of manufacturing and the offshoring of jobs has come the perception that the future of decent work in the West is high-tech and white-collar—that the only alternative to high-powered careerism is "Do you want to fries with that?" As a result, internships now wear much the same halo as higher education, while apprenticeships are overlooked by comparison, still struggling with their blue-collar stigma. To an economist, the logic goes like this: if white-collar firms are increasingly organized around their intangible human or organizational capital—whether it be their brand or their "culture of innovation"—then this is what interns have to learn, just as much as any specific skill set. From this standpoint, says Kaplan, "it's possible to learn just by being there, as opposed to formalized training. But in many situations this is hard to distinguish from "firms just taking the easy way out, taking advantage of the fact that there's a huge demand for jobs" to cut training costs.

Young people are acutely aware of the gulf that separates the blue-collar and white-collar worlds, and how internships can bridge that gap—one reason that so many self-funding interns denigrate the paying retail, fast food, or bartending jobs that support them through an unpaid position. "They're working at Jamba Juice, or Anthropologie, or at Abercrombie—jobs that they see as completely unconnected to their careers," says Gina Neff of how her students make it through unpaid journalism internships. They don't understand how these "dead-end jobs" could "help them get to where they want to go," she adds, or how the skills they're gaining might be useful—they save their real energy for the internship.

Under the influence of human capital or signaling theory, most economists assume that the short-term sacrifice of an internship will be rewarded with a future payoff: an internship bonus that has never been proven to exist, but may be supported by anecdotal evidence. Yet however rational a step in terms of economic theory, neglecting paid work in favor of unpaid and doubling down on debt are risky strategies. For many, the return on investment never comes, the economic landscape changes in the meantime, or an incomplete investment spells disaster. In *Generation Debt*, Anya Kamenetz describes how the prospect of a six-month, full-time, unpaid internship—required to obtain a Bachelor's degree—finally tanked the finances of one student, who ended up with $55,000 in student loan debt, $1,000 in credit card debt, and an unfinished degree.

Staking everything on a career-launching internship, as sociologist Mark Granovetter points out, is not unlike working unpaid for shares in a Silicon Valley start-up: "There are a surprising number of people willing to work just for 50 or 60 thousand shares of a company that may never see the light of day ... Unless they think that what the company is doing is the best thing since sliced bread, then they probably have no better alternative." Interns at start-ups, such as "Nora," often work for the *possibility* of getting an equity share in a company. After earning her MBA, Nora had put in several months, full-time and unpaid, at a New York City start-up, as a way to transition from accounting (her pre-MBA work) into marketing. "If I'd had another avenue to go down to try to make the switch, I probably would have," she says. Now she believes that the start-up—consisting of two founders, two interns, and a friend of one of the founders who pitches in—represents her best shot for launching a high-powered career and climbing into the winners' circle, however risky. "Honestly, it's an investment," says Nora, adding that in just a few more months she'll have burned through the savings of many years' work, but at least she has "a cushion with my fiancé supporting this venture." After the official launch of the start-up's website, Nora hopes there'll be "some movement" towards giving her shares of the company or a salary, but she remains cautious: "I don't want to step on their toes too soon to ask for that."

Of course it's not that young people don't want to be paid for their work—it's just that most paying jobs in the youth labor market are vulnerable, alienating, pitifully paid, and seem to lead nowhere. Against this backdrop, internships (like college degrees) appear to be a light at the end of tunnel, a way to escape from the basement of the American workforce—something worth sacrificing for. As a brief investigation demonstrates, students are understandably hungry for meaningful, career-oriented work, even if it's without pay, by the time they reach college age; most have had enough of the minimum-wage basement of the youth labor market.

"The vast majority of American youths engage in some labor market activities while enrolled in school," reported the Bureau of Labor Statistics (BLS) in 2000, focusing on paid employment, and "work activity is substantial even among fourteen- and fifteen-year-olds." The proportion of American teenagers who work is notably higher than in other developed countries—though it bears no comparison with the 115 million children performing hazardous labor, almost all in the developing world, according to the International Labor Organization (ILO). U.S. teens who work—many of them in the familiar modes of camp counselor, baby-sitter, or yard worker mowing the lawn—actually tend to be from more well-off backgrounds than those who don't, perhaps because the children of less affluent families are expected to do more around the home, helping out a single parent or taking on more chores. According to the BLS, "Most working teens spend their earnings as discretionary income, rather than helping to meet family expenses."

In 1997, BLS researchers took a random sample of 9,022 young men and women, all born between 1980 and 1984, and began to track their work experiences—ever since, these researchers have continued to follow up, creating a detailed, longitudinal portrait of how a generation enters the workforce. More than half of respondents reported having held some type of job at age fourteen, mostly occasional, "freelance" arrangements on "an as-needed basis or for multiple employers" such as neighbors or family friends. Approaching college age, the picture changes substantially —a census report in the late 1990s found that 39 percent of seventeen-year-olds worked regularly during the school months and 48 percent held jobs during the summer, averaging around twenty hours per week. Retail work in fast food restaurants, clothing stores, and the like accounts for a substantial chunk of this seventeen-year-old workforce, as any mall-goer knows.

Workforce participation only increases with college; in fact, college students are *more* likely to be employed than their friends who are not in school, as Marc Bousquet reports in *How the University Works*. Any perceived dichotomy between workers and students is a false one, writes Bousquet: "In the United States, only 20 percent of undergraduates do not work at all. About 50 percent of all undergraduates work an average of twenty-five hours per week. The remaining 30 percent work full-time, more than full-time, or at multiple jobs approximating the equivalent of full-time, averaging thirty-nine hours a week." With two-thirds of students now borrowing money to pay for college—up from just under half in 1993—and with the average student loan debt for graduating seniors over $23,000, jobs during college are no longer about discretionary income: they're about staying afloat. Perhaps the principal reason that college graduation rates have been stalled for decades, and why they remain catastrophically low at community colleges in particular, is the ongoing struggle of working students to make the grade and hold on to their jobs. Nonetheless, working students identify and are identified as students first and foremost; their social status is sharply divorced from what they actually do with their time.

Many jobs worked by teenagers, and even by some undergraduates, actually earn less than minimum wage, given FLSA exemptions (food service jobs, for instance) and training wages. There is even a "youth minimum wage," instituted in 1996, which allows employers to compensate those under twenty years old at a lower rate during their first three months of employment. Turnover is sky-high, given the compounded effect of poor working conditions, particular vulnerability to economic swings, and young people's desire to try different things. From a longitudinal study two decades ago, we know that men held an average of 8.9 jobs and women an average of 8.4 jobs from age eighteen to age thirty; if anything, this incredible degree of churn, long a feature of youth job markets, seems to be increasing. The exhaustion and uncertainty involved in entering the American workforce are substantial. According to one study, the job changes that young men make during their first ten years in the labor force represent two-thirds of their lifetime total—apparently, as many as half of these changes involve a switch of occupation or industry, rather than just a simple change of employer.

Increasingly, as we have seen, internships have become a conduit for just this kind of mobility between careers.

On the positive side, economist Derek Neal points out that job switching early on can be crucial for increasing lifetime earnings; young people may be deliberately positioning themselves in the workforce, trying to match their skills and interests to high-paying roles in stable or growing industries. Indeed, those who seek stability too early on and fail to job-switch when they're young may remain stranded on the lower rungs of the class ladder. In a now-famous study, economist Lisa Kahn found that the earnings of young people who start their careers during a recession are permanently depressed, possibly because of their understandable reluctance to maneuver between jobs and careers in a difficult economic climate. For these unlucky graduates, Kahn found that every percentage-point increase in the national unemployment rate lopped as much as 7 percent off their starting salaries, and the wage gap with those who got their start during an economic boom still persisted decades later, with the gap growing as large as 10 percent.[6]

Today, youth unemployment is at an all-time high, hovering near 20 percent for sixteen- to twenty-four-year-olds and exceeding the jobless-ness rate for any other group; if the recession persists, the scarring effects on the youngest generation of workers may be profound. Already the major coping mechanism, decades in the making, is for young people to delay or permanently jettison the traditional milestones of adulthood. Judging by five such milestones in particular—leaving home, finishing school, becoming financially independent, getting married, and having a child—researchers have found that only 46 percent of women and 31 percent of men had become "adults" by age 30 in 2000, compared with 77 percent of women and 65 percent of men of the same age in 1960. Taking just one of these indicators, the percentage of twenty-six-year-olds living at home is now 20 percent, double the figure for 1970. Without stable, decent-paying jobs, internships—now seen by many as a strategy for waiting out economic downturns—are clearly part and parcel of this phenomenon of "prolonged adolescence," of delayed independence and the postponed assumption of "adult" responsibilities.

"No one person decides the structure of the labor market, it's something that evolves, or is decided by policies," says Greg Kaplan—as a group, young people might be better off steering clear of unpaid or low-paid internships, but realistic individuals have no such luxury. For many, the breakthrough opportunity offered by an internship may be a real one, making it pragmatic to work temporarily for free—at least for those who can afford to do it, in a labor market where there's no other option. At the same time, the internship signal may already be losing its force and its meaning due to "systematic overinvestment," and employers keep upping the ante: increasingly it takes a prestigious internship, or a string of internships, to put you over the top.

It's all about delayed gratification: interns and their families are making a risky, potentially high-yield investment (whether in human capital or in a labor market signal), ponying up for a payoff in the near future. Although many firms described in this book see interns simply as a way to save money, some companies—mostly top-flight, brand-name multinationals in highly skilled industries like finance and technology—also take an investment view. They are justifiably proud of their formalized, well-paid, HR-run programs, which are not only legal but exemplary. These programs have substantial associated costs, including dedicated work-spaces, office computers, sometimes even background checks and institutional subscriptions (to services like LexisNexis). Programs with a strong training or mentoring component must factor in the value of regular employees' time, although full-time internship coordinators are a rarity at all but the biggest and most professional programs—usually this is another hat for someone to wear, typically a junior employee or an HR staffer.

What's the calculus for these employers, and is their investment in interns worth it? The principal cost savings for well-paid, corporate internship programs comes from hiring—hence their focus on conversions. "Our department was judged on the numbers: offers made, offers accepted, conversion (or 'yield') to full-time hire," says Natalie Lundsteen of the time she helped run Gap's corporate internships in San Francisco. According to one study, quoted in a *Management Review* article about the boom in corporate internships during the mid-1990s, employers save $15,000 per person by hiring from their intern pool.[7] A Human Resources VP at a Michigan construction firm seconded this number to *Crain's Detroit Business* in 2010, saying that headhunters may charge a fee equaling 30 percent of a position's salary—at a $50,000 salary, sourcing that position will cost $15,000 before a day's work has been done.[8] (Of course, in glamorous industries where the competition is intense, headhunters and recruiters may only be called on to fill executive positions.) Having an intern pipeline, which can usually be bundled with existing campus recruiting efforts, also means that new hires will know the ropes from their internship days and won't require much hand-holding at the outset.

When times are good, the scale of an internship program will be closely tied to hiring projections. "It was all about talent sourcing, that's how we looked at it," says Teri McCaslin, an HR executive who oversaw the Monsanto program. According to Howard Curtis, who also managed the program, a company like Monsanto would consider a 50 percent conversion rate a successful use of internships as a recruiting tool—that is, if half of the interns join Monsanto in a full-time capacity at some point following the internship, given available positions. By that metric, Curtis adds, the company's internship program was successful for science, engineering, and agronomy students at the company's plants, because "at that level, much better supervision was provided" and young people "could see how they would get in at the ground floor." At the corporate level, however, retention was notably weaker, says Curtis, in part because many managers "would say, 'I really don't have time to sit down with them, talk to them, mentor them.'" One of the biggest complaints from these managers, he adds, was that the presence of interns detracted from the time they had for their primary responsibilities. As a result, Curtis was under pressure to find interns able to work on their own.

At a very select number of companies—mainly high-tech, consulting, and finance—the calculus around internships has a second dimension: they represent a highly effective way to capture and woo the best talent early on. Some companies, like consulting firm Deloitte Touche, run model programs that receive positive publicity and burnish the company's reputation on college campuses—they also pay an average wage of $24.50 per hour. Other firms use internships to recruit certain types of employees in particularly high demand, such as minorities and women, as we'll see in Chapter 9. Especially during the salad days of the dotcom boom, some talent-obsessed companies lavished many of their famous employee perks on the interns as well—one example being the massive "Gates barbecue" hosted by Bill himself each summer for Microsoft's 1,000-plus interns. Before they've even donned their cap and gown, impressionable students can be bowled over by corporate generosity. These interns do work for their perks, however: in her close study of London investment banking internships, Lundsteen found that bank interns "were expected to respect the hierarchy, to defer to and agree with more experienced colleagues, and to accomplish successfully without guidance any tasks assigned by a person of authority."

"A lot is expected of you when you start because your co-workers often don't remember how little a college student actually knows!" according to "Tina," a former engineering intern at two ExxonMobil refineries. "People at the refinery were ridiculously nice and accommodating of a student who wanted to learn," she adds. Hers was a high-value, well-paid experience, focused mostly on "silver bullet projects"—situations where her colleagues "had an interesting project or issue that they were too busy to deal with, so they let us work on them to see if we could come up with something novel." In one case, the refineries "needed to start a new system of compliance with EPA regulations," so Tina and a fellow intern analyzed computer models of the different refinery units in order to understand their waste streams, then spent time at the actual refineries, and finally found themselves "creating electronic tools which could be used to better-understand the refinery systems under consideration." Not bad for a summer's work.

Of course, the calculus for these companies can change drastically when business dries up—which explains why recessions hit the well-paid, high-quality internships hardest. "Unfortunately when times get tough, training is one of the first things that's cut," says Howard Curtis, "and it's been that way for quite a while." Having a hiring pipeline suddenly becomes a lot less important during a hiring freeze, and top talent is much easier to come by in an economic downturn. Reeling from the Great Recession, Microsoft recently cut its intern class by 20 percent, and many banks have also made deep reductions—or switched to unpaid internships, as with some positions at Merrill Lynch and Smith Barney. A broad survey tracking the number of blue-chip corporate internships, almost all of them paid, registered a 21 percent drop in 2009 alone.[9] Steven Rothberg, founder and president of CollegeRecruiter.com, reported that his site had only 10,000 internship listings, half of the total a year earlier. "The number and quality of internship opportunities are significantly down," said Rothberg, adding that a majority of them now appear to be unpaid. Drawing on conversations with employers, Rothberg says, "They are either eliminating the program entirely or they're eliminating the compensation." Senior Vice President of BankAtlantic Tom Triozzi cagily explained a switch at the major Florida bank, which has billions in assets: "We used to pay, but we're not doing that anymore. We ask them to work for free for a great work experience." All this volatility highlights the pitfalls of relying on internships as an educational tool or a school-to-work strategy: when the economy sneezes, decent internship programs get pneumonia.

A far cry from the world of Gates barbecues, unpaid internships usually thrive in a bad business climate, because the cost savings—especially when full-time positions can be axed or left empty because of interns—seem immediate and obvious. If well-paid internships more often represent a considered, nuanced investment in talent, unpaid positions may simply be stopgap measures, a way of plugging operational holes. In addition, the economic rationale for offering unpaid internships can easily backfire, as employers grapple with hidden costs and low returns from dispirited, less productive interns.

It's a vicious cycle, as unpaid internships attract a narrower range of applicants, only able to work for shorter periods of time; conversion rates are nonexistent, as the interns are much less likely to become full-time staff, meaning that any training by the firm would effectively be wasted, being of no more than short-term utility. Not to mention that having a revolving door of inexperienced employees illegally performing operationally vital work, without financial motivation and struggling to get by, can be a recipe for disaster. Consider the widespread use of interns to manage web content and social media initiatives. Despite the perceived generational fit, it delays the hour when full-time employees have to learn the new tools of their trade, and puts people who know and care least about a company's brand on the front lines of communicating it.

Making a paid internship program unpaid involves more than flicking a switch—there are costly and meaningful adjustments to be made. Ryan Krogh, of *Outside* magazine in Santa Fe, spends twenty to thirty hours per week running the magazine's internship program; the other half of his time is devoted to editorial responsibilities. The recent decision to do away with intern pay "was driven entirely by money," says Krogh—with three to five interns at a time, working for Santa Fe's $10/hour living wage and often asked to put in overtime, "it was just so hard to contain those costs." Himself a former intern, Krogh has done his best to make the program "more educational ... to compensate for the lack of monetary compensation," resulting in more work for him as the coordinator. The interns' main role is to fact-check everything that *Outside* prints, "one of the most important things you do at a magazine," says Krogh (industry-wide, fact-checking used to be a paid, entry-level position). Interns also conduct research for editors, write articles for the website, and perform other, miscellaneous tasks—like securing satellite phones for reporters off to Sudan or Antarctica.

The decision to stop paying has had other impacts, says Krogh: "The first thing I noticed was that the quality of the interns definitely took a nosedive. You could just tell [the applications] were stock cover letters, stock résumés ... Before, when they were paid, it was more graduate students from journalism schools, and they knew what was going on. They had no problem hopping in and going to it, and now it's people fresh out of college who may not have a whole lot of experience." Pay or no pay, the interns are still there, fact-checking their little hearts out in what the full-timers call Internia—"their little cubicle downstairs where they get too loud and piss off the accounting staff because they're laughing too much." If they disappeared, Krogh explains, "it would dramatically change the way everything works. The interns are pretty integral to what we do here."

Why have so many companies given up on dedicated training programs and internship conversion rates, instead treating young people as more or less disposable? One commonly heard answer, loosely drawing on economic thinking, is simple supply and demand—with so many interns clamoring for positions, companies can afford to set the bar low. If there's some truth to this, however, it's largely because of how skewed and manipulated the internship marketplace actually is. Consider a product flogged, and sometimes even required, by over 4,000 colleges to nearly 10 million students across the nation. And given the globalization of internships, now factor in the triple-digit surge in the number of college students worldwide since 1990, with a 22 percent increase at North American schools alone.[10] Then there are the massive, hidden subsidies that boost the supply of interns, in part because internship costs are bundled, often almost invisibly, with ballooning college-related expenses, and in part because of the misguided generosity of families, schools, and governments. The near-complete absence of any law enforcement only compounds matters, meaning that internships, unpaid ones especially, don't follow the normal dynamics of the rest of the job market.

In short, nothing could be less natural than the patterns of supply and demand in the internship marketplace. Unwittingly or not, industries that virtually depend on unpaid internships, backed by pricey academic credit, are fixing the price of entry cartel-style: pay up or stay out. Discouraging the use of scarce funds to subsidize internships, especially from taxpayers' pockets, removing the pressure and coercion currently applied by schools, and placing internships on the level playing field of the broader job market are all necessary steps to restore a fair, competitive system.

One place to start should be the minimum wage that is owed to most interns, in part for legal reasons described in Chapter 4. Enforcing or reinforcing interns' right to minimum wage would have no more catastrophic effect than any minimum wage legislation has ever had—and bring internships in line with other forms of work. "From the economics of it, it's almost the same," says economist Greg Kaplan, "because an internship is essentially a way of getting around a minimum wage for a firm. Firms want to drive wages down as far as the market's going to let them do it." The "minimum wage literature" in economics, adds Kaplan, "often quickly becomes ideological"—but no one, not even the most committed free-marketer, can pretend that minimum wage laws around the world have had any particularly dramatic or obvious effects, aside from the intended one of guaranteeing workers a wage floor. The endless unemployment lines, vertiginous inflation, and economic collapse predicted by some have never materialized—in fact, despite conventional wisdom to the contrary, many economists are now questioning whether there has been any downside at all to increasing the minimum wage.

This is the conclusion of a range of recent academic analyses, drawing on different data from the last half-century and a variety of econometric methods: especially important has been the research of economist David Card in a long series of influential studies.[11] "It is widely believed that the imposition of a binding wage floor will reduce the employment of younger and less-skilled workers," writes Card. "Although the theoretical arguments underlying this consensus are simple and compelling, the empirical evidence is surprisingly limited"—despite decades of studies relentlessly searching for such effects. Even those studies that have purported to discover increased unemployment due to minimum wage regulation admit to tiny effects on only the most marginal group: "a reduction of between 1 and 3 percent in teenage employment as a result of a 10 percent increase in the federal minimum wage," according to an authoritative survey of the literature. Moreover, as Card and Alan Krueger revealed in an influential paper, even these findings relied on a questionable methodology and have since been superseded by studies that "have estimated negligible or even marginally positive employment effects of the minimum wage."

Card's research has taken advantage of the "natural experiments" afforded by various minimum wage increases over the past few decades— in California in the late 1980s, when the state boosted the earnings of low-wage workers by 5–10 percent; in April 1990, when a federal increase of 13 percent failed to have a clear downside even in the low-wage states where tremendous numbers of workers benefited; in Pennsylvania and New Jersey in 1992, where hundreds of fast food restaurants, notoriously dependent on the federal floor, took an adjustment completely in stride.

With even the most vulnerable employees basically unaffected, suffering neither in terms of layoffs nor reduced hours; with prices showing little appreciable rise; and with no apparent rash of business bankruptcies, an increasing load of evidence indicates that employers have simply been able to absorb these relatively minor costs. Indeed, they may have even benefited from the increased spending of workers, as Henry Ford did by paying his autoworkers $5 a day in 1914. When the federal minimum wage increased to $7.25 in 2009, the Economic Policy Institute estimated that consumer spending would increase by $5.5 billion over the following year.

Card holds that "a minimum wage increase can be expected to cause some firms to reduce employment and others to raise employment, with these two effects potentially canceling out if the rise in the minimum wage is modest." According to another theory, "a higher wage forces employers to invest in their employees and figure out ways to make them more efficient (i.e., valuable)," thus benefiting everyone. Economist Madeline Zavodny speculates that the conventional wisdom about negative impacts from a wage floor relies on a very blunt caricature of a labor market "with many identical firms and homogeneous workers."[12] There is evidence, she writes, that "a minimum wage will lower employment among low-wage workers but may not lower total employment," with skill or, among teenage workers, age possibly playing a key role. The true overall effects of minimum wage legislation are still poorly understood, but one thing is clear: the sky has not fallen in. It's not for nothing that the minimum wage is a nonpartisan issue backed by a broad consensus—67 percent of Americans support it, according to one poll, *and* would like to see it increased to $10 per hour. In 2005, initiatives to boost the minimum wage were voted on in six states—Arizona, Colorado, Montana, Missouri, Nevada and Ohio—and passed in all of them. Women in the workforce, and single parents in particular, have benefited.

Raising an intern's compensation from zero to minimum wage would be a more significant step, and might well occasion some reductions in the intern ranks, but the relative brevity of internship stints, the wide distribution of interns across firms, and their small numbers overall would all act as countervailing pressures. Initially, policymakers could move slowly, at least ensuring interns a "training wage," a familiar concept already used in many countries (including the U.S. to a limited extent), which allows for sub-minimum wage salaries in recognized training situations. Inevitably, economic cycles will continue to play a decisive role for interns, as for almost all other young, low-wage, and contingent workers. Nonetheless, visions of internship opportunities disappearing en masse and forever are wildly overblown, empty echoes of employer warnings against the minimum wage that haven't come to pass.

For interns and employers both, counting up the costs and benefits of an internship situation may be far from straightforward, and understanding the wider economic causes and effects of the internship explosion is harder still. But for one particular group of people, the profitability of internships is beyond question—they hawk hope, sell unpaid labor for a fee, and peddle in human futures.

CHAPTER EIGHT

Futures Market

DEAN JONES: I've been reviewing Darren's internship journal: doing laundry, mending chicken wire, high tea with a Mr. Newman.
KRAMER: I know it sounds pretty glamorous, but it's business as usual at Kramerica.
DEAN JONES: As far as I can tell, your entire enterprise is nothing more than a solitary man with a messy apartment which may or may not contain a chicken.
KRAMER: And with Darren's help, we'll get that chicken.
—*Seinfeld*, "The Voice"

"Every day, we're changing people's lives," Eric Normington tells me, welcoming me into his office. "We're giving people access to opportunities, we're doing something that can really impact somebody ... I realized that in organizations I have a unique ability to pull people together, to take things that are your biggest challenges and make them your best opportunities. That's been my secret to success." Built like a college athlete and brimming with a sunny evangelism that is half Silicon Valley entrepreneur and half door-to-door salesman, Normington isn't pitching a new alternative energy start-up or a hot social networking website. The commodity on offer here at the University of Dreams—a ten-year-old private company enjoying explosive growth, just down the road from the likes of Google, Apple, and Facebook—is familiar and cutting-edge at the same time: Normington is selling internships.

"It's who we are," says Normington of the company's name, admitting that the word "university" sometimes throws people off. After all, no teachers teach here, no students take notes; there are no grades, no home-work assignments, no varsity teams. Normington's university is an unmarked building in the historic district of Redwood City, California, its interior transformed for a youthful, aggressively casual, tech-driven start-up: the nerve center for fifteen internship hubs around the globe, from Hong Kong to Costa Rica, from San Diego to Dublin, from Chicago to Sydney. University of Dreams, which runs year-round, boasts of having arranged 10,000 internships and having worked with over 3,500 employ-ers in 30-plus industries ("from exciting start-up companies to some of the biggest multinational conglomerates in the world"). From an initial group of fewer than a hundred interns in 2000, the "university" now plays middleman for more than 2,000 internships each year—a number that has been growing 50–100 percent annually, with full-throttle acceleration coming since 2005.

An eight-week summer with the University of Dreams typically costs $7,999 (as high as $9,499 for the London program)—that's right, you pay "UofD" $1,000 per week to work, which makes college tuition look cheap. In some cases, the company you intern for may pay something, but the program makes no particular effort to find paid positions or get employers to pay: indeed, UofD provides a fig leaf of academic credit so that employers will feel comfortable not paying. Normington is quick to point out that tuition costs include housing and food, as well as "program gifts," "orientation," and "lifetime alumni networking events." "Students paying for internships is the headline," says Normington, referring rue-fully to negative press attention, "and the whole subtext is 'I can't believe students pay this much for an internship.' Our story can get boiled down to that headline, but the experience we provide, what we do, our organization, isn't that." Yet the company also provides a straightforward "internship placement service," without any housing, food, "experience," or other bells and whistles, for $1,500–$2,000 a pop. It's clear that there is a market for internships, and University of Dreams knows the going rate.

With over 2,000 interns each paying close to $8,000 in tuition, annual company revenues could easily top $16 million, though neither Normington, who is Chief Marketing Officer, nor Eric Lochtefeld, the company's founder and CEO, will comment on the financials. "I'm not going to give you any hardcore specifics on that kind of thing," says Normington, his voice beginning to crack, "but I will tell you we are a homegrown company, organically grown, self-funded in every direction. We don't have other people's money, it's not VC-backed, 'let's hit the accelerator and roll this thing forward'—and that's by choice." With the "boom in the education space," he adds, "we've had people who've come to us and said, 'Let's push this thing to the nth degree, whatever that could be,'" but the company wants to remain "very holistic," focused on its "core"—"inspiring, equipping, and challenging individuals to pursue and follow their dreams."

Who are those individuals? Normington answers before I've even finished asking: "Have we had rich kids that have done our program? Yeah … But these aren't silver-spoon kids. Some of them might be, but the percentages, as a group, it's exactly the same as you'd see in any walk of life, in any university setting." This strains credence—how many people can afford to get their kid an $8,000 summer job? "There are students who have to take out loans, either federally backed, academically backed or privately backed," he adds. "And there are students who also have a support network: friends, family, etc. that help pay for it." Support network, that's what we're calling it these days. Helpfully, UofD does offer various ways of paying on installment, for hefty associated fees— and it offers "full or partial scholarships" for some students, amounting in total to just over 1 percent of the tuition it charges.

At a time when the internship business had barely begun, Lochtefeld hit upon his formula almost by accident, thanks to the dotcom bust: "I had seven of the biggest companies in Silicon Valley paying for every penny … for over 600 students in our first year, and it all went away in a blink of an eye. I went on vacation to Bali for two weeks, and returned to learn that I lost half of my clients." A "recession-proof" business model, Lochtefeld discovered, would lean on the student and her parents, "as they require our kind of assistance in a good or bad economy." He says, "We prefer the student as the customer and I know this makes [college] career centers angry, but it really is in the best interest of the true customer—the intern." Brilliantly, with slick marketing and advertising and a customer-friendly approach, Lochtefeld has convinced families to pay for something that career centers say they offer for free, cutting out the colleges and going directly to students and parents. Although Lochtefeld has in some ways simply extended the trade in internships, started by colleges and nonprofits like the Washington Center, he is clearly innovating the trade in young people's futures as well—contracting out UofD programs to be run by "licensees" (in Sydney, Chicago, and Costa Rica, for example) and buying academic credit in bulk.

The academic credit wholesaler is Menlo College, a small, business-focused college just a few miles away from Normington's office, which reportedly provides University of Dreams interns with academic credit at $45 a head, grossing $50,000 for the Menlo career center in 2008. Normington says it's "a core credit," "transferrable, depending on the home institution" and that "it can be used either as an elective credit or a core credit towards their major." On the other hand, Michael Smith, of the Washington Center, which prides itself on academic rigor and its connections to academia, calls the arrangement "silly": "I think Menlo did it to make some money, and University of Dreams did it because otherwise they may have problems with the fair wage and standards law." Questioned by the *Chronicle of Higher Education*, Menlo Provost (and now President) James Kelly backpedaled, saying Menlo was not selling "true academic credit," but instead a continuing-education credit, "useless credit," according to Kelly, "because I would not accept it here."[1] Menlo's director of career services was more defensive: "It's a service to the community, because we're getting college students out into the business world."

Part of the appeal for young people is precisely that they are treated as customers, at least at first, rather than prospective employees. "If students aren't having a great experience," says Normington, "who do you think they come and talk to? They come to us first." But surely it would be healthier for an intern to talk to her boss about a work issue? Not on the UofD model, where nothing is expected of employers. Despite having many participants with previous internships, Normington says, "the one thing that interns all have in common is that they have no experience." Of the notion that an internship is just "making copies and getting coffee," he says "that doesn't really happen." University of Dreams—and the budding internship industry more generally, aping the travel, education, and self-help businesses founded by self-actualized Baby Boomers—claims to sell something "transformative" and "life-changing." A favorite statistic, derived from a multiple choice survey given at the end of the program, is that 85 percent of the interns rank their UofD junket as the best summer of their lives.

So where do I sign up? Should it be finance with Smith Barney or Merrill Lynch in New York, or something I, like, *really care about*, like the Salvation Army (in LA) or the American Red Cross (in Chicago)? A fashion internship in Barcelona or PR in Hong Kong? "Employers work with us because we're good people," explains Normington, guffawing, and adding that UofD aims "to make a love connection right away." In reality, it's the fact that companies can so easily outsource their entire intern recruitment process to University of Dreams, without spending a dime or making any commitment—in the end, the company is simply presented with an interested, minimally presentable candidate. "It was a way to get some good, qualified, pre-screened candidates, without doing a lot of the recruitment ourselves," one HR executive told me, who has since dropped the program "mostly because we had a tremendous number of applicants just reach out to us directly." The fact that companies give "exclusives" to University of Dreams and similar operations, in all of which high "tuition" freezes most young people out, is a sign of laziness, cynicism, and the work of personal connections. As Willy Franzen, author of One Day, One Internship, says, "Companies aren't scared to take on bad interns, I guess."

Famous dreamers stare down from the walls of Normington's office, silently imparting their approval of his rhapsodies on the transformative potential of paying to work. There are framed photos of Mother Teresa and of Winston Churchill—"dreamers" both, apparently—and of the Imagine Mosaic from Strawberry Fields, the John Lennon memorial in Central Park. The word "Inspire" is emblazoned on a door's lintel, a mezuzah for the interning faith. Staffers, many of them strapped into their Skype headsets and ready for battle, dutifully don their gray University of Dreams fleece jackets, which sport a quizzical logo: angels' wings bearing aloft a college graduation cap. For a moment, Normington's elevated rhetoric comes back into focus: "We're going to college students and saying look, this is really an incredible and pivotal life-changing moment in your life. You have to think about what your dreams are, what you want out of life. Maybe for one moment in time unleash the pressures of parent influences, social influences, peer influences." But then comes the real message: "Internships are no longer an option, they're a necessity."

The captive audience is only growing larger—international participants, high school students, and recent graduates are all big segments for growth. University of Dreams—which recently changed its name to Dream Careers, Inc.—continues to cash in on a "fundamental shift that's happened with universities themselves." As Normington puts it: an internship is now often "not only an elective, it's actually a requirement, and that's awesome … We get students that come and call us and say, 'Look, I need an internship to graduate, but I can't find an internship.' " Lochtefeld sees a bright future for what he calls "destination internships," which he equates "with the study abroad industry thirty years ago, but I think it will be at least three times as big." What are we talking here, Eric? "I see at least a million college students serving in destination internships. We are in the second inning of a nine inning game."

After taking on fifteen internships in four years, Lauren Berger crowned herself the Intern Queen. "I'm really interested in branding and marketing," she explains, "and figured 'The Intern Queen' would be a great way to brand myself." A posh-sounding title was probably the least that Lauren deserved for her troubles—out of all fifteen gigs, she earned a $100 stipend, once. Now she tours the country, relentlessly trying to turn her internship obsession into a business and a source of niche celebrity, all but raising pom poms in the air and doing back handsprings for the internship grind.

The Intern Queen—who would not grant an audience to this author —instructs her followers to dive in and offer their labor to the lowest bidder, accumulating fancy-sounding stints and bursting the bounds of the one- or two-page résumé. There is something sinister and distressing about the litany of the Intern Queen's *res gestae* and the image she projects as the ultimate self-deprecating, preternaturally cheerful intern, brandishing brand-name internships like trophies. All hail the Intern Queen! She has reigned from the throne of a Television Department internship at Trans Continental, and as a Promotions intern at a comedy club; she smote enemies as a casting intern at the WB Television Network and at NBC; she was the resplendent Content/Production intern at *The Daily Buzz*, a morning news show, and shed her grace on Showtime as a Production Assistant (intern) for *The L Word*. She conquered New York as an Editorial Intern for *Backstage* newspaper. She towered over PR: two internship gigs a piece in Tallahassee (Moore, Zimmerman) and in LA (BWR, Warren Cowan and Associates). Most miraculous of all, the Intern Queen did the internship trifecta, three at once, just *because*: On-Air Promotions at NBC, Drama and Comedy Development at Fox, and radio at MTV. Among the royal exploits recorded: clerical tasks, cold-calling media, making press kits, controlling audition lines, running scripts to talent, dubbing tapes, collating scripts, attending press conferences, coordinating staff trips, and so on.

For teens and twenty-somethings, internships are at least a source of social capital (if not actual capital), and this shared generational experience demands spokespeople and stars, and apparently tee shirts. Intern Queen seems to have had a modest success in making a business out of her internship overdose—her company, Intern Queen Inc., dishes out internship advice (on the blog "I AM INTERN"), helps jittery kids secure glamorous unpaid posts, polishes CVs for a fee, and has its own clothing line, called Intern Ethiks—all part of the Intern Queen's efforts, at last, to monetize. She has promotional partnerships with University of Dreams and with the personal branding website OneCubicle. She claims to have worked with over 500 employers across North America, to have spoken at thirty-five colleges in sixteen states, to have arranged hundreds of placements, and to receive 40,000 visitors on her site each month.

The Queen's intern boosterism quickly begins to sound like a relentless harangue. Her sometime advice column in *Seventeen* magazine—"five secrets to help *you* to get the most out of your experience"—praises and perpetuates all that's obsequious and careerist in the intern experience. Under tip #4, "Know your place," she lets her readers in on what she learned through hard experience: "As an intern, you should always keep quiet unless someone asks your opinion … I made sure not to overstep my bounds." So much for interns as "fresh voices" or enfants terribles. Tip #2, "Get coffee skills," admits that it's "lame" to talk about the coffee maker and copy machine aspect of internships, but goes on to do just that. Not knowing how to use a coffee maker in her early days as a serial intern, Lauren writes, "I made myself look inexperienced—and had to work *twice* as hard to get [my boss] to trust me with tougher tasks." These hackneyed tricks of the intern trade are never held up to any scrutiny. The ever-smiling, unquestioning, and well-made-up intern is held up for our admiration and emulation.

The Intern Queen is extreme even as internship cheerleaders go, but she may also be a frightening bellwether. Hundreds of high school and college students, dazed by the scramble for internships, write to her for advice and heed her manifestos, groping for a role model. The Queen hears from more and more teens looking to land internships early on. She hears from companies laying off employees in the current downturn and hoping to replace them with a patchwork of interns. The tee shirts she sells proclaim in bold letters: "I spill coffee for a living," "All work, no pay," "I'll do anything for connections." She's confident that the future belongs to people like her—savvy kids from well-heeled families, able to underbid and out-network the competition: serial interns.

The Intern Guru takes a more critical approach, but his underlying goal is the same: to be at the center of the internship gold rush, directing traffic. He is Matthew Zinman, a self-described "educational activist and social entrepreneur," who controls a hot-air empire that includes the Internship Institute, an umbrella non-profit organization; Apprenti-Corps, a service learning program; the impassioned "Intern Guru" blog; and his own Z University, "an educational affiliate." His most recent, high-minded endeavor, Businesses for the Ethical Treatment of Interns (BETI), calls for mandatory internships at all colleges and a network of Internship Readiness and Job Placement Centers across the country, managed by universities and corporations. Never mind the nod to animal rights: Zinman is in the business of selling instructional DVDs, hand-books, and consulting services to companies that hire interns. Like many in the internship industry, he moves seamlessly from the vocabu-lary of education and social justice to that of business, preaching that internships are "THE solution to improve workforce readiness and 'right-careering' college students."

Then there's the Intern Lady, Cindy Morgan-Jaffe, who hawks "starter kits" like "Find an Internship" ($59.95) and "Make Your Internship

Count" ($29.95), welcoming students to "the Intern Lady Talent Pool" for a cool $350: that gets you a brief interview with the Lady herself, a cursory review of your "portfolio" (résumé, cover-letter, and online profiles) and her certification that you are "job ready." "Over 80 percent of jobs are found through networking," counsels the Intern Lady, promising that she'll direct the many internship leads she hears about to her "talent pool."

Other free agent career coaches trying to make a buck off internships —and usually off entry-level jobs as well—are powering their start-ups with, you guessed it, unpaid interns. Heather Huhman, a frequent propagandist for internships, claims to be "passionate about helping students and recent college graduates pursue their dream careers," but runs her career-coaching company Come Recommended on unpaid labor: at one point in 2010, six of Huhman's eleven employees, in every area from editorial content to corporate relations, were interns. J. P. O'Donnell, who runs the career advice blog Careerealism (with its tagline "Because EVERY job is temporary"), recently hired twenty "virtual twinterns," unpaid virtual interns to "increase the visibility" of her site via Twitter. Is that a good career move for college students—to spend eight hours a week promoting somebody's blog via 140-character messages?

More thoughtful are young ex-interns like Richard Bottner, who calls himself "The Intern Advocate." After an internship at a well-known company in Boston that "wasn't what they said it was going to be," Bottner established Intern Bridge, which has since produced the most detailed and comprehensive statistics on college internships in the U.S. The principal customers for Bottner's research and consulting services are companies and college career counselors; products include webinars, research reports, how-to books, and advice on everything internship-related, from how to select an internship supervisor to how to evaluate the success of a program. "Our clients range from small- and medium-sized businesses, mom-and-pops, to Fortune 500 companies," says Bottner. "There's definitely a marketplace. There's more and more people that are seeing opportunity in the internship space."

That's the space that Robin Richards, a serial entrepreneur from southern California who has already brought the world Tickets.com and MP3.com, intends to dominate. Dismissive of the "thousands of micro marketplaces," he intends to establish the new Internships.com as "the world's largest internship marketplace," ultimately capable of listing a million positions (there were under 22,000 on the site as of mid-2010). A bevy of job-listing sites like MonsterTRAK, Vault, and WetFeet—which do quite a bit of internship business, but don't focus on it—had better beware. The massive trade in internship guidebooks—there are thousands that cover the topic, and hundreds that focus on it—may be at stake as well, as more and more of the resources move online.

Tiny companies are scrambling to occupy their own particular niches. There is now a legion of them just trying to play middleman between interns and start-ups, which can always use the free talent. Urban Interns, based in New York, charges employers $39.95 for one job posting, active for thirty days, and hawks a premium feature for interns. "Business owners are increasingly relying on a variety of part-time, flexible paid and unpaid hiring solutions ..." says the company's co-founder, explaining the demand. Across the Atlantic, a group of Oxford graduates coined the term "enternship" for the entrepreneurial internships listed on their website of the same name, promising maximum flexibility for the "enternship provider." Proclaiming itself "in alpha" (not even beta, like these other efforts), the freshly minted YouTern offers a similar service. Fast Track Internships takes a sneakier approach, charging $799 to land you unpaid work (or your money back!), essentially by authoring and editing your application materials without employers knowing. Co-founder Steve Rodems, a former powdered soap salesman, claims that 10 percent of his clients are college graduates, marooned by the recession. Another new service, Jobnob, has thousands of listings that explicitly target recent graduates out of work, encouraging them to take on part-time stints at start-ups, primarily unpaid. Jobnob-hosted Happy Hours, some held on elite college campuses, have attracted hundreds of eager attendees, as the *Atlantic* reported.[2]

Between specious content, stock photos, and broken URLs, it's clear that many websites in "the internship space" are fly-by-night at best, bits of business culture ephemera dreamed up by former interns and hucksters on the make. Are dedicated "internship search engines" like internalert.com and thinkintern.com likely to ever take off? How can internsforyou.com promise to supply interns for any need within thirty to sixty days, offering companies "a flexible pool of people that are already trained and can be called in the future on an 'as needed' basis"? Is it better to charge employers or young people for "resources," be a matchmaker, or sell internship positions outright? No one knows yet. Whether it waxes or wanes, consolidates or multiplies, the internship industry points a dark way forward—internships are hot commodities on the open market. Someone is building a business, offering up your free labor, right now.

What is an internship worth? If you have already evolved beyond the outdated notion that people should be paid to work, let your imagination run free. In actual practice, a typical internship has all the accoutrements of a low-level job, albeit usually short-term and ill conceived, but the social meaning and economic function of internships, as we have seen, is something else altogether. Interns are positioned as "investors" with cash and time to burn, or customers, conspicuously consuming internships to adorn already extravagant résumés. Employers, eager to give back, are the friendly people who allow interns to take up office space and perform a bit of cheap labor. After years of being flooded with applications, and patting themselves on the back, employers are finally realizing the extent of their power—why not sell internships outright?

Internship auctions are apparently an innovation of the late Subprime Era, but they are thriving equally well, perhaps even better, in the pits of a recession. The practice is as straightforward as it sounds—an organization puts one of its internships on the auction block and the position is awarded to the highest bidder: there is no question of advertising the position, reading applications, conducting interviews and the rest of that meritocratic nonsense. The money goes to charity, at least at this stage in the evolution of internship auctions: this is what justifies the buying and selling of a job. "I didn't think twice," says a PR executive, who now auctions off an internship in her office each year to benefit a charity she supports. The president of the charity asked her to do it, she says, and "every year it goes for a higher rate."

Hundreds of such auctions have taken place, if not more. Leaving aside private school benefits and charity galas, the website CharityBuzz.com alone has sold well over 100 internships at nonprofits, fashion houses, media outlets, and so on. On average, even less glamorous internships tend to go for several thousand dollars—but in the upper stratosphere a Versace position in New York City sold after nineteen bids for $5,000; a blogging internship with the Huffington Post went for $13,000. (The website Gawker quipped afterwards: "If this thing succeeds there is no limit to the number of internships we personally expect to be auctioning off, on the side. This new revenue stream could save the once-new media.") It goes without saying that these companies won't be paying their interns any time soon, not now that the *companies* are being paid.

While even fairly pedestrian paid internships and entry-level jobs melt away, internship auctions are setting new records all the time; prestigious positions have moved way out of reach. In April 2010, a one-week internship at Vogue, with fashion doyenne Anna Wintour, was snapped up for a cool $42,500. The money will benefit the Robert F. Kennedy Center for Justice and Human Rights; it's better not to ask if the auctioning of job opportunities is a fitting tribute to the liberal icon.[3] According to the CEO of CharityBuzz.com, half of the internship bidders are parents looking to snap up these experiences for their children.[4] The auctioning of full-time jobs would seem a foolish and unfair hiring practice, but somehow bidding on internships passes muster. Even short-term internships can provide crucial access to a profession or a mentor—it's no wonder that the wealthy are willing to pay significant sums for their progeny to vault over the competition. Access to internships is often restricted enough as it is—to enrolled students (sometimes at particular schools), to those with connections, to those who can afford to work for zero or no pay. Internship auctions, whatever good causes they may benefit, are a crowning absurdity.

Even internship boosters find much to criticize in University of Dreams, the excesses of the Intern Queen, and the prospect of internships placed on the auction block—they commit the cardinal sin of cutting out the schools. For non-students without personal connections, paying to land an internship may seem like the best available option; after all, students taking for-credit internships often pay their schools significant sums for the same privilege. The Academy originated the market in student futures and still runs the largest of them all, spreading the internship gospel and selling students academic credit by the pound, as we saw in Chapter 5. If the marketplace is now increasingly beyond the control of colleges and universities, they have only themselves to blame for monopolizing opportunities, sanctioning illegal work situations, and letting the academic legitimacy of internships wither.

The growth of the internship business, and the transformation of internships into both a commodity and a status symbol, is relatively recent: only a decade ago, there was little, if any, commercial activity surrounding them. When they first emerged, career centers saw internship businesses as filling a useful niche, handling a surge of interest especially in overseas opportunities—an internship counselor at a small college in Ohio, after all, may not be prepared to help a student find an internship in Barcelona or Buenos Aires. (Larger and wealthier schools now often do have one or more career counselors dedicated to international internships.)

Now, even domestically, businesses may often have an edge, giving students the exact kind of internships they ask for, bundling them attractively into larger "experiences," and aggregating internship postings from all over, while career offices remain focused, by choice or by necessity, on opportunities in the college's immediate vicinity. And this is perhaps the most sinister advantage—many internship businesses offer the luxury of direct placement, virtually securing an internship for their client, who may apply only in name or show up for a final interview. At career centers, says John Charles, an internship advisor at American University, "the great bulk of the work is assistance, resources, preparation, coaching. For various reasons we don't try to place students." The reality, says Charles, is that "individuals have to be able to learn how to find their own jobs and internships, because it's a life skill, and we want them to develop those skills"; at the same time, he adds "there's also a fairness issue, because if we want to target students to get certain opportunities, it means that we're giving them advantages that we're not giving to other students." A third consideration is that it's not practical, in most cases, for a small career office to place the hundreds or thousands of students who are seeking internships; as a career counselor at an elite private university says: "We have no way to do placement in the way it used to be done. Employers don't act that way."

Will the internship industry remain a relatively minor player, or will it effectively muscle out schools and take on the massive proportions predicted by Eric Lochtefeld? If an organization is selling internships, does its tax status—profit or non-profit—really make much difference? With few exceptions, neither businesses nor career centers have demonstrated much willingness to check the spread of unpaid and illegal internships. When employers are unwilling to pay, there are no efforts at any scale to guarantee access for those without money behind them, whether working-class university students, community college students, or those outside higher education altogether. Making an industry out of internships simply renders tangible a fait accompli long in the making: internships are becoming the face of privilege.

CHAPTER NINE

What About Everybody Else?

Simply holler, "Internships are not racist and elitist!" as loud as you can; repeat as necessary until you believe it.
—Jim Frederick, "Internment Camp"

"I enviously saw them toil in their chosen field for no money," writes Lucy of her college friends, "while I was desperate to get any job I could that would pay my rent and bills, as I was responsible for *all* of my own costs in college—rent, food, bills, and tuition … [I] needed to work full-time while attending school and sixty to seventy hours a week in the summer just to pay bills … Of course their connections through the glamorous world of unpaid internships got them much farther than my 'real job' did."

Siyu, still in school, tells his college newspaper a similar story: "While a lot of my friends have taken unpaid internships in the summer to boost their résumés, I can't afford to do that. With each internship experience of theirs, I notice the increasing gap between them and me. They are able to afford experiences that I cannot at this point, and these experiences definitely serve as bonuses for their future job searches."

A Master's student in Oregon sees little chance of working in politics. "My parents and I immigrated to this country fourteen years ago with little but the clothes on our backs," he wrote to his local public radio station. "Since I entered college as a freshman many years ago, I have found that I do not have the option to work a full or even a part time internship which is unpaid. For years now, I have been restricted to looking for only paid internships in order to contribute my share to the family's finances. As someone who is very interested in politics and has studied political science, I have found that this means most of the internships in Washington, D.C., for example, or even some internships at the state level, are not ones that I can afford to participate in simply because they are unpaid. This is essentially a kind of economic stagnation: because I cannot afford to take unpaid internships, I have less experience than some of my more well-off friends and because I am less experienced, I am less employable."

Then there's Caitlin, who has plans to be a journalist but can't afford to take on unpaid work—she spends her summers earning money as a lifeguard: "I love hearing about the unpaid internships my friends have taken, and I don't resent the fact that they're able to take them, but I definitely recognize the growing gap between me and them with each internship they take." Or take Rebecca, who had set her sights on an unpaid consulting internship, before her mother was laid off and part of her college scholarship axed by state budget cuts. She had no choice but to take a paying job. As few consulting firms are now taking candidates without "relevant experience" (read: a consulting internship), Rebecca is justifiably worried: a door may have just closed in her face.[1]

Lucy, Siyu, Caitlin, and Rebecca are not isolated individuals—most young Americans, in most circumstances, cannot afford to work for free or less than minimum wage for any appreciable period of time. It's not by any means true that all interns are rich—many, if not most, are making a serious sacrifice to take on unpaid work temporarily, when there's no other option. However, there is another sizeable, as yet invisible group: the non-interns. It's impossible to estimate how often a young person's career ambitions are blocked by the financial hardship of an internship. "You can be whatever what you want when you grow up" is a childhood fairy tale for all but a few. Everyone, at some point, gets a mental map to the realm of the possible, in terms of work and career—everyone gradually internalizes the fact that some professions are for the children of the well-to-do. It's a conclusion drawn by observing who's involved, where the jobs are located, what the pay is like, and what the other barriers to entry are. "People reshape their ambitions to fit the situation at any given time," says Anya Kamenetz, mentioning a friend who toiled as a fact-checker without pay, hoping to break into journalism. When financial reality forced him to throw in the towel, he found work at a library and gradually convinced himself into a new career.

Still intimately linked to four-year schools and well-to-do segments of society, internships are often a pipe dream for the 70 percent of young Americans who don't graduate from college. For this group, any career path that mandates internships is effectively off limits. High school internships, still relatively unusual, are concentrated at wealthier, typically private schools. In communities where college attendance is rare, internships are not even on the radar; among college dropouts, they are a rarity. The overwhelming percentage of community college students have to work paying jobs alongside their classes, leaving many internships out of reach. Who's left? Even among college undergraduates, 80 percent of whom work, unpaid or low-paid internships are often a serious stretch—and the ability to undertake them far from a given. Ben Yagoda, a professor of journalism at the University of Delaware, states the case succinctly: "The pressure to complete an internship before graduation backs many low-income students into a corner: they can either take a paying job during the summer to earn money and not go further into debt, or they can take out additional loans to finance a summer internship. Both options hurt them in the long-run, by either limiting their experience and therefore marketability as a job candidate, or by accruing more debt."[2] Rising tuition, the cost of textbooks, student-loan rates, and cynical credit card marketing, Yagoda points out, have all been denounced for their role in holding young people back, but unfair internships have largely escaped scrutiny.

For students already exhausted from the climb, internships are the newest rung on the ladder, the latest lap in the credentialing race, as more and more professions require college degrees, special training certificates, special types of experience, and graduate degrees. The connection between class and educational attainment has solidified in recent years, but at least a massive public and private effort has gone into providing financial aid and establishing government-supported schools and universities. Internships, with only the faintest beginnings of such a broad support network, threaten to erase these achievements, leaving scholarship kids and graduates of state schools and community colleges stranded. Although rigorous calculations are impossible, internships are an increasingly potent factor in the disturbing trend of widening social inequality in America—a process four decades in the making that lines up tellingly with the timeline of the internship explosion.

The argument is straightforward: many internships, especially the small but influential sliver of unpaid and glamorous ones, are the preserve of the upper-middle class and the super-rich. These internships provide the already privileged with a significant head start that pays professional and financial dividends over time, as boosters never tire of repeating. The rich get richer or stay rich, in other words, thanks in part to prized internships, while the poor get poorer because they're barred from the world of white-collar work, where high salaries are increasingly concentrated. For well-to-do and wealthy families seeking to guarantee their offspring's future prosperity, internships are a powerful investment vehicle, an instrument of self-preservation in the same category as private tutoring, exclusive schools, and trust funds. Meanwhile, a vast group of low- and middle-income families stretch their finances thin to afford thankless unpaid positions, which are less and less likely to lead to real work, and a forgotten majority can't afford to play the game at all.

How significantly this process exacerbates efforts to build a more meritocratic society is unknown; with better data collection and a longitudinal economic study, we might have an answer. Besides, it's probably too early to gauge the deepest effects—the internship explosion has only gone fully mainstream, integrated into every white-collar field, since around the turn of the millennium. If current trends hold, today's interns will dominate critical professions and hold positions of substantial power in a few decades, even more so than today; today's non-interns will remain trapped in the basement of American life. By the time a proper accounting is possible, the damage to our meritocratic ideals will have been done.

We know how racist and sexist hiring policies, education practices, and work conditions have long perpetuated significant pay differentials between white men, on the one hand, and women and minorities on the other, only recently beginning to narrow under intense legal and social pressures. We know that workplace practices, from the hiring process to the subtle games of office politics, have drastic impacts on social equality. Despite the battle against pay discrimination, income inequality between social classes continues to increase, with Gini coefficients ballooning around the globe—although still rooted in demographic differences, income inequality today is increasingly bound up with age and educational attainment. And, as a recent government-commissioned report in the U.K. discovered, with internships as well.

Reporting on "fair access to the professions" in the U.K., a team of policy-makers led by Alan Milburn, a former cabinet minister from a working-class background, devoted a chapter to the role of internships. According to the panel's report, "Internships are accessible only to some when they should be open to all who have aptitude. Currently employers are missing out on talented people—and talented people are missing opportunities to progress. There are negative consequences for social mobility and for fair access to the professions. A radical change is needed." The authors of the Milburn report make three recommendations: internship recruitment should be made transparent; programs should be run according to a set of humane and common-sense standards (given that "many internships, perhaps the majority, are not run so well"), and industries and employers should work towards "the removal of financial barriers for interns."[3]

The Milburn report, however diplomatic and cautious its language at times, galvanized opposition to unfair internships in the U.K.—in particular, it attracted attention for noting that, in several fields, "students are now highly unlikely to be able to progress into the profession without a minimum amount of relevant work experience," i.e. an internship. For example, Britain's National Union of Journalists told the panel that "under 10 percent of new entrants came from working-class backgrounds, with just 3 percent coming from homes headed by semi-skilled or unskilled workers." If the link between internships and social inequality remains only a compelling hypothesis, the connection between internships and access to certain professions is unmistakable.

To an equal, if not greater, extent in the U.S., internships have become a barrier to entry, particularly for professions that have broad and authoritative roles in the wider society, such as entertainment, journalism, and politics. A half-century, or even a few decades ago, people of working-class backgrounds were at least able to fill the lower and middling ranks of these professions; the face of discrimination was more likely to be gender- or race-based. Intense competition to break in, bone-deep funding cuts, and the erosion of a culture of paying for work have altered the landscape, with disturbing consequences. As Daniel Brook notes, "a whole host of middle-class careers that are often enjoyable and fulfilling—teaching, writing, music, art, activism, government service—no longer buy the lives they once did." We now take it for granted that enjoyable professions need not pay well, or perhaps at all—the satisfaction comes from the work, right? "As a result," writes Brook acidly, "these fields have been relegated to a mix of moral giants, mental midgets, and trust-fund babies."[4]

Imagine if people of wealthy backgrounds were disproportionately represented in accounting or racecar driving. If poor inner-city kids never become star polo players. What's the worst that could happen? The broader social impact of such skewing is likely to be minimal—some amount of demographic determinism may be inevitable, after all, as people figure out their careers. It might be a loss for polo as a sport, drawing from the limited talent pool of toffs, but policy-makers could keep their distance. Yet with internships the case is often altogether different—income issues aside, many of the professions that they unlock matter deeply to the broader society. Film and television shape our hopes and dreams, our stereotypes, our views of history and the future; journalists are opinion-makers, wielding access to vital information day-in and day-out; politicians are at the helm of our economic and social infrastructure, often responsible for matters of life and death. Even if individual filmmakers, columnists, or mayors don't impinge on our days, the aggregate effect matters; the overall direction of these professions plays a decisive role in the lives of us all.

It's easier for a working-class kid to enter the business or military elite, writes anthropologist David Graeber, than to penetrate the cultural elite, heavily concentrated in the internship-crazed professions. "A mechanic from Nebraska knows it is highly unlikely that his son or daughter will ever become an Enron executive. But it is possible," writes Graeber. "There is virtually no chance, however, that his child, no matter how talented, will ever become an international human-rights lawyer or a drama critic for the *New York Times*. Here we need to remember not just the changes in higher education but also the role of unpaid, or effectively unpaid, internships … It has become a fact of life in the United States that if one chooses a career for any reason other than the salary, for the first year or two one will not be paid." Graeber points out that in many professions—charitable work or literary criticism, for instance—"structures of exclusion" have existed for a long time, "but in recent decades fences have become fortresses." The political implication is a recipe for red-state paranoia: the mechanic from Nebraska comes to resent and mistrust the human rights lawyer more than the Enron executive.[5]

In a straw poll taken at a summer intern lunch in Washington D.C., writes Laura Vanderkam in *USA Today*, she found that "more than 60 percent of these mostly unpaid interns had parents earning more than $100,000 a year." She adds: "Only about 20 percent of all families of college students earn that much." If interns face daily indignities, as we have documented in previous chapters, many are also fundamentally privileged. For all their abuses and contradictions, internships are often effective at furthering careers, although not always. Indignities and mindless work may or may not be worth enduring. But work that is recognizably work, undertaken without wages in return, is like a virus in the labor force, spreading quickly to other sectors—it should be illegal no matter the net worth of the worker. *Not* having access to an internship can be the kiss of death if you want to move up in the world.[6]

Access to an internship involves not only being able to afford it, but also being able to get the position in the first place. If personal connections grease the wheels of the job market, they are the motor powering the trade in internships. Drawing on testimony from across the U.K., the Milburn report confirmed that, despite the rising importance of internships, "by and large, they operate as part of an informal economy in which securing an internship all too often depends on who you know and not on what you know." Few in the U.S. would disagree—and personal connections are only the tip of the iceberg, when academic programs, internship businesses, "experiential education," non-profits and even auctioneers are all getting in on the act. An individual on her own may stand little chance.

"It's almost on an endless basis that people ask me for help with internships," an executive at a well-known company told me. "I'm bombarded with requests and I tend to say yes. I have found them for a lot of people in my network—friends who have kids … If I got a request from someone I didn't know, to be an intern for me this summer, and it wasn't coming through a friend or a network, I'd probably turn it down." In any case, she adds, an internship is "a definite easier ask" for parents (as opposed to a job), "and it's easier for me to say yes, all I need to do is find a desk, a computer and a phone and that person is on board. I don't need to make the case that I need to bring another salary in my P and L [Profit and Loss Statement]." She considers it an "informal favor," "helping people whom I know get access to this experience"—"I'm not going through any corporate channels to do it." The quality of interns obtained this way has been "diverse," as she politely phrases it. They were not top-flight talents that she would trust with core functions: "We had a report, and someone stapled everything upside down for me."

The circle of favors, moreover, is always expanding. "We do work with a Catholic school around the corner," the executive told me, "because some things that we do for our clients involve curriculum, and we're always looking for a school to test a curriculum. The nuns called us up and said we've tested your curriculum, we've been happy to do it. As a favor for us, will you bring in our kids as interns?" Then there's the senior executive at the firm with strong ties to his ethnic roots: "Every summer he comes to me with kids from his homeland who want internships. Every year it's so hard to refuse him, we just try to find a space for these kids to sit."

Until this year, the executive usually employed three or four interns in her office each summer; they would work regular hours "at the basic jobs of the industry" without pay and without academic credit. However, the old policy was dropped recently when the firm's practices came under scrutiny: "In the past, we had unpaid internships and this year we did change that," an HR executive at the firm told me. "The reason why we changed to a paid internship is not that we've had any difficulty in finding candidates. To the contrary, we have lots and lots of interest in unpaid internships and always have. But there has been particularly this year a sharp increase in media attention and Department of Labor attention to whether or not unpaid internships are truly legal." The gentlest and most generalized reminder, in other words, was sufficient to make plain the risks that the company was taking—and the interns were worth keeping.

As far as she always knew, added the executive, internships were "one of those gray, gray areas under the law," but it's "better to stick with the letter of the law than to push the boundaries," especially given the recent legal clarifications. Reform of the firm's internship practices—paying minimum wage is also likely to lead to increased HR involvement with the interns—was a way for the executive to make her mark as a prudent manager, as she's new to the company. With between twenty-five and thirty summer interns across the entire firm, the move from unpaid to minimum wage will hardly have a traumatic effect on the bottom line. Although this step is something the company should be proud of, the executive's caution in wanting to remain anonymous is understandable. "Not that I think anybody from the Department of Labor is going to be reading your book and trying to identify companies that might have been in violation in the past," she said to me, "but I don't want to take any chances, if you can understand what I mean."

"We have this advisory board, very high wealth individuals, heads of hedge funds and whatnot," says "Tom," describing a well-known poverty alleviation nonprofit founded by a Nobel Prize winner. "They send their nephew in and so we have no choice but to take him." One summer, he adds, an individual office had six full-time staff, five graduate student interns, and four to five "nephews or nieces of important people" interns. "It happens to us all the time," says Tom. "Who are these kids? They're totally ineffective, they take up space, I have to redo their work products—but at the same time, you have to smile and say, 'Great, thank you so much.' It's like babysitting, we have to keep them happy. I get frustrated—I just want somebody who does their job." The nonprofit gets ten to fifteen résumés a day, he says—"People will do anything for us, they love our founder. People want to be inspired, especially our generation." But inspiration is for the well connected. Tom says that he has developed a new theory about the NGO world while working there: "I think nonprofit work is for the rich."

Nonprofit work, fashion, film, the arts: perhaps more than ever before, the rich are working—and dominating particular industries. This is where "the rock-star jobs" and the glamor internships are—the more glamor is perceived, the more vital the connections are and the less likely it is that pay will ever enter the equation. Yet rich kids aren't the only ones who want the dream careers: according to a national survey conducted a few years back, one out of eighteen college freshmen expected to become an actor, musician, or artist. "The policy at almost all the auction houses, museums, the whole art world, is that internships are unpaid," "John," an art history major, told me matter-of-factly. At the auction house where he interned, many interns who had previously received (meager) pay had just lost it, and a new rotation of interns (there are five rotations each year) had been added, "mostly because they had experienced a whole bunch of layoffs and just needed manpower." During John's academic-year stint, he edited an entire catalogue for his department, which he called a positive experience overall, although admittedly in a very particular work environment: "Almost everyone I was working with was privileged in some sort of manner. And one of the other interns I was working with was literally royalty. The amount of work that she was ready to do was next to nothing. Her father is a customer."

Elite auction houses, fancy galleries and prestigious museums are already closely associated with wealthy elites, who steer and support them: perhaps some skewing in their workforces is not surprising; in any case, they represent a fairly small niche. But a wide range of lesser-known careers now emanate at least a local glamor, from book publishing to public relations, from sports management to graphic design, and even some areas of the law. "I noticed that summer I interned with the judge that all the interns were rich kids: all the interns were driving Lexuses, Mercedes, like all leather, fully loaded cars," a young lawyer told me of her internship on the Ninth Circuit Court. "I realized that the only way people in law school can work for judges is by being from wealthy backgrounds. By working with a judge, you get to network with that judge and other judges, and you just get an insight into the process that no one else does. We got to see why they picked applicants to interview for a clerkship. We got to know the reputations of judges—what do they want, what do they not want. Clerkships are so hard to get that any little bit helps."

In small professional worlds like animation, theater, and photography, between the overproduction of the relevant academic degrees and the high demand to break in, conditions continue to worsen significantly for interns. Floods of family-supported interns have brought the bargaining power of young professionals in these fields, minuscule to begin with, close to zero. "These internship opportunities no one would be able to accept if they didn't have the money to support themselves while learning about their craft," says "Sandy," referring to the twelve- and sometimes fifteen-hour days she's spent on the dream of becoming a stage manager, every hour well below minimum wage. Interning and apprenticing at four theaters across the country (in Maine, New Jersey, Florida, and California), three of them unionized, Sandy has never been able to earn more than $150 per week, though sometimes housing and food have been covered. Nor has she ever been able to take on other jobs simultaneously. With three college internships under her belt, Sandy is more than five years into the intern trap, with no end in sight—she's still in the game thanks to family support.

Considerable online controversies have recently broken out around the extent of the unreasonable demands now made even by the most famous and flourishing employers. A recent case in point: the studio of photojournalist James Nachtwey posted an intern-seeking ad, looking for candidates with an impressive range of specialized skills for a minimum of three months of unpaid work. The backlash was intense for Nachtwey, perhaps particularly so because he is a photographer considered to be at the apex of his profession, with prestigious, six-figure monetary awards to his name—especially well known for creating work in war zones or during epidemics that makes transparent appeals for social justice. "It is insulting, and frankly should be illegal in that it discriminates on the basis of class," wrote one commenter on Jamie's List, a website for professional photographers. Another called such unpaid internship postings "especially shameful when they're attached to individuals—such as Nachtwey —and institutions that claim to be working in the interest of social justice." Everyone understands that the next generation of Nachtweys is not to be found among the Third World victims he photographs. A well-educated elite from well-to-do backgrounds will stand behind the camera.[7]

"Because cultural work is prominently featured in popular discourse, especially in visual images, and associated with trendsetters, beautiful people, hipness and cool," writes Gina Neff, unpaid internships, freelance arrangements, and other forms of precarious "entrepreneurial labor" become "a model for how workers in other industries should also behave under flexible employment conditions." And perhaps the ultimate model of this type—where everyone is now a free agent, where projects coalesce and dissolve without cease, where a few hits subsidize a heap of failures —is the entertainment industry: the vast penumbra of brand-name studios, production companies, television networks, record labels, and so on that stretches over the endless offices of Hollywood, Burbank, and Manhattan. What happens when glamor internships—and the resulting socioeconomic skew in the workforce—become part and parcel of an industry that employs millions, is heavily unionized, and exerts enormous influence around the world?

It's no secret that the world of entertainment, particularly film and television, is an unlikely cocktail of highly skilled, unionized professionals mixed in with the wealthy and well connected, basking and dabbling in the scene. What effect does it have when only the well off can afford the internships necessary to become producers, directors, or screenwriters? These figures wield a massive influence; the nature of their background matters. The personal socioeconomic background of studio heads, film-makers and television producers is manifestly influential in the projects they pursue and the way they pursue them. The "new Hollywood" of the 1970s, ushered in by ethnic, working-class directors like Martin Scorsese and Woody Allen, championed realistic, countercultural work over vapid, feel-good musicals. Since then, a concerted effort around increasing Hollywood's ethnic and racial diversity has left questions of class behind. What might we expect of a grown-up "intern generation" defining taste in film and television a few decades hence? On a guess, a homogenization of taste, a preference for the lavish over the shoestring, plot settings endlessly recurring in southern California suburbs and New York City, upper-middle or upper-class heroes and heroines, unrealistic and unrepresentative portrayals of American life, and a lack of pointed social commentary. In short, we're already halfway there.

Indeed, to some extent, the idea that you need to pay your dues and work your way up is already deeply rooted in the entertainment business, with foundational myths like Steven Spielberg's "unofficial, on-the-fly internship," seven days a week unpaid at Universal Studios. According to a *Vanity Fair* profile, the young Spielberg simply "showed up on the lot wearing a suit, his dad's briefcase in hand" and "settled into an empty office … making himself known to the cinematographers and directors." George Lucas' internship at Warner Brothers landed him on the set of a musical directed by Francis Ford Coppola, who mentored the young USC graduate.[8]

"In this industry, if you aren't willing to debase yourself for free, you're in trouble, because someone else will," according to Matt Singer, who has written on his multiple internships in the film business. "A bad internship is a slippery slope of degradation and exploitation. When I quit several months later," Singer writes of a film-editing internship, "I hadn't edited a single piece of film, but I had spent an afternoon visiting every Vitamin Shoppe in midtown on a futile quest for a discontinued flavor of Power-Bar." At another internship, Singer writes, "I spent an entire week ineptly assembling a large tape cabinet" and was then "scolded for my lack of carpentry skills"; at a third, he was "a pro bono valet to a producer who would not make eye contact with me, and who routinely demanded I pour her soda into a mug so that she needn't sip it from the can."

"Tyler," an eight-time intern and now an independent comedy writer, saw internships as the only way into entertainment: he was a suburban kid from Long Island, without family or friends to plug him into the scene. "I really was convinced," he says, "that having more than a half dozen internships on my résumé before I graduated college was going to seal the deal wherever I went, but it wasn't the case." No deals were sealed, no offers were made, and he looks back with some amazement on it all. "Everybody was gunning for a job—it was near impossible," says Tyler, but people would keep hoping against hope and making more and more sacrifices. There's the illusory sense that one more internship, or one more month on a job, might put you over the top. Interns, like actors, are betting on a long shot, waiting to be discovered.

Almost all of his intern colleagues had parental support behind them —more than that, says Tyler, "especially at the bigger places, so much of it is based on nepotism." Particularly "over the springs and summers, the interns were so often comprised of nephews or nieces or cousins of higher-ups." He stayed afloat thanks to paying jobs on the side, finding temp work, tutoring, squeezing oranges at a downtown juice bar. It hardly mattered to Tyler as long as the work supported his interning habit.

In the world of TV—Tyler had successive unpaid gigs at *Late Night With Conan O'Brien* and *Saturday Night Live*—interns give the big-shots "the ability or the opportunity to be lazy, and feel better about themselves, by dumping tasks on kids who are just trying to figure things out." Still, there was no other way, he reasoned—and a twenty-year-old doesn't have the time, not to mention the clout, to change the whole system. At *Conan*, he was answering phone calls, running errands, and delivering mail. The hierarchy was strict and beyond question: "The writers were treated like kings and we weren't allowed to talk to them without being spoken to." At *SNL*, the atmosphere was better, or at least someone as experienced and driven as Tyler was able to make the best of it: "I forced my way into sitting in on writers' meetings, seeing scripts that were going to be tossed, or sketches that were going to be canned, just taking in as much as possible, even if it was somewhat under the radar."

At *SNL*, errands and menial work were nonetheless always the norm. "I had to take a car to New Jersey to pick up a sumo wrestler's outfit, and I was just like, what am I doing? What, this is really teaching me a lot about comedy writing and television production?" Worse for his morale was an errand he was given during a major blizzard, when he had to deliver a script to a writer's home on a Saturday night. "I was freezing, there were piles and piles of snow, and I had this wet envelope, and all I wanted to do was get to a place that's warm and maybe use the bathroom." After arriving at the writer's apartment building in Chelsea, he trudged up four or five flights of stairs, "so exhausted, a wet mess," and rang the bell, only to have the voice of the invisible writer dismiss him summarily: "Throw it in front of my door. Have a nice day." "That was definitely a degrading and infuriating moment," says Tyler. Yet these opportunities are desperately in demand.

"So many of them are executive referrals," admits "Laura" of her interns—she is a television executive at a major studio, running one of the most formal internship programs in the industry. Diversity is "absolutely" a problem in television, she says, and internships exacerbate it. A decade ago, she says, connections were everything; interning was so informal that the studio's legal, safety, and labor relations staff didn't even know about it—"Then I think there was an incident where somebody [an intern] got hurt," says the executive, "and it was like, 'What do we do? What intern? Why didn't you tell us you had an intern? You can't be doing that.'" Now the studio advertises with local colleges, sometimes receiving up to fifty applications for one spot; and there are typically thirty interns per semester, a third of them working in corporate (paid $10 an hour, supervised by HR) and the other two-thirds on individual shows (unpaid, unsupervised, required to receive academic credit). "We have to check the paperwork," says Laura, in regard to students receiving credit—the studio has no other responsibilities in this respect. "Especially with the economy the way it is, and here where we've had a reduction in workforce, [the interns] fill a very important need," the executive adds—they cover phones, alphabetize files, make deliveries, and sometimes do the work of coordinators as well, handling budgets and call sheets. "When we have a lot of people on vacation or who are out sick, we deploy the interns," she says. With the recent layoff of multiple production assistants, interns filled the breach.

Without money or connections behind you, it's a serious uphill battle, says "Sally," who calls herself "one of the fortunate ones who rose from intern to PA [production assistant]". "I've seen a lot of people that came here [to LA] that couldn't get a job, or couldn't afford to work for free, so they went back to Utah, or Colorado, or wherever they're from. You have to be able to sacrifice, take a risk, live in a studio, or live with six people. If you don't know anyone, then you've got to hustle." Sally knows what she's talking about—having grown up in a poor, single-parent family and working multiple internships during college, just barely scraping by.

In many cases, the thankless unpaid labor doesn't necessarily end even after a string of internships. "Working for free as a PA is something you need to do—a lot of them work for free, or they work for mileage or they work for food," says Sally, adding that "mileage" in Hollywood often does not include commuting, only driving on the job in one's own car. Indeed, conditions for PAs are not unlike those faced by interns, although the former are generally in their mid- or late-twenties, already college graduates, sometimes with substantial work experience. Long-time showbiz journalist David Robb writes that you can recognize PAs because "they wear earpieces on the set so they can be yelled at from afar—and they all have stories of abuse." They are "the lowest-paid workers on the set—if paid at all—and the only ones without a union, the only ones no union even wants to bother with. In Hollywood's caste system, they are the untouchables." Robb cites a Craigslist ad, representative of the vital, highly skilled labor that companies are trying to scoop up for free: "Looking for experienced production assistant for upcoming feature-length film shoot in Missouri. Great for your résumé! We are looking for those who feel comfortable with/and have: Camera/equipment knowledge; camera set up, working closely with DP; lighting set up; transporting equipment and heavy lifting. Compensation: no pay." Increasingly, such ads also use the word "production intern" or "intern PA," in an attempt to skirt the law.[9]

Sally at least may have finally broken through; she's just started a production company of her own. Now that the tiny start-up is just moving out of stealth mode, says Sally with a laugh, she's planning to go back to her old campus and get some interns.

"Jim" considered himself lucky—at least he had an internship. The summer after his sophomore year, already feeling "behind the eight-ball" in the internship arms race, Jim marshaled college connections to score an unpaid, full-time position at NBC in New York. But there was a last-minute catch—a friend from school, who had promised Jim a place to sleep for the summer, backed out of the arrangement. Jim spent the rest of the summer effectively homeless, crashing on more than twenty different couches in the tri-state area and exhausting his extended network. "It was harder to get people to commit for the weekends—I'd usually end up traveling really far," remembers Jim, who hefted his duffel bag everywhere the entire summer and bought six-packs of Brooklyn Pennant Ale to thank his hosts. It was his first time ever in New York.

"It definitely hurt my confidence, in terms of who I am as a person," says Jim, who grew up in a small town and is the youngest son of two public interest lawyers. "I went back home and my dad is angry, he's in tears, insecure that he can't provide a place to live for his son, to try to further his career. That was tough, to see that." Jim learned that General Electric, NBC's parent company, with its market capitalization over $160 billion, declines to pay minimum wage to many of its youngest workers; that only the well off and well connected can land a prestigious internship and afford to take it. Three years later, Jim says he figured out "the whole getting-a-job thing is completely bogus in the upper crust of society." Still, he's not sure how he could have done anything differently: "I don't know how anyone ever explains multiple summers with huge divots in your résumé. What, you worked at Walmart? A gas station? It's a joke." For the vast majority of students who are not top of their class or graduating from top-tier schools, he says, internships are one of the few ways to distinguish yourself: "Unless you have 4.0 or 3.9 [GPA], who are you? The kids at our school that did jobs that are meaningless in terms of learning or progressing your career were just laughed at."

There is an increasingly stark divide between interns who coast along with the help of their parents and interns like Jim, possibly a much larger group—crashing on couches, taking out loans, working serious side-jobs that pay, even going on food stamps. These ways of coping with internship pressures do allow the less well heeled to play, for a time, and perhaps even win the internship game—but rarely can they go as far, or hold out as long, as the kids with parental backing and open checkbooks. Intern Bridge, in cooperation with Phil Gardner, alleges that unpaid internships in most fields "skew towards low-income families," indicating just how much of a sacrifice many interns and their families are making.

According to Intern Bridge reports, some three-quarters of students report that they need a paying job in order to work an unpaid internship. Even full-time "jobs on the side" are not uncommon: in two cases I have come across, unpaid interns at ABC and MTV worked as full-time bartenders, from 6 p.m. to 2 a.m., to support themselves—one still had to take out extra student loans to cover academic credit costs. The *New York Times* described Susan Lim, an undergraduate taking an unpaid internship doing public policy research, as working eighty-nine hours a week one summer, and well aware of the gulf between her and her wealthier fellow interns: "I have to do the same things they do plus more to get to the same place." Phil Gardner sees the negative academic effects of students' piling on both unpaid internships and paid work: "In that scenario, something's got to give. And I tell you what, it's more likely to be my class than the workplaces—because they need the income and they need the credential of the internship to get where they want to go, and the hell with the classes they're taking."[10]

One in nine Americans, to give the most conservative estimate, now rely on food stamps, meeting the income requirements of the federal relief program—and evidence is mounting that many of the new recipients (over 500,000) are in their twenties and have some college education, according to the Department of Agriculture. Anecdotally, it appears that more than a few of them are interns. In one case, an unpaid, full-time intern at a literary magazine had to go on food stamps and Medicaid a year after graduating with honors from a renowned college; in another, a directing intern at a theater, receiving an "exceptionally modest" stipend, relied on food stamps to get by. *The Pursuit of Happyness*, starring Will Smith, dramatizes the real-life story of Chris Gardner, who was forced to live on the streets, homeless with his young son, during a six-month unpaid internship as a stockbroker at Dean Witter. If such stories are relatively rare, they nonetheless make a point: internships leave us vulnerable, allowing no room for error, and forcing some, in extremis, onto the mercies of the welfare state.

Few of the teenagers and twenty-somethings from Jim's small town take on internships, he says, lacking the connections to beat the competition and the wherewithal and the mentality to live in a big, expensive city. And even though he pulled it off, Jim found himself a second-class citizen, barely able to keep up. Because of the low-quality "journal entries" he submitted, he didn't even earn the dubious 0.0 credit offered by his college, which NBC required: "I'm miserable because I have to work for free, and I'm having to then write journal entries about it just so that my college can vet me for the company, so I just sent crap over."

That was Jim's first and last summer in journalism—after graduating, he found work at a tech company. He's one of many middle-class kids from small-town America effectively shut out by a journalism profession that now asks its entrants to work for free and earn expensive graduate school credentials—all for an uncertain future. In print journalism, paying your dues used to mean a few low-paid years at a small-town newspaper; now it just as often entails an expensive graduate degree and unpaid stints. A significant percentage of the editorial staff at any given newspaper, magazine, news radio or television station got started this way, although the chances of any given intern converting to regular employment remain abysmally low. "It certainly weeds out a certain percentage of people who would be interested in it," says Ryan Krogh of *Outside* magazine, where eight of the twelve editors began as *Outside* interns, including those at the top of the masthead. At *Harper's*, nine of eighteen editors are reported to have started there as interns.

"Every single person on the editorial staff did one internship somewhere," says Anya Kamenetz of *Fast Company*, the business magazine where she works and where interns have outnumbered staff writers since the recession. Historically, in part because of strong unions, newspaper interns were once more likely to be paid than their counterparts in television—this is no longer the case. The New Media platforms replacing failing and struggling newspapers are even less likely to offer fair compensation for work. "I have a friend who has a small gossip website," one disillusioned Hollywood intern told me, "and he was able to get six summer interns responsible for updating digital content, tweeting, and updating their Facebook status updates."

As in other fields, the growth of credentialing in journalism has fed directly into the rise of internships—many "j schools" now require full-time internships during the degree, charging substantial tuition and providing relatively little support in return. "Unpaid internships are discriminatory," says Howard Schneider, a former editor of *Newsday* (which uses unpaid interns) and now the dean of the journalism school at SUNY–Stony Brook. "You are basically eliminating students who can't afford to do these." Schneider is one of the few at least asking the right questions: "At what point are we just feeding this beast that continues to use these students as surrogates? At what point do we wind up helping these news organizations defer ever deciding to hire anybody?"

"Sarah," like many of her 150 classmates at Northwestern's Medill School of Journalism, already had a magazine internship under her belt when her junior year rolled around—the usual semester for required full-time internships, many of them outside Illinois. "A huge ripoff," says Sarah, "I had to pay almost regular tuition to have a full-time internship," primarily fact-checking for a small monthly. Northwestern provided two brief internship check-ins and helped some of the students secure their positions. This is the same program in which MaryBeth Lipp, another Medill student, "felt vulnerable, fearful, disrespected, alone, and powerless" when sexual harassment began a few weeks into her internship, as described in Chapter 4.

Sarah ended up doing five internships in journalism, she told me, before realizing that she had to switch fields to find paying work. She blames herself for not realizing that simply having had internships in journalism put her in too broad a category to land most journalism jobs: specialization starts early. The last journalism stint—a year after she had graduated from college—involved moving back to Chicago, on an editor's insistence that the internship was a temporary measure while he arranged a full-time position. Then "about a month into it," Sarah told me, "he got fired/resigned, and then I was stuck at this internship with no prospect of a real job there ... So I was like, well shit, back to square one. What can I do? So I looked for internships again"—only this time in the world of environmental non-profits. Four months later, an internship became a full-time position, thanks in part to deft maneuvering on Sarah's part: "It was my first salaried job ever, two years after graduating. That was a big deal for me: I'm getting benefits, I'm going to have health insurance!"

The same struggle that kept Sarah out of journalism is something she also recently witnessed in her new field, while speaking on a panel about international nonprofit work: "The room was full of people with Master's degrees, some people with ten years of experience, and they were all unemployed ... There was seriously a desperate vibe in the room. And the panelists, including myself, kept encouraging people to get an internship: 'Why don't you just pack your bags and volunteer at an organization you really love?' Some of these people got really frustrated and they raised their hands and they were like, 'Look I don't know what your situation is, but I could never pack my bags and leave. I just could not afford it. Do you have any more practical advice?' " "It's pretty brutal," she adds, for "people who are knee-deep in student loans from getting their Master's and can't get a job" to have no option but unpaid work.

Sarah saw these effects on the field she left behind: "Journalism is not diverse—in the newsroom there are a lot of men, a lot of white men. I personally found it unfair that a lot of my classmates were able to take these unpaid internships in New York or D.C. at all these really prestigious publications—they all offer unpaid internships: the *New York Times*, the *Washington Post*, the *New Yorker*, the *Wall Street Journal*. I know that some of these kids' parents were helping them with the cost of living. I can't even consider that as an option; it wouldn't work; I couldn't do that. Meanwhile their résumés look really prestigious." The annual Newsroom Census of the American Society of News Editors (ASNE), which has tracked diversity in journalism since 1978, confirms what Sarah saw first-hand—despite some improvement, minorities still represent only 13 percent of the workforce (although they constitute more than a third of the U.S. population).

"Isabel," who completed two unpaid public radio internships, sees broad ramifications for a profession whose members increasingly hail from upper-middle-class and upper-class backgrounds: "Almost every-one I knew doing internships were white upper-middle-class people who went to private universities. It narrows the voices of who we hear, it narrows the kind of news that we hear. Obviously you can have people from an upper-middle-class background who interview poor people, but they're not going to cover it in the same way and there's not going to be as rich a dialogue … That's something I've felt in general that public radio does lack, it tends to cover upper-middle-class issues." Adelle Waldman echoed this view in her *New Republic* article "Intern or Die": "when news is delivered by people who harbor such similar ambitions and come from such similar backgrounds, people who have spent their summers in the same cities and have worked at the same types of organizations … they are likely to keep spotting and writing about the same types of issues—and keep missing different ones."[11]

The same principle is coming to apply in many of the glamorous and creative fields where internships are ascendant: public interest lawyers drawn to the same kinds of cases, artists influenced more by aesthetic rather than political or class considerations, politicians sharing the same tired perspectives on how to defeat poverty. Politics in particular should give us pause for thought, although we have already examined the fright-ening internship hierarchy of Washington in Chapter 6. Where does that wise injunction "follow the money" lead us in the world of unpaid politi-cal internships? What are the consequences of relying on the voluntarism of the well-to-do, rather than a professional system of payment for work, open to all who are qualified?

First and foremost, a system of unpaid or underpaid internships is inherently limiting: any field in which it takes hold is trading away access to the best, most diverse talent for short-term, small-time savings. Instead of bemoaning the fact that many of the best and brightest now choose the private sector over public service, and attributing it all to high salaries and dazzling opportunities, we should ask a more basic question: is it even possible for a poor kid to break into politics anymore, at least without a serious champion, an enlightened university, or a dedicated nonprofit plucking her out of the crowd?

In a fascinating case study, the *New York Times* analyzed the nearly 1,500 interns who have worked unpaid at City Hall under New York City Mayor Michael Bloomberg, a fierce critic of nepotism. According to a mayoral spokesman, one in five interns was directly recommended by someone in the administration. Sometimes still in middle school, the children, grandchildren, and stepchildren of prominent political, business, and media figures all figured prominently (from the progeny of Goldman Sachs, CBS, and Blackstone Group executives to the scions of well-connected wordsmiths Tim Russert, Neil Simon, and Robert Caro).[12]

A truly representative politics is almost beyond our comprehension: a politics in which people of different professional backgrounds all took part, for instance, instead of the current tyranny of lawyers. Or a politics that included some leaders who had not graduated from the usual four-year colleges, to take another example. Internships are now another hoop to jump through for this homogenous mass of leaders, who have largely lapped up the same experiences and the same perspectives already. A stale, elitist politics is practically inevitable under such circumstances. A political system built on free, well-connected labor is a shaky edifice, an even more dire playground for the rich than Hollywood—at worst, the system becomes a tool of their interests, tinkered with or maintained at their beck and call; at best, it is a well-intentioned club of those born luckily to wealth, struggling to overcome the narrow viewpoints of their own class.

Kunda Musambacine was born in Zambia, attended school in England, and moved to the U.S. at age sixteen, thinking he wanted to be an artist. He took a marketing job, in deference to his family's encouragement to be more practical, but was laid off as the dotcom world went up in flames. As the next bubble began to form in real estate, Musambacine found work in construction, mostly as a carpenter, before he decided to complete his Bachelor's degree. "Internships were not part of my vocabulary at that time," says Musambacine, who considered becoming a teacher. Now internships are what he lives and breathes.

From a small, anonymous office in downtown Oakland, Musambacine is working to bridge the internship divide for minorities. He is a manager for INROADS, a St. Louis–based nonprofit which recently celebrated its fortieth anniversary and is dedicated to placing minority college students in high-powered corporate internships. With approximately 100 employees in twelve different offices around North America, INROADS has arranged over 26,000 internships at hundreds of blue-chip companies since its founding. "Our goal is that at the end of their college career that student actually gets a position with the company," says Michelle Neal, regional director for the Pacific Northwest—and the organization claims a 50 percent success rate, operating "one person at a time, trying to change the landscape."

Musambacine and the other managers in Oakland work with local employers such as healthcare giant Kaiser Permanente, Google, Target, IBM, and Traveler's Insurance, helping them fill internship slots with top-flight African American, Hispanic, and Native American college students. INROADS actively recruits students across the country through minority student business clubs, career centers, and campus events, at four-year colleges only; there are some 10–15,000 applicants annually, around 15–20 percent of whom will ultimately make the cut. Those selected are actively mentored by INROADS staff before they start work, provided with mock interviews, helped with their résumés, evaluated, and trained in skills like "impression management." Students and companies have the final say concerning placements, but INROADS does the matchmaking—on average, the organization sustains itself by charging companies $4,000 per intern. For companies, INROADS is a diversity pipeline.

All INROADS interns are paid, usually between $15 and $20 per hour, and the students are expected to complete at least two summers with the same firm. "We require the company not only to have a supervisor, but to have a mentor for that student," says Neal. "What we try to do with an internship is to make these students ready not just for an entry-level position but for something higher … The company is saying, 'We are investing in you to move you on a fast track of management.'" Nowadays, INROADS often finds its internship placements through its own alumni, who've been climbing the corporate hierarchy ever since Father Frank C. Carr was inspired by Martin Luther King's "I Have a Dream" speech to found the organization. "He realized that minorities did not have the same footing as their white counterparts," says Neal, "and that these talented students may have done well in school, but once they got into the real world, they didn't necessarily have the foundation to help them progress in the corporate world." At its height a decade ago, the program had 6,000 interns in a single year, but "the economy has had a big influence," according to Neal—the annual number is now a third of that.

"INROADS got her out of her shell, polished her up, and got her prepared for the corporate world," Neal says, citing a young woman who immigrated from Mexico at age thirteen, barely able to speak English, graduated high school near the top of her class, and is now a rising star in the field of healthcare. "It's changing, but it's not something most minorities know is a step you need to take," says Neal. "Internships are something that minorities have not had ingrained in them. I think it's very much an expectation in the white upper-middle class … but for a minority student, it's almost vital for them to be competitive," in particular to counter advantages such as nepotism and personal connections. At the same time, Neal admits that the program includes the "relatively privileged," and Musambacine says that the socioeconomic profile of INROADS students is "more middle class" than when the program began.

INROADS is not alone—a small group of other organizations, mostly focused on fast-tracking minority students into positions of corporate leadership, have also chosen internships as their weapon of choice. Sponsors for Educational Opportunity (SEO) focuses on helping minorities break into Wall Street; the Hispanic Association of Colleges and Universities works on placing Latino students in paid government internships;

Management Leadership for Tomorrow takes a broad approach to train-ing "the next generation of African American, Hispanic, and Native American leaders." Tellingly, all these organizations have focused on internships as a crucial bottleneck; leveraging the diversity commitments of Fortune 500 companies, they have managed to spread the internship wealth a little further. The number of interns who benefit is tiny in the scheme of things, but at least the model focuses on well-paid, actively mentored internships and galvanizing employer interest—though it remains to be seen if such enthusiasm would extend beyond elite minority recruitment.

As an intern for the Hispanic Heritage Foundation, Emanuel Pleitez helped create Latinos on the Fast Track (LOFT), another program along these lines, supporting internships for students who had already received scholarship money from the foundation. "If you fund organizations that have reach into communities that are underrepresented," he points out, "then you're helping to level the playing field. If you're just making paid internships, the same networks will find those paid internships. You're just paying the interns that have an in." In other words, pay is secondary to access in the grand scheme of things—a point that is reasonable enough for short-term internship stints and is supported by the fact that high-income students are heavily represented in paid internships. Pleitez sees minority families as being relatively more skeptical about the value of working for free, particularly post-graduation. "At the end of the day," he says, "the parents will be supportive of their kids, but they're not exposed to the possibilities. They just look at their balance sheet every month and say, 'Hey, can you help out with this or that?'"

Pleitez himself, having gathered the importance of internships early on, gradually convinced his family that there might come a period when he wouldn't be able to contribute his share to the family finances. For one of his internships, at a nonprofit community organization near his uni-versity, Pleitez was also able to use funds from the Federal Work-Study Program, which gives schools substantial latitude in supporting the work of students on financial aid. (Essentially, the federal program pays most of the student's wage, while the community organization contributes a small portion and is able to say it has "paid internships.") "Someone from my background," Pleitez sums up, "would be willing do an internship if they're told in advance that they're going to have to prepare for this, and they're at least given housing and food."

How long could these interns hold out—for two or three years and through a variety of career possibilities, like some serial interns? Are middle-class minorities more deserving than non-minority working-class students? Are those not enrolled in four-year colleges simply beyond help? Do we always want more internships, regardless of their fairness and quality, as long as they provide nebulous "opportunities"? Affirmative action–style internship organizations raise as many questions as they answer. Their approach is understandably pragmatic, accepting internships as an established force, a lever to move the world. For any one of us, an internship, if we can secure it and afford it, may well be the way to launch a career—perhaps stultifying, but necessary. Yet internships are spreading faster than we can reform then, and "internships for all" cannot save the day—just as "college for all" has not.

So what about everybody else? What happens to the non-interns? Some will succeed anyway, of course, but many more will languish in an underworld of menial, low-wage work, trapped under a new glass ceiling or spirited away from particular professions. Internships are dividing us.

CHAPTER TEN

The Rise and Rebellion of the Global Intern

I'm courteous and affable, my name badge is retractable / You other
interns laughable, your thermos must be half as full.
　　—Greg Justice, Cisco Systems, "The World's Most Interesting Intern"

In France, unpaid interns take to the streets in a large-scale strike,
masked so that their employers won't recognize them on TV. In Sweden,
Pakistan, and South Korea, governments announce the hiring of tens of
thousands of interns as a desperate measure to alleviate youth unemployment; in Australia, where a relatively modest 19 percent of university
students do internships, the government mulls a national internship
scheme to meet skilled labor shortages. In Germany, a gang of activists
dressed as superheroes raid luxury food shops, redistributing Kobe beef,
Ruinart Champagne, Serrano ham, and Valrhona chocolate to unpaid
interns, among others. In India, the nation's best-known company, Infosys,
institutes an elite, well-paid internship program, personally overseen by
the company's CEO and attracting participants from all over the globe. In
China, 100,000 students are mobilized, by order of a provincial government, to serve as three-month interns in factories that have recently seen
a spate of worker suicides.[1]

There is no single body of experts, no famed multinational corporation, no particular institution or government that is pushing the relentless
global expansion of internships—a process occurring so rapidly, and at

the instigation of so many different actors, that its contours seem almost impossible to gauge. The dynamics vary substantially from country to country, with particular labor laws, different industries, and specific values surrounding work all coming into play, but the overall direction is clear: internships are pushing into the workplaces of middle- and high-income nations the world over. What took four decades to materialize in the U.S. has rapidly become a global fact of life: internships are at once a significant source of cheap, flexible white-collar labor and a major steppingstone to affluence and professional success. They grant access to those who can afford them, and block further progress for those who cannot.

The internship explosion in the European Union and in the Commonwealth countries has followed the American example in many respects, despite the reputation these countries have for strict labor laws and strong unions. Tacitly, and sometimes explicitly, business leaders and government officials have understood internships as one more component in a suite of American-style or "Anglo-Saxon" business practices, "bolstering competitiveness" by normalizing informal, short-term, and unpaid/underpaid work for a vast swath of the youth labor force. The same factors that have made internships appealing in the U.S. have proven persuasive from France to Australia: for employers, the ability to deploy personal contacts blamelessly and save labor costs either directly or through entry-level hiring; for young people, the chance to sample a range of professions, distinguish yourself from your peers, and enjoy a semblance of social mobility. Internships, as both cultural phenomenon and business practice, now spread wherever the new spirit of capitalism spreads.

Yet these are early days for the global intern—many companies and even countries have heard nothing of the concept or have so far remained impervious to it. For all its useful ambiguity in the U.S., "intern" is an even murkier concept in the rest of the world, trailing far fewer immediate associations or pop culture references in its wake. In France, they are *stagiaires*, in Germany *Praktikanten*, in China *shixisheng* (a word which can also mean "trainee")—but the English term is increasingly understood, and its connotations are becoming more and more dominant. Yet generally speaking, the lack of understanding, research, and clear public policy surrounding internships is as glaring around the world as it is in the U.S.

In the blue-collar trades of Western Europe, where apprenticeship reinvented itself even more successfully than in the U.S. (as discussed in Chapter 3), the internship is seen simultaneously as its white-collar equivalent and as a drastic departure, known for execrable training and inhumane terms of employment. Universities have kept their distance, much more than in the U.S., often taking the perspective that students should spend their college years as students and that labor market maneuvers are beyond their ken—some Oxford colleges, for instance, have gone so far to forbid groups of students from taking internships. Even more so than in the U.S., the internship system is a rude awakening for European youth, upending traditional notions about how one enters the workforce and jettisoning from the get-go any illusions that work should bring a living wage and basic security. Yet unlike Americans, Europeans have not accepted these changes in silence, as we shall see.

In the developing economies of Asia, the Middle East, and Latin America, internships are more concentrated, by and large, wherever multinational corporations have hung their shingles—in the largest and wealthiest cities, in government offices where connections are the order of the day, in organizations that pride themselves on following global norms. They are, perhaps, a telling index of how globalized a country's organizational culture has become. The wealthy and well connected have long found ways to get their offspring into promising positions, but the first recognizable interns in places such as Jakarta or Johannesburg have tended to be young foreigners employed by foreign organizations—a growing tribe that is half-backpacker, half-expat, and bears the lack of pay far better under friendly exchange rates. No expat packages are necessary —multinational companies and nonprofits, which increasingly amass international teams to run their English-speaking offices, have learned that internships are a cheap way to bring in young, Western-educated talent. Such interns may not need our pity, but it's interesting to know that they actually exist: a French computer geek, backpacking through Laos before beginning an internship in Chennai, designing Facebook apps; a young English woman, fed up with her corporate job in Hong Kong, heading off to a do-gooder internship in Harare.

The annual number of American students traveling abroad for internships has almost doubled in the last decade, surging from 6,950 in 2000 to 13,658 in 2008, according to a survey of some 1,500 educational institutions conducted by the Institute of International Education. And this figure only includes enrolled college students who received academic credit, leaving aside those who did it on their own, and all the recent graduates and career-changers flocking overseas. A new perception has locked into place: if you want an international career, get an international internship first. Never mind that the nature of the work is often identical to what's done on Main Street at a local business. "There isn't going to be a lot of difference for many career fields in the actual tasks and duties," says one college career counselor, who advised students seeking international internships, "and so you have to ask yourself why do you specifically need to be in Germany to do that? Predominantly it's just because people want to be abroad."

Indeed, the spread of international internships has taken its cue from the explosive growth of study abroad programs; boosters often pitch the two in the same breath. Both present compelling business opportunities, given the limitations of most colleges to run programs overseas, and a slew of companies have rushed to cash in—heeding the prediction of Eric Lochtefeld from University of Dreams that a million college students will eventually undertake "destination internships" each year. These companies typically bundle together an internship placement, housing, visa help, and other services for a hefty fee, counting on families' ignorance of the real costs on the ground in, say, Beijing or Berlin. A San Francisco company, Intrax Internships Abroad, charges between $6,000 and $8,000 for arranging eight-week gigs in four European countries, as well as China and Japan. Other organizations include Global Intern, Global Experiences, Global Placement, Internships International, as well as country-focused organizations like Masa Israel (which saw a 51 percent increase in 2010, placing nearly 1,500 participants), and non-profits like the Association for International Practical Training, which boasts that a third of the 2,500 interns they place (working in twenty-four time zones) are young professionals already out of school. It goes without saying that these opportunities are by and large for the well heeled, with scholarships few and far between: such internships are almost never paid and airfare is usually not included.

And you often don't get what you pay for. Companies like Intrax and University of Dreams are busily evangelizing for the internship idea, but many organizations, especially in hot new destinations, simply don't get it, despite their enthusiasm. "The idea of an internship isn't terribly widely used around the world," says the career counselor who worked on international internships. "I also think culturally, in a lot of places, as a student you're supposed to be in school." Another international internship advisor adds: "It might be necessary for students applying for opportunities overseas to use the word volunteer with an employer to get an internship overseas, simply because that language is more understandable … Expectations, while they're a problem here [in the U.S.] of course, can be even greater in a place where internships are not understood in the same way."

The biggest problem in these cases, typically, isn't about long hours bent over the photocopier or substantive, uncompensated work on vital projects: it's boredom. "People were scared of me, they didn't know what to do with me," says one American of her internship at a Chinese law firm in Shanghai. A Canadian student, seeking an internship in the second-tier Chinese city of Nanjing, was referred by her dance teacher to a magazine editor who then referred her to an "investor." He liked the prestige of having a foreign intern working in his private residence and at his beck and call, but he barely knew what to do with her: her work was mostly Googling, she says, when there was anything at all. Says another intern of a stint at a United Nations office, "I got to Brazil, and on the first day they were like 'Well, we don't really have anything for you to do. What are you interested in?'"

"I didn't actually do much or accomplish much while I was there," says "Jeff," an American student, of his internship at the diesel engine division of the Russian company Kazanka, in Chelny, a mid-sized city in Tatarstan. "Two months is not even long enough to get used to being there, to adjust to such a different place." The connection was made through AIESEC, a student organization that claims to arrange 4,500 international internships for members each year, as part of its mission to promote cultural exchange. Jeff simply went on the AIESEC database, "got an email from this girl from the middle of nowhere in Russia, in Tatarstan," and soon found himself in Chelny, tasked with marketing diesel engines to China. Language was a serious problem, even though he had studied Russian: "I was able to understand most of what people said, but not necessarily able to talk back."

A state-owned enterprise that dominates the city of Chelny, Kazanka was glad to have Jeff, and forked over some rubles for the trouble, but they weren't particularly hip to the internship concept. "I was the guinea pig, so things were just trial by fire," says Jeff. "I was basically just sending out emails and making phone calls to different factories or potential partners in China … I couldn't even make phone calls that frequently, because I had to go to this special phone to make international calls, so most of the time I was just sending hundreds of emails and not getting any response, or just a few." The company basically had no marketing materials, aside from a picture of the diesel engine with some vital stats, and certainly nothing in Chinese. "By the time I got Photoshop on my computer, I only had a month left," says Jeff. Still, it was an experience—he got to know the local AIESEC members (two of whom later decamped for internships in India), chatted with old Russian ladies at the factory, and was featured on a local TV program as one of the only three foreigners in the entire city.

Wherever they have gone, interns like Jeff have introduced this new category of short-term, student-focused work. Brought by multinational companies, well-known universities, visiting professors, or theorists of work or education, the prestige of the concept is all the greater. Just as they have emulated American and European practices surrounding higher education, elites in other countries have taken notice of internships. Organizations like the Washington Center and University of Dreams report that intern traffic is now increasingly going the other way, with the children of Pakistani generals, Saudi royals, and Chinese industrialists interning on Capitol Hill or on Wall Street. A company like Intrax—"an official sponsor designated by the U.S. Department of State" to administer the controversial J-1 visa (that Disney favorite), as we saw in Chapter 1—can place 300,000 participants from over eighty countries in positions with American companies. Internships don't count as work and don't have to include training when companies can spin them as cultural exchange.

How quickly is the internship idea spreading internationally? What are the vectors of transmission? The effects on the ground? By examining these dynamics in China, where internships in their current form were virtually nonexistent a decade ago, we can hazard some general answers, gauging the impact of study abroad programs, multinational companies, globalized business practices, and the expansion of higher education—all intermingled with local labor markets and ideas about work. We can witness the internship explosion that unfolded over decades in the U.S. played out in fast-forward: the panicked student race to amass credentials and the gradual realization, on the part of firms, that all this eager labor could be put to use.

Thousands of miles from Beijing and located in the remote borderlands of the country's southwest, Kunming is a small city by Chinese standards. With little industry to speak of, it remains virtually unknown outside of China. It's the last place you'd expect to find a crop of international interns—at least until 2009, when "Rick" helped pilot what might be described as Kunming's first internship program. The cohort is still small, only about a dozen at a time—but Rick now brings young participants from around the globe, including the U.S., Canada, England, Hong Kong, and Dubai, to work in this remote mountain city. Most of the interns are eighteen- and nineteen-year-olds, recent high school graduates whose parents are paying over $1,000 per week to land their progeny an impressive-sounding gap year experience.

"These people are looking at China as a good place to invest in, whether that be with your child or your own money," says Rick of the parents, who are more heavily involved than in any other international program he's worked on. "I'm getting chains of emails from dad in Dubai, who is saying, 'This is what I want, this is why we're doing this … Working in China is the kind of experience I want my son or daughter to have.'" Many of the students have never worked before, either at home or abroad; have never written a résumé; and speak no Chinese. "The students are totally different," says Rick of those who choose his company's China internship program in Kunming, rather than, say, one of the organized treks of self-discovery over the Tibetan Plateau or down the Mekong.

To the companies, it can be "a very hard sell," admits Rick, "having fairly inexperienced foreign kids coming to Kunming, especially for those who want to work in a Chinese organization." Nonetheless, Rick is making inroads, and has been able to go through previously established connections, since his company has operated its other study abroad programs in China for eighteen years. "I think there's a certain cluster of organizations that are suitable for this kind of thing," says Rick of the approximately thirty companies and nonprofits he has contacted, from Chinese law firms and businesses to international environmental NGOs.

About a dozen of them have agreed to take interns, but few know what to do with the kids: "some of [the internships] were really nonexistent: there was a lot of dead time and loitering around the office." Not only does Rick not even mention the issue of pay, he says that "if push comes to shove, we need to talk about how much *we'd* be willing to pay" for a placement. The commitment is still fairly modest, scaled down to only a month's worth of work, four days a week, for a few hours at a time. Because of massive language issues, even in offices with English-speaking staff, Rick is now hiring local students to work as part-time translators for the interns.

Being located in Kunming, he thinks, might even be a strength for the program, given all the competition for internships now in major cities like Beijing and Shanghai. In 2008, for example, Harvard launched the China Student Internship Program, offering its students dozens of internships at a range of name-brand Chinese companies and well-known Western firms with China offices—numerous other schools and organizations have recently started offering similar programs. Not to mention the thousands of foreigners who have found internships in China through other means, such as "Ben." Through family connections he's managed to land plum summer gigs in both Shanghai and Beijing, with an international law firm and a major American healthcare provider respectively. All this foreign activity has not failed to have an impact on Chinese students, families, and employers.

"Everyone's parents all have their own relationships and networks," says "Jessica," a Chinese management consultant in Beijing, "so their kids, on summer or winter vacation, will often have opportunities to do some kind of internship work." During school vacations a major provincial TV station, says another Chinese student, typically has four or five unpaid interns translating news from English-language sources into

Chinese—the positions are secured through connections, never advertised. Informal arrangements like this have existed in Chinese workplaces for a number of decades, says Jessica, but that only makes the recent shift all the more significant: internships are now spreading everywhere, many of them significantly more formal and rigorous; they tend to last longer; and are now a vital piece of the career puzzle. "When I was an undergraduate, there were still very few students doing internships, mostly at very good companies, like foreign investment firms," says Jessica of her time at Peking University a decade ago. "But by the time I'd become a graduate student, the outlook had changed a lot. In 2002, 2003, 2004 it really started."

Even prestigious, well-paid internships—like the one Jessica landed in the Beijing office of U.S.-based consulting firm Bain & Company in 2004—were "relatively sporadic, not very systematic," she adds. In many cases, interns were more like temps, paid by the hour and performing support work as needed for particular projects. The growing size of the program recently prompted Bain's Beijing office to "design a more American-style program," at first targeting MBAs from the U.S., but now also including "lots and lots" of Chinese undergraduates going into their senior year, says Jessica. With offices in twenty-seven countries, it's not surprising that Bain has developed a set of global norms surrounding its "culture of apprenticeship"—the firm now has internship positions in Tokyo, Toronto, Stockholm, Sydney, Amsterdam and other business capitals around the world. Other multinationals in Beijing and Shanghai have been following suit, giving internship programs unprecedented exposure at China's top universities. On-campus career development centers, on the American model, are also making headway.

Not all internships in China pay or are well organized. "A lot of companies now, when you're applying for a full-time job, will take a look at your internship experience," says Jessica. "And because employers are really looking at what type of experience you have, a lot of students, in order to gain that experience, agree to work for free." There are "a lot of cases" of companies not paying, says Jessica, including well-known investment and securities companies, which can ask young people to do unpaid research "because they have so many applicants." There is apparently little awareness about relevant labor law, despite the fact that Chinese cities and provinces have minimum wage legislation. If something goes wrong, one Chinese intern told me, "I can tell my father."

"Let me put it like this," a Chinese intern says, describing the undergraduate population at his university. "Basically you can divide us into three categories: people doing an internship; people preparing for all kinds of exams (e.g. GRE, TOEFL and so on) and taking the related summer course; and people who are just playing around," since they have a job secured already. Han, an undergraduate at Renmin University in Beijing, tells me that 90 percent of his college friends are doing internships or something similar. He himself has done four—two with the Beijing offices of U.S.-based organizations (a well-known PR firm, which paid, and a start-up nonprofit, which did not); one, unpaid and informally arranged, in a powerful government office; and the fourth, more like an unpaid training program, at New Oriental, a major provider of private educational services in China.

Differing office environments aside, American interns would find most of the work familiar: answering phones, typing, translating, printing, photocopying, and the Chinese office equivalent of making the coffee: *duancha songshui*, which literally means "carrying tea and bringing water." By and large, domestic companies are less demanding of interns, but also less likely to pay; although almost all of the bigger ones have interns somewhere or other, major firms have not developed formalized, large-scale programs that they advertise openly; and government offices shy away. The internship business is in its infancy, with the wealthiest sending their children to intern abroad, but efforts like the Hong Kong China Internship Association (HCIA) have sprouted up, charging students from mainland China the small fortune of 9,000 renminbi ($1345) for an "internship week" in Hong Kong: essentially pay-to-play networking for the children of the wealthy.

On the opposite end of the spectrum, the China Labour Bulletin, a Hong Kong-based organization that defends and promotes the rights of workers in China, reports a sharp rise in the number of "internship contracts" taken up by college graduates with few other options. Law school graduates, for instance, are now mandated by law to undertake a year-long internship. An engineer entering the petrochemical industry needed "an internship certificate" to get a foothold in the industry; despite a very low salary, he signed on with a company that promised the certificate within a few months, only to discover that he had to wait six months before converting to staff status and a full three years before receiving the credential.[2]

Others, with their expensive and hard-won degrees, are simply desperate to avoid the hellish world of factory work—there are no longer enough entry-level jobs to absorb the vast streams of new graduates produced by the rapid expansion of the country's higher education system. According to China Labour Bulletin, which typically reports more on sweatshop conditions and coal mine deaths, "many of the internships offered by companies in China provide minimal training for little or no pay, no benefits and no protection under labour law, and no guarantee of future employment." Interns "can be dismissed by their employer with virtual impunity"; some have to work eighteen months before they are entitled to any time off. These internships with Chinese characteristics are a white-collar world reflection of what Andrew Ross calls a "descent into precarious circumstances [that] has occurred within a generation and on a much more momentous scale [in China] than anywhere else."[3]

The Bulletin reports on companies' heavy use of internship contracts, very low-paid even by Chinese standards, as open-ended "trial" periods for new employees. An engineering graduate named Wang, promised "on-the-job training overseas for eight months" along with ten others, instead found himself assigned manual work, such as cleaning and haulage —if he dropped out, the company threatened, he would have to pay back the costs of this "training." In another case, an intern at the National Theatre in Beijing, fired after testing positive for Hepatitis B, attempted to sue the theater for damages, but was rejected by a court, which held that he was not a true employee. A whole other class of internships may be required to earn a college degree, with the placements essentially dictated by professors. To take only one example, a Language and Literature student was required to spend two months supervising students at a rural elementary school, working from 5 a.m. to 10 p.m. six days a week.

In the most egregious case along these lines, the provincial government of Henan recently deployed 100,000 interns in an attempt to woo the huge Taiwanese electronics manufacturer Foxconn—which is mulling the possibility of establishing a factory in the province. After a widely reported string of employee suicides in its Guangdong factories, Foxconn found itself with a labor shortage, which the Henan government was happy to fill. Even the state-run newspaper *China Daily* had a hard time masking its surprise: "In a striking development, up to 100,000 vocational school students in Henan province have been ordered to leave for Shenzhen over the weekend for a three-month internship at Foxconn." The students were given nine days' notice to pack their bags; regardless of their fields of study, they'll be assembling iPhones, Playstation systems, and Kindles. By order of the government, "the only option aside from joining the scandal-plagued manufacturing giant is to drop out of school," reported the newspaper. Within a few weeks, another Foxconn death was in the news: an intern, whose age was reported as either eighteen or nineteen, had "fallen" from the window of a six-floor company dormitory.

Nor was this mass migration an isolated case—out of nowhere, Foxconn seems to have become one of the world's biggest abusers of internships. According to a detailed report recently compiled by university researchers in mainland China, Hong Kong, and Taiwan, the company uses interns extensively in at least five of its major plants, compensating them at the lowest possible pay grade (under $200 per month) and often forcing them against the law to work nights and overtime. In order to avoid paying for the medical and social welfare owed to regular employees, Foxconn has in some cases reportedly filled *more than half* of its assembly line jobs with interns—usually with the cooperation of hundreds of schools that stand to receive a fee in return. Even the company's unconvincing attempt to exonerate itself is damning enough: responding to the report, Foxconn claimed that "only" 7.6 percent of its 937,000 current Chinese employees are interns—and that this never exceeds 15 percent. That's right: 70,000 interns, or 150,000 at peak times, manning the assembly lines to pump out iPods.[4]

On February 29, 2004 in a Milan supermarket, the patron saint of interns and casual workers made his first appearance in the world. According to his traditional prayer, San Precario (Saint Precarious) gives succor to the "chain store workers" and "call center angels," to "flexible employees hanging by a thread" and "temporary and contingent workers," to "those souls whose contract is coming to an end" and to "undocumented workers." He performed a miracle at the deli counter, granting customers an immediate 20 percent discount on all products, unbeknownst to store management. The famous image of San Precario, since paraded and venerated by hundreds of thousands of young Europeans, summarizes in holy form the pervasive condition of "precarity": kneeling, with hands clasped in prayer, a fresh-faced and earnest fast food worker beseeches the world for a modicum of security in work and life. Emanating from his hopeful heart are the saint's five attributes, rays of light that spotlight the clip-art icons of his dreams: income, housing, health, communication, and transport.

San Precario is the creation of Chainworkers, a crew of Milanese activists known more for media activism and anarcho-syndicalist organizing than for Catholic devotion. He is a satirical *détournement* of popular tradition, a postmodern figurehead for a movement against the precarious working conditions and eroded living standards of neoliberal ascendancy. More than socioeconomic uncertainty and the inability to earn a stable living, precarity is also spiritual aporia: "being unable to plan one's time, being a worker on call where your life and time is determined by external forces," stresses Alex Foti, one of the movement's organizers. "The saint appears in public spaces on occasions of rallies, marches, interventions, demonstrations, film festivals, fashion parades, and, being a saint, processions," report Marcello Tari and Ilaria Vanni. "San Precario is also transgender, and it has appeared also as a female saint. A 'cult' has spread rapidly and has led to the development of a distinct and colorful iconography, hagiography and rituals." Officially, the saint's day is February 29, the only intermittent day on the calendar—but his iconic power is never more in evidence than on May 1: the new EuroMayDay.[5]

From modest beginnings in Milan in 2001, when some 5,000 people were involved, EuroMayDay has grown to include hundreds of thousands of participants in dozens of cities. Overwhelming the stale and dwindling May Day commemorations of worker solidarity and old-fashioned labor muscle, EuroMayDay is a carnival of loosely organized and unorthodox political activism. The target is precarity, which many European activists see as the central labor issue of the twenty-first century. In forging a movement against the disappearance of decent work, activists also see the possibility of creating a new coalition that joins immigrants, a working class hollowed out by downsizing and offshoring, and a shrinking middle class stuck in internships and temporary work arrangements. "The bet, the political bet," says Foti, "is to have the hackers helping the cleaning ladies."

Little-noticed by the mainstream labor movement—which appears to have scant interest in, and even less aptitude for, organizing non-standard workers—the anti-precarity movement nevertheless represents the most concerted, eloquent rebellion against contingent labor and unprotected, unjust arrangements such as internships. In a recent documentary, a member of the group Generation Précaire, which is spearheading the movement in France, succinctly explained why interns have become involved: "Interns are the symptom of something much more vast and that is the Precarious Generation."[6] While certain other groups of contingent laborers (temps, migrant workers, freelancers) have achieved some degree of self-organization, interns have remained beyond the pale—too inexperienced, too transient, too accepting of the system— at least until the rise of anti-precarity activism.

The movement's dream is for "casualized, sessional, intermittent, temporary, flexible, project, freelance and fractional workers" to establish common cause together. Numerous groups have mobilized—from the Precogs (a network of "precarious and cognitive" workers, their name inspired by the film *Minority Report* and the story that it's based on) to the Madrid-based feminist collective Precarias a la Deriva (Precarious Women Adrift). In 2004, London hosted Precarity Ping Pong; 2005 saw the International Meeting of the Precariat in Berlin and the Precair Forum in Amsterdam. In most of Western Europe, the combined ranks of contingent workers now account for nearly a third of all workers; as we saw in Chapter 2, the non-standard workforce in the U.S. is similarly massive, comprising some 30 percent of the total. Yet despite this huge potential audience, and the possibility of a broad-based movement, it remains unclear whether all contingent workers can actually constitute a natural or even practical coalition. "Precarity is unevenly experienced across this spectrum of employees," explains Andrew Ross, "because contingent work arrangements are imposed on some and self-elected by others." Although often under enormous pressure, interns are usually on the more voluntary end of the spectrum—many come from privileged backgrounds, as we have seen. While there is ample evidence of solidarity in many individual internship programs, is there any hope of a broader intern identity, however fleetingly interns partake of it, let alone of interns rallying against an abstraction such as precarity and empathizing with migrant workers or temps?

Thanks to the government of Prime Minister Dominique de Villepin, France provided a hopeful test case in 2006 with a now notorious proposal: a new type of employment contract called the CPE. Known in English as the First Employment Contract, the CPE, desperately desired by French companies, would have decisively casualized all employees under twenty-six, allowing employers to fire them for any reason whatsoever during a substantial "trial period" of two years. In the months when the government was building support for the CPE, interns staged a series of small, spontaneous strikes in Paris and forced the government to admit, in a report by its Economic and Social Council, that many of France's 800,000 interns work for years on end, for little or no pay. The CPE, threatening to erode the few decent jobs left for young people, unleashed passionate protests, with millions taking to the streets, a large number of them interns. Forced to back down on the CPE, the French government simultaneously took more notice of internships—in a small sign of progress, interns working longer than two months must now be paid at least a modest stipend, approximately €400 ($520), or about a third of the French minimum wage.

In Germany, pressure from the so-called internship generation of struggling twenty-somethings has likewise forced the government to pay attention. In 2008, a survey of 2,600 young people found that more than half of interns were not paid at all, despite having college degrees, and that most internship stints did not lead to full-time employment. Anti-precarity demonstrations, a petition with over 60,000 signatures, and increased media attention all prompted Labor Minister Olaf Scholz to call for new regulations to end internship abuses.[7] Taking matters into its own hands, the so-called Robin Hood Gang in Hamburg has targeted *Prekarisierung* (German for "precarity") by raiding classy delicatessens and Michelin-starred restaurants, redistributing the loot to the city's precarious underclass. A recent German film in the radical chic tradition,

Aufstand der Praktikanten (Uprising of the Interns), briefly played out—and then dashed—the fantasy of an intern general strike.

"Now in the U.K., the growth and interest [in internships] mirror what happened in the U.S." says Natalie Lundsteen, who has researched internships at Stanford and Oxford. "They are just about five years behind," she says, adding that the word internship referred until recently to "a paid, structured, corporate opportunity." The mass emergence of unpaid positions—and American-style internship auctions—has stirred up serious resentment, although the rhetoric around precarity, so prominent on the European continent, is largely absent. Setting an important legal precedent, an employment tribunal forced London Dreams Motion Pictures to pay a former unpaid intern over £2,000 in back wages and expenses—making it clear that the intern was in fact covered under the country's National Minimum Wage Act. The excuse that interns are volunteers, no matter where they work or what they do, rings hollow. A host of online campaigns have emerged—from Intern Aware, which is building momentum around the findings of the Milburn report; to Internocracy, "a social enterprise passionate about changing the culture of internships"; to Interns Anonymous, a forum for eliciting the lived experiences of interns and aggregating intern-related news.[8]

If examples of intern rebellion are multiplying across Europe, partly inspired by a wider movement against precarious work, what about the U.S.? Why so little perceptible backlash at ground zero of the internship explosion? Alex Foti has framed the precarity movement as being distinctively European, stating in an interview, "If we don't act now, we're looking at a future of precarity for all Europeans. Because the idea is to make us a new Asia or a new America—not a new Europe." As many have pointed out, the concept of creeping precarity implies a former sense of stability and guaranteed social welfare, which few industrial societies have enjoyed outside Western Europe in the decades after World War II. Despite a possible reflection in Generation X discourse, writes Stevphen Shukaitis, an American observer of the anti-precarity movement, "In some ways arguments around precarious labor emerge out of, and are based upon, certain latent assumptions and conditions concerning the role of the welfare state and social democracy that are fundamentally different from those that exist in the U.S."

In Western Europe, government reports have brought widespread awareness of internship abuses, forcing politicians to act. In contrast, in the U.S. the problem is grasped impressionistically and, without experts or numbers or direct testimony, is likely to remain outside the ambit of public policy. In the U.S., sharply worded complaints and critiques, from college cafeterias to online forums, have achieved little traction and found no channels for reformist activism. The lack of a broader principled stance against contingent work, tremendous youth unemployment, and the phenomenon of "prolonged adolescence" leaves internship critics sounding isolated, petty, or spoiled. Yet the connections are unmistakable. When labor laws go unenforced, employers can push for unpaid interns in the white-collar workforce and practice wage theft in the low-end service and manufacturing sectors. When the concept of fair pay for a hard's day work disappears, workers are pressed into a vicious cycle of underbidding each other, all the way down to zero. Shared most of all is the existential condition—precarity—of working completely at an employer's will, of burning through savings in hopes of a better future, of lacking the resources to protect and develop yourself, let alone a family.

Besides the coalition-building concept of precarity, American reformers and activists might also turn for inspiration to another characteristically European demand: flexicurity. The portmanteau term reflects the fact that most anti-precarity activists aren't advocating a return to the comfortable alienation of Fordist job security. They recognize that flexible work arrangements are not always dystopian, especially for younger workers who are still maneuvering in the labor market and exploring their own capabilities, interests, and earning potential. Thus far, the security part of the arrangement demands more of governments than employers: higher pay and social welfare provisions for flex workers, and measures to cushion the gaps between gigs. "The overall emphasis is on employment security—as opposed to job security," writes Andrew Ross, "and, in its strongest versions, flexicurity preserves and extends core labor rights to all workers, regardless of contractual status."

Nor is flexicurity purely a vision of San Precario's—a number of governments across Northern Europe, beginning in Denmark and the Netherlands, have implemented just such a policy, beginning in the 1990s, with notable successes. Arguably, a recent provision of President

Obama's healthcare bill—allowing parents with healthcare coverage to insure their children until they reach the age of twenty-six—mirrors the same philosophy. Indeed, flexicurity remains one of the few proven ways to protect workers against the vicissitudes of a radically deregulated labor market, although with some justice, critics point out that this policy of mutual accommodation has its limits. Flexicurity still allows companies to casualize workers with impunity, for instance, and may do little to protect workers in the very bottom rungs of society, who face wage theft and unsafe conditions. It is notable, however, that the countries that have embraced flexicurity have also substantially resisted the culture of unpaid internships.

Globalizing at light speed, compelling and catchy, haphazard and half-understood, the internship idea has come a long way. Laws and conditions vary considerably around the world, and there is as little information on internships globally, and as little organized wisdom about them, as there is for any particular country or city. If the need to provide young people with meaningful training and a bridge into the workforce is unquestioned, not so the new workplace norm—that intern means "free for the taking," that working for nothing is a way of paying your dues. Some acquiesce, holding that red-hot global competition and economic stagnation demand the sacrifice, while others fight back—one internship at a time or all at once, through protests, petitions, pranks, opinion pieces, a million splintered efforts. San Precario smiles down. There is nothing inevitable about unpaid fashion designers in London, Chinese engineers on brutal internship contracts, and the endlessly prolonged, barely compensated *stages* and *praktika* of the European continent. There is still time to get internships right.

CHAPTER ELEVEN

Nothing to Lose but Your Cubicles

"Do the interns get Glocks?"
"No, they all share one."

—*The Life Aquatic With Steve Zissou*

Picture unsorted mail forming menacing towers; websites, newsletters, and contact lists growing increasingly out of date. No one to get coffee, make Xeroxes, or run errands, but also no one to be mentored, no one to cover vital work during staff vacations, and no one with timid, bright ideas about reaching the youth demographic. The magic of Disney World would become a nightmare, and the iPod assembly lines of Foxconn would grind to a halt. Capitol Hill would grow hushed, as junior staffers took up administrative tasks and a slower pace of work set in. Nonprofits would make hard choices, focusing on core programs and pondering necessary hires. Companies would bring in temps and ask employees to put in overtime; eventually, some might even go out of business or never get off the ground. A general strike of all interns would show all that they contribute for the first time. Bringing a delicious, low-level chaos to the world's work, it would demonstrate forcefully just how much intern labor now sustains a wide array of industries and offices.

For young people, the sheer scale of the internship arms race has made the raw credential unremarkable, a box to be checked, in economic terms a broken "signal" for college graduates just starting out. Its shelf life is short. Its power is largely negative—it seems risky *not* to have done one, it teaches you what *not* to do. Employers are increasingly aware that these experiences can mean just about anything: your parents are well connected, your school required it, you barely showed up at the office. Even elite internships turn on opaque, connections-based hiring processes and astronomical odds. An internship may occupy your days, but it's hardly a summer break or a year off: more likely it's a pressure cooker, another system of praise and censure. It keeps you out of trouble, but maybe "the organization kids"—the earnest, ever-striving millennials, aspirationally if not actually upper-middle class—could use a little trouble.[1]

A whole generation has been utterly professional about their pre-professionalism, forfeiting the more relaxed jobs and leisurely summers of old, ignoring other paths of self-development. These young shock troops of the New Economy keep parachuting into the workforce, bristling with the armor of their credentials. They endured, even lapped up, the hyper-programming of childhood, every waking hour filled with karate sessions, piano lessons, after-school Spanish classes. Juiced for competition by parents and teachers, they keep blazing through private schools, magnet schools, and "gifted" programs, collecting Advanced Placement exams and chalking up extracurriculars, beating the curve with SAT tutors and gaining polish with foreign travel and study-abroad programs. Self-programming almost comes naturally by now, carrying to extremes every homily about work imbibed from relatives, friends, acquaintances, professors, and career advisors. Most interns cast a small vote for careerism over curiosity, for networking with contacts over hanging out with friends, for the office over the open road. Internships are boring us and they're making us boring.

A set of century-old traditions aim to grow well-rounded citizens—laws against child labor and the exploitation of young workers; summer camp and summer vacation; a civic-minded, liberal arts education in high school and college. How much of that will we give up for enhanced competitiveness and a foot in the door? With good reason, eighteen-year-olds talk of feeling "burnt out," and young people at every stage pine for a "year off," a "gap year," or indeed any kind of socially acceptable halt to the relentless credentialing slog. Having jettisoned months and years of their free time, they're reaching to reclaim it, looking for breathing room to forge something distinctively theirs, something creative, liberating, and self-defining.

Some internships *may* fit the bill for original, autonomous self-definition, but on the whole they fall far short of meeting that description. As education, they pale in comparison to our schools. As training to work, they compare unfavorably with apprenticeships. As a form of work, they are often a disappointment, and sometimes a rank injustice, failing our expectations and violating our laws. They have come to embody the ethos that all free, unstructured time should be harnessed for résumé-building and career development. Dreaming of becoming a comedy writer, Tyler the eight-time intern wishes he had worked on his own material, "rather than just picking up people's lunches and trying to see what they were doing." The three-time intern Andy, who felt that "maybe the real answers come from staying with things," would like to have slowed down, found a long-term mentor, learned a subject in depth, taken a real trip somewhere—but his intern years sped by in a desperate blur.

You can opt out—take back your time, boycott the busy work. You'll probably be in a cubicle soon enough. Well-intentioned, jittery parents should not lend blind support, moral or financial, to anything labeled an "internship," that magic word which suspends judgment. There have been decades of deliberate but half-baked efforts to help young people transition from the world of school to the world of white-collar work: and truly it's a miracle that anyone can make the leap from Psych 101 to being gainfully employed. There is no single road. Paid work experience, personal projects, foreign-language mastery, community service, job shadowing, freelance work, academic research, registered apprentice-ships, and just plain old living and learning are all possible ways forward.

Remember Henry, in Chapter 4, who ultimately found his career from doing what he loved as a camp counselor, not from an exploitative intern-ship. Consider the entrepreneurs and artists who have tinkered with new ideas and inventions and then taken a risk. Figure out how to turn a job at the mall into something with a future: talking honestly about your ambi-tions to your supervisor, interacting with customers, pressing for better work conditions and career advancement. Strike out and develop a new skill—whether it's taking a Spanish class or learning from a friend how to fix cars—and turn it into a career opportunity. Refusing to join the internship arms race need not mean losing your edge, resigning yourself to a second-tier career, or ending up on the unemployment rolls. Even in the fields where internships now seem a dominant prerequisite, employers will notice if driven, bright, and creative young people are finding other ways to break in. Young people need intense, structured learning opportunities *and* the space to be entrepreneurial. Why champion a one-size-fits-all way into work? You can make it without an internship.

Starting out, no one knows how many way stations, how many purgatories, await them. Twists and turns are expected—no road through life is straight, no career path is normal—but not the distorted logic of work without reward, of needing to working for free to have a career. Exploration should not be confused with self-indulgent indecisiveness. If you hadn't interned, what could you have done? What happens to all the lost time?

I wrote this book to explore a single theme: internships are a new way to work, a novel and dynamic practice in the workplace with huge implications for higher education, access to the white-collar world, social inequality, and the future of laboring. These questions have taken me from Disney World to Silicon Valley, from Ivy League campuses to Chinese factories, from medieval apprenticeship to the New Deal and the New Economy. Call it experiential education, volunteer work, participant observation, training, or apprenticeship—but most interns are now workers. Concocting all these different labels provides only the thinnest justification for taking away the rights of interns *as workers*, for keeping them from understanding what work itself is all about.

The first intern, confined within the four walls of his hospital, was a medical apprentice, updated for the modern age by a profession seeking to burnish its reputation with standardized forms of practical training. By mid-century, Corporate America, in high Fordist fashion, was finding internships to be a rational form of workplace planning, guaranteeing a sufficient supply of skilled, credentialed labor to power economic growth. The transformation and massive expansion that has followed—the ever-accelerating explosion of the last few decades—now positions internships as the gateway to all white-collar work, in an era when decent jobs outside that charmed circle are increasingly hard to come by. Fired by this incentive, interns have become a craven, flextime labor force sanctioned and even mobilized by academia, available in two principal flavors: the privileged and the precarious. Not to mention those who can't pay to play.

Despite changing priorities, firms have found interns to be well worth the trouble—old motivations like standardizing the abilities of employees, guaranteeing a steady supply of skilled workers, and saving on labor and hiring costs are easy to grasp. The indifference and even collusion of government is unsurprising: non-enforcement of the FLSA is part of a larger pattern of allowing New Deal protections to decay in the name of deregulating labor markets. The failure to measure or address the internship explosion is symptomatic: laws and regulations are simply not keeping up with the times. The indifference of unions bespeaks their own torpor, their inability to combat the rise of contingent labor, and their lack of a foothold in the white-collar world.

Refusing to offer or take internships in their current form is a feasible option, but many internships are already ethical and well paid, with strong mentoring and real opportunities for advancement. These model internships—fast-track positions for minority students arranged by INROADS, well-paid corporate internships in finance and engineering, life-changing stints at small companies and nonprofits that invest in training and mentoring, and so on—may still represent the best way to enter the workplace for many young people. "When an internship program is done right, it kind of sings," says Gina Neff, the professor who studies communications internships and manages a program in Olympia, Washington. "Everybody knows and feels it." As Tina, the former ExxonMobil intern, told me: "the pay was excellent, the training was good, and I was able to live in different parts of the country while doing something pretty unique, that I liked." Yet the better internships are, the more competitive they seem to be, unfortunately.

Any thoughtful approach to fixing the current system must proceed along two separate tracks: rectifying the indignities faced by current interns and ensuring greater access to internships that are worthwhile and meet basic criteria of fairness. The current system generates more and more opportunities—of increasingly lower quality. High school students and college freshman are eager for the chance to indulge their curiosity and try out a profession early on—an understandable feeling, especially given a dearth of targeted, short-term job shadowing opportunities and a school system that is still substantially disconnected from the world of work. Although many interns I spoke to complained bitterly about their positions, they worry that exposing illegal or exploitative internships would result in fewer opportunities across the board.

Although widespread, this feeling has little evidence to support it. Why jack up the quantity of internships before we've made a concerted effort to improve their quality? While it's true that some individual employers might balk at paying minimum wage and feel moved to cut their programs, this would only separate the wheat from the chaff—the internships that are least valued by employers and interns alike are the ones that would disappear first. The excuse that a firm "doesn't have the money" rings hollow: in the scheme of things, internships are never particularly expensive, and the question is simply whether they are valued enough to make it into the budget. And at least two important data points attest that raising the alarm and fixing abuses are unlikely to bring about an appreciable decline in internship offerings. First, as we have seen, mandating pay for interns is equivalent to closing a minimum wage loophole, and a substantial academic literature on the minimum wage has shown few adverse effects from instituting wage floors in the labor market. Second, as we'll see below, the architecture profession moved decisively to combat unpaid, illegal internships and witnessed no apparent drop-off in the number of available positions.

No silver bullet is likely to solve all the issues outlined in this book: recall that the term "intern" is a handy bit of marketing spin, covering a whole range of quite different situations. Employers *do* need sufficient incentives to give young people a shot. No one would suggest employee status for a high school student shadowing a petroleum engineer or a banker for a week or two. Putting in fewer than ten hours a week at a nonprofit, on a flexible and occasional basis, may resemble volunteering or freelancing a lot more than regular work. Supply and demand will inevitably play a role in the internship aisle of the labor supermarket, and different norms will continue to prevail in different industries. But let's insist on one simple principle: you shouldn't have to work for free to break into the white-collar world. To allow that is to devalue work, threaten regular jobs, and exclude the less privileged. To enact this princi-ple, companies, industries, schools, governments, as well as interns and their families, should try several different measures and see what works. Initiatives and experiments are needed from all quarters; together, their combined effect could be decisive, ending an unethical, inefficient drift with a sensible, professional, and humane approach to entering the workforce.

What employers can do is not a mystery: open advertising of positions; a strong training and mentoring component; discrete and manageable projects; a duration of at least a few months (for internships—less time for shadowing), allowing intern and supervisor to adjust to each other. What about the nature of the work? Most interns don't and shouldn't expect immediate glamor, writing legislation and designing the summer fashion line. Nearly everyone staples reports and makes coffee some-times, but interns should not replace administrative assistants, janitors, couriers, or temps, for a dozen obvious reasons. College student plus work does not equal an internship. The term "intern" should be applied ethically and transparently to opportunities that involve training, mentoring, and getting to know a line of work—internships should reflect what a given industry is all about and what the organization actu-ally does. Tasks should play to an intern's strengths and account for the training she's receiving. Academic credit, supervised by a professor, can be a valuable enhancement and a useful safeguard, if there is a genuine academic tie-in—but this applies to a distinct minority of internships.

A project-based model allows interns to focus on achieving something tangible, instead of becoming a gofer or doing the work of a regular employee, only with lower standing. More geared to future managers, a rotation model can be equally effective, granting access to different areas and functions of an organization—but should not be confused with doing "a little of this and a little of that" dependent solely on the short-term needs of a firm. Virtual internships and home office internships should be treated with suspicion, unless there are sufficient guarantees. Having large intern cohorts can mean camaraderie and quality control, while individual situations may offer close mentoring and the chance to work on more momentous projects. When things are clicking, interns can do big things: unlock energy savings for companies, help start-ups get off the ground, lend serious technical expertise, and run marketing strategies and ad campaigns, to name just a few real examples.

Whatever work the interns are performing, the question of pay is central. There's a reason that money issues have been a key theme of this book, and why I have cast a much harsher light on the hundreds of thousands of interns, probably millions around the world, who receive less than the local minimum wage each year. All research indicates that pay radically changes the equation: broadening the applicant pool, providing powerful motivation, allowing interns to focus on their work, enabling longer and more fruitful stints, and publicly marking the seriousness of the position. Pay is about respect and livelihood—only the thinnest sliver of internships can, and should, be exempted from the FLSA by meeting the Department of Labor's six-point test, providing such vital training, in return for so little labor, that pay need not be an issue.

People have asked me: if interns are from the elite to begin with, why bother paying them minimum wage? Aren't companies being rational in spending their money on other things, when interns don't seem to need it? These are valid and important questions—although it should be emphasized again that a clear majority of unpaid interns come from middle-class backgrounds, and they are likely making a sacrifice to be where they are. Indeed, even when a given group of interns is more privileged, these questions put the cart before the horse: if the firm *did* pay wages, they would attract a diverse, normal group of young people who certainly could use the money. An equally important point is that it is simply not possible, or ethical, for employers to discriminate about compensation in this fashion—the wage should match the work, not the family background of the worker. Nor is any employer in a position to decide who needs to be paid: especially in this day and age of long credit-lines and easily maintained appearances, one never knows when a well-dressed, cheerful young man is deep in debt.

Internships save firms money, as we have repeatedly seen, but these savings can easily be dwarfed by the risks inherent in the current system—from bringing people who are mediocre or worse into an organization (if their parents win an auction, for instance) to blackening a firm's reputation and attracting the undesired attention of employment lawyers and government regulators. A much safer and more reasonable strategy for saving money through internships, already pursued by many blue-chip companies, is to use them as a genuine recruiting tool. Even if there's little hiring in the offing, consider that you're ushering someone into an industry and may well do business with them again down the line. A firm's best interests will be served by kick-starting the careers of its high-performing interns and helping them find work inside or outside the company.

A firm can start by getting its own house in order, consulting, if in doubt, with HR professionals, legal counsel, and university career centers about what goes into a sound internship program. (In the interests of accuracy, the word "program" should only refer to cases where an organization, or one of its departments, is demonstrably working to shape a standard experience for all of its interns.) If an executive says a firm's program is all about "giving back," and boasts about the important work that interns do, let him put his money where his mouth is.

That's just what the Atlantic Media company did, announcing in April 2010 not only that it would immediately start paying its interns, but also that the previous year's intern class would receive retroactive pay. The company said in a statement that it had previously worked with outside counsel to develop an unpaid program where "interns work side by side with our editorial and business-side staff" and can experience "a strong academic program with a formal curriculum including lectures, case studies, homework and exercises." Nonetheless, a *New York Times* story about the proliferation of illegal internships and Department of Labor concerns brought about a rethink: "We had thought this was the way to structure unpaid internships but if it sits near a gray zone, it's not for us." Especially in the wake of the national discussion prompted by the *Times* story, the company reaped good publicity from the announcement—and the interns, of course, were thrilled. As Ross Eisenbrey of the Economic Policy Institute says, "Some companies will be scared into it. Other companies will do the right thing because it's the right thing."

Calling things by their proper names is another major step that organizations can take. Bosses who want to give back but can't pay for work should consider setting up a shadowing program, so that students from local high schools and colleges can experience something of what it's like to sell insurance or write software. Nonprofits should call on volunteers when that's genuinely what they need—not full-time six-month interns, doing the work of regular employees without pay to further their careers. Offices committed to their interns should be publicly recognized and perhaps even rewarded—even calls for an "internship tax credit" (a measure of this kind was recently passed by the Philadelphia City Council) may be worth heeding.[2] As it stands, feckless employers enjoy a dual benefit by not paying: a short-term competitive advantage over firms that do pay, and an outrageous exemption from recognizing interns' other workplace rights, as discussed in Chapter 4.

U nderstandably, many firms are unwilling to take a chance and make reforms while their competitors continue to cut corners. But what if an entire industry changed its practices? The sky didn't fall in when the field of architecture did precisely that in the mid-1990s, taking a powerful and effective stance against the mistreatment of unpaid, over-worked interns. At the time, Thomas Fisher, dean of the architecture school at the University of Minnesota, wrote of a "cycle of exploitation that gets passed from one generation of architects to the next," that "mis-understandings about the wage and hour law abound in the profession, and that non-compliance with the law, especially regarding interns' over-time pay and consultant status, is widespread." Architect Fred Stitt estimated that as many as half of small architecture firms were in violation of the law.[3]

"There were a lot of problems with star architects," says Kevin Fitzger-ald of the American Institute of Architects (AIA), and interns would "be going to work for them basically for free, for nothing. They wouldn't get paid, but they worked these crazy hours." These firms, adds Fitzgerald, weren't "budgeting projects very well and [weren't] willing to pay for the real costs of having an employee." The "ignoble tradition" of architects demanding free labor was considered deep-seated in the profession, wrote Fisher, with an impeccable pedigree dating back at least to Frank Lloyd Wright's unpaid Taliesin Fellowship in the 1930s and the work-place practices of legends like Le Corbusier and Bruce Goff. "My office runs on unpaid interns," said one noted architect to Fisher. "A bit," replied three young employees of another prominent practitioner, when asked by Fisher if they were paid. Summing up the different forms of exploitation still popular in the 1990s, Fisher notes that "some of the best-known firms do not pay interns at all" while others "engage in less obvious forms of exploitation, much of which is illegal and all of which damages the profession"—including misclassifying interns as independent contractors or consultants, not paying for overtime, and discriminating in the studio. "There is nothing unusual about such experiences," wrote Fisher in 1994, although "it's scandalous that the architectural community has looked the other way for so long."

Compounding matters was the fact that a multi-year internship (termed an IDP, short for Intern Development Program) is virtually required to become a licensed architect in the United States. Since 1976, when the structure of IDP was first established, the program has become an indispensable career move for graduates of architecture schools who want to continue into the profession—typically a three- to five-year period spent working full-time at a firm, learning every aspect of the field. Small firms with under ten employees, quite common in architecture, might have one or two such interns; larger ones with multiple offices could have as many as thirty or forty young architectural interns at any given time. And not all architecture internships are structured IDPs—it's still common for students and recent graduates to do more informal stints, not geared specifically towards becoming a licensed professional, undertaken for a summer or longer.

The fact that unpaid and barely paid interns were patently performing vital work, sometimes for years on end, stoked anger among many young architects, which finally boiled over during the recession of the early 1990s. The involvement of professional associations like the AIA in creating and managing the standards of IDP afforded a certain amount of leverage for reform; the understanding that these firms also violated federal labor law added further urgency. "We were the first to cry out," says Je'Nen Chastain of her organization—she is currently president of the American Institute of Architecture Students (AIAS), an independent nonprofit that represents 30,000 architecture students and interns. First building its case at industry conferences, in journals and in newsletters, the AIAS Board of Directors then passed a resolution in 1993 strongly condemning unpaid internships. The student group lobbied other key professional organizations to follow their lead in establishing a strongly worded policy on the issue—which the AIA soon did, along with the organizations that represent architecture schools and the profession's state licensing boards.

"The AIAS maintains that employers must properly compensate all employees," states the policy, which is still in force today. "Compensation must be in compliance with the regulations for the jurisdiction in which they are working … In the past, it had been considered appropriate to 'hire' students or recent architecture graduates to work for an architecture firm for little or no compensation until they had obtained a sufficient amount of experience"—a practice that "ignores and belittles the contribution that each participant adds to an architecture project." AIAS "denounces those firms, organizations, and individuals that do not properly compensate their employees" and "supports the efforts of interns who refuse to work" for such firms. Any student, intern, or architect wishing to participate in any AIAS event—as a speaker, awardee, jury member etc.—must sign a statement that they are neither engaging in nor making use of unpaid work.

Other key professional organizations in architecture soon endorsed the policy and sought a means of enforcement, ostracizing architects who continued not to pay—effectively making fair compensation part of the ethical code that all upstanding members of the profession are expected to follow. Deans of the different architecture schools began to scrutinize the postings for unpaid positions that came their way; a prominent architect, Peter Eisenman, was pointedly barred from speaking at a major conference after refusing to verify that his studio only arranges lawful internships. Five detailed surveys of young architects, undertaken since then, have enabled the profession to better understand what works and what doesn't about internships in architecture. As a part of its ongoing mission, AIAS distributes a toolkit to members about "why unpaid internships harm students and the reputation of the profession and what to do to deal with those situations," according to Chastain. The discussions of the mid-1990s even opened up the possibility that an offending architect could lose his membership in the professional organizations or his license to practice architecture.

But such drastic measures haven't been necessary. "I think it is a different world out there now," says Kevin Fitzgerald of the AIA. "I think most architects would shy away from not paying people these days: they're wiser than that." Brett Roeth, vice president of AIAS, adds that "it has become a part of our professional culture that internships should be compensated," that anything else is "just not acceptable in architecture." According to Roeth, "The early 2000s were a boom-time for interns," with some even earning signing bonuses—clearly the need to bring fresh, still very affordable talent into the profession hasn't gone away, despite a changed professional culture. Only lately, with the deepest recession in memory and 40 percent unemployment in the profession, have a small number of postings for unpaid architecture internships quietly reappeared.

Those in the profession are remaining vigilant—from professors of architecture to the bloggers who flag such postings to student leaders like Chastain and Roeth. Strongly supported by the major professional organizations in the field, AIAS remains "an independent, student-governed organization that represents the voice of emerging professionals in a strong way," says Roeth, explaining the group's success in spearheading the campaign. What architecture has achieved proves that a profession can take a practical and ethical stand against abuses—and win. Other student groups and professional organizations should follow suit.

There's an old joke among architects, says Chastain, that the profession "eats its young," who still face long years of demanding apprenticeship, challenging standards, and overtime work. But the worst is clearly over, and at least now an ever more diverse crop of young architects can stop worrying about basic issues of livelihood and get back to designing the world around us.

Like professional associations, educators are in a position to initiate positive, momentous changes. Why have they allowed the casual exploitation of their charges, who are just on their first, fledgling attempts at self-discovery? Why do they encourage their students, already burdened with the need to find paying work, to take time away from school to work without pay, subsidizing the operations of cheapskate companies and spineless nonprofits? Evidently, schools believe they can control a system they have done much to create and have learned to benefit from. To a certain extent, the issue has simply flown under the radar. Although internships vetted by schools at least have some oversight, this doesn't change the fact that American colleges and universities have disgraced themselves by pushing unpaid and illegal internships and by squeezing credit money from students while providing little in return.

Just as damning is the fact that, although perhaps unwittingly at times, economists, sociologists, psychologists, education theorists and career counselors have all provided intellectual justification for the internship explosion, attacking the idea of substantive training and helping to over-turn the once deeply held concept of fair pay for hard work. Regardless of whether their students are tens of thousands of dollars in student loan debt, or come from impoverished backgrounds, they cynically assume that students can work for free, or pay their college to work for free.

Take sociologist Dalton Conley, who doesn't think it's worth the sub-stantial effort to make internships transparent or investigate their role in widening social inequality, since "there'd be an uproar" and both nepo-tism and connections-pulling are only natural. Otherwise, he told the *American Prospect*, "it gets to where, for anyone to be in a summer intern-ship, you have to do an ad in the newspaper and vet all résumés"—surely more effort than it's worth, despite the decisive impact that internships are supposed to have on the rest of our lives. He arranged academic credit and some associated readings for a student's internship at *Vogue*, which the magazine required and for which NYU received tuition, although he finds such situations "ridiculous." Pointedly, Conley notes how the internship explosion is one of the "unintended consequences" of "a very progressive view of education from the '60s that life experience is equally valid as classroom experience. And that was meant to help the working class."[4]

Past theories aside, schools must face up to their current responsibility for shaping the internship landscape—there are several steps they can take. From the perspective of interns, the most urgent of them is to stop the practice of making students pay to work. Charging tuition for a rele-vant, optional seminar is perfectly valid, as is assessing a fee for administrative services performed by the school. But directly assigning costly credit units to work that students undertake off campus, typically running into the thousands of dollars, is a heinous practice. The excuse that it's just part of normal tuition simply doesn't hold up. Schools are anxious about internships becoming a cheap way for students to rack up the credits they need to graduate—but the problem is one of the schools' own making. If need be, they can exclude internship credits from the required total, or rethink the purpose of granting credit in the first place, but levying outrageous pay-to-intern fees is not the answer. The fact that many schools have earnestly raised small pools of money to support some unpaid positions, as discussed in Chapter 5, is sadly overshadowed by these practices.

The use of academic credit to justify unpaid labor is poisonous, as many faculty and career center staff have started to recognize—the Department of Labor, which has discussed academic credit as a possible proxy for an internship's educational and training content, risks making a serious mistake by doing so. Credit, as we have seen, is bought and sold with consummate ease and zero oversight—for the Disney program, for University of Dreams, for international students on countless J-1 visa schemes. Some institutions are awarding credit to students knowing nothing but their name and address and that a check from them has cleared at the bank. As described in Chapter 5, companies require students to get credit, and they in turn pressure their schools to help indemnify those employers, who are acting illegally. The least that schools can do is not penalize their students for being caught in this vise, not force them to subsidize an employer's flimsy indemnification. In the long run, college presidents have to take a stand against the complete subversion of academic credit and the way that firms abuse it to hide from the law— instead of writing petulant letters to the Department of Labor, daftly averring that they have the situation under control.

Higher education also artificially inflates the supply of interns, weakening their negotiating power in the labor market. (Likewise, schools blithely create new degree programs, leading to an overproduction of credentials in fields that have few jobs: recipe for a desperate labor market.) At the same time, colleges effectively endorse thousands of internships, between career counselors touting them, professors arranging them, and university websites formally posting them. The promotion of illegal work opportunities in higher education must stop. It doesn't take an employment lawyer to make these judgment calls, even a basic algorithm could do half the work: any unpaid internship that fails to lay out a clear training program should be summarily rejected or slapped with a warning label. Internship handbooks, internship fairs, and info sessions of various descriptions should go beyond describing the networking techniques and fawning flexibility needed to squeeze into the workforce—they should cover the workplace rights of interns and the concept that work demands reward.

Requiring internships is often tantamount to outsourcing part of a student's education—in many cases, schools themselves should offer the applied opportunities if they're really that vital, just as chemistry departments are expected to have lab facilities for hands-on work. Still, there may occasionally be educational grounds for a given department, or even an entire college, to require an internship for graduation. Yet it's still a stretch to mandate that students pay the school to do this off-campus work and to disallow credit from appropriate, well-documented internships that students might have arranged on their own—as we saw in the case of Sarah, a student at Northwestern's journalism school. Schools requiring internships should pledge to find paid positions for their students, negotiating with employers if necessary—and only charge when the school is providing something clear in return. If relevant, paid work proves impossible to find, schools should contemplate the use of shadowing or participant observation techniques instead, where learning can take place with no strings attached.

In short, schools should either keep their distance from the Wild West of sketchy internships, however much that might disappoint students, or take a few lessons from cooperative education, as described in Chapter 5. A century old, that movement still represents a thoroughgoing approach to bridging the gap between education and work. Its collapse and comparative irrelevance are ascribed to its being *too* vocational, stressing work experience over a well-rounded education, and the fact that it relied financially on the changeable support of schools and governments, rather than the eternal anxieties of students and their families. Yet not only did coops provide career paths accessible to students of all backgrounds, they also by and large guaranteed honest wages for an honest day's work, humane working conditions, and real training.

For too long, governments have informally counted on schools to form a first line of defense. After all, the original Supreme Court decision outlining the six-point test likened a proper trainee situation to vocational school. Yet the reality is that learning at school and learning at work are two entirely different things, pace Hamburger University—the first occurs because the institution is directing all its efforts to that end; the second comes as a byproduct of the economically useful activity that the worker is performing for an employer. The number of internships that are really school-like, full-time, dedicated training programs is vanishingly few. Overwhelmingly, the expectation of employers is that interns will labor and (somehow) learn simultaneously, and that their work will bring clear benefits to the firm.

There's a reason that the Supreme Court understood an unpaid trainee to be someone who brings "no immediate advantage" to a firm: immediate advantage is something you should pay for. This criterion for FLSA exemption alone lays bare the fact that trainees and interns hail from different universes. Of course, employers expect to derive a material advantage from their interns—the interns are workers, often indistinguishable from regular employees, as we have seen. On the other hand, National Public Radio's "Intern Edition" is a "fully featured," intern-produced "program," brilliantly demonstrating that it is possible for employers to give interns serious, nonexploitative work that introduces them meaningfully to a profession. Employers who actually want to train the next generation, and not just squeeze it for cheap labor, should consider intern editions of their own.

The Department of Labor must start by enforcing the law—the same goes for governments around the world. Investigators should respond to all plausible hints or allegations that a firm is failing to pay minimum wage, but also actively seek out abuses, recognizing that interns feel understandably timid and have little incentive to come forward. As things stand, few firms will be able to pass the six-point test absolving them of employer responsibilities, even under the reasonable "totality of the circumstances" interpretation where interns are permitted to provide their employers with "immediate advantage," but still must get at least as good as they give. Labor law tests of volunteer status should apply to those nonprofits that want to continue using unpaid interns. With overwhelming numbers of interns now doing the work of regular employees, the law should assume that the word "intern" means a type of employee, not a type of student. Legislators should start with interns in the political system, ending the unholy FLSA exemption for congressional interns, who should receive at least the same consideration as the high-school-age congressional pages. Elected representatives, perhaps even more than judges and DoL investigators, must close the significant loophole that permits the discrimination and harassment of interns at work, leaving interns like Bridget O'Connor in legal limbo.

If wisely used, federal, state, and local money used to support internships in government could have a dramatically positive effect, as the Economic Policy Institute (EPI) indicated in its 2009 proposal "Paving the Way Through Paid Internships." Over four million college students aged sixteen to twenty-four come from working families whose combined income is three times the Federal Poverty Line or less—that is, under $67,000 annually for a family of four. When they're even able to shell out thousands of dollars for a single summer of unpaid work, these families are making a considerable sacrifice. Alex Hertel and Kathryn Edwards of EPI have estimated conservatively that 22,000 federal interns each year would fall into this category and be eligible for income assistance under their proposal.[5]

Providing as little as $3,500 for a low-income student to take a summer internship in D.C. or the state capital could significantly broaden the range of young people able to break into politics. According to EPI, an annual $500 million outlay could subsidize as many as 100,000 public service internships, harnessing for administrative needs the Federal Work-Study Program offices already installed at some 3,400 schools. Indeed, a much more significant portion of existing work-study funds could arguably be allocated to internships meeting certain criteria—as Gardner writes, "This sacred cow for institutions needs to be revamped to help students reach their career goals." Any such programs would have to do better than AmeriCorps at ensuring that existing and potential full-time jobs aren't axed in favor of these government-subsidized internships. Even at the level they propose, say the researchers at EPI, only 4.3 percent of eligible college students would be covered—but it would be a good start.

If these fixes don't improve conditions more broadly, members of Congress and state legislators should pass an Intern Bill of Rights (see Appendix A), or companies themselves should take the initiative by endorsing such a code of conduct. Recall what the Fitzgerald Act did for apprenticeships—a brief, straightforward piece of legislation and a tiny office in Washington D.C. have largely been able to set the standard for what constitutes a high-quality apprenticeship. The law's success demonstrates that there *are* sufficient reasons for employers to participate in well-structured programs, held to a high standard and involving on-the-job training of young workers at a living wage. The past few decades have shown that demand for internships is more than robust, from young people and employers alike—and not just because it's a lawless free-for-all. With the right incentives, a Fitzgerald Act for interns might just work, providing firms with the best interns, still at a relative bargain, and placing them in situations where they can "earn and learn" at the same time. It could galvanize a political demographic that is famously lethargic, seeming to awaken with the 2008 election only to slumber again soon after. An Intern Bill of Rights would recognize internships as a distinctive and important form of work, worth taking on its own terms, measuring and evaluating, improving and protecting. Interns would enjoy the same rights and privileges that apprentices do today.

A fter the titanic struggles of the early twentieth century, the industrialized world reached a surprising degree of consensus about work —a consensus which still remains substantially intact today. Whatever people think about politicized issues such as taxes, welfare, abortion, or gay marriage, they generally agree that ten-year-olds should be found in school, not in coal mines; that weekends and vacations should be available to all; that a minimum wage and basic workplace protections are part of a fair and just society; that workers should be able to organize around their common interests. Perhaps most of all, we continue to believe in the power of an honest day's work, and in the virtuous imperative to spend some of one's time in productive activities that require more than casual attention. William Faulkner wrote that "the only thing a man can do for eight hours a day is work. He can't eat for eight hours; he can't drink for eight hours; he can't make love for eight hours. The only thing a man can do for eight hours is work"—and we had best make the most of it.

As practiced today and documented in this book, many internships represent a slow drift away from this firm, humane consensus about work. Along with the explosion of contingent labor and much scarier trends such as the resurgence of sweatshops in our midst and a global race to the bottom around labor standards, internships are turning back the clock. They are symptomatic of a drastically unequal, hypercompetitive world in the making—one in which, as so many Americans rightly fear, succeeding generations will work harder for less reward, for a lower quality of life with fewer avenues for getting ahead.

Present, former, and future interns, listen up and take action. Whether any particular internship is life-changing or completely forgettable, a month long or a year long, paid or unpaid—attention must be paid. We've had the professional mindset, believing we could defend ourselves, parley with the boss, complain to the career center, take the problem to mom and dad. Knowing nothing of grievance procedures, collective bargaining, or severance packages, all we could do was quit. Intern dropout rates would be shocking if anyone tracked them.

Up until now, young people have ceded everything, asking only for a foot in the door in return. It's time to stop spreading the internship gospel without a second thought. Stop thinking your labor is, was, or will be worthless. Just because you have a student ID and live in a dorm doesn't mean you're not also a worker. Identify and organize *as interns*, and form alliances with like-minded groups such as temps or freelancers. Even if you've moved on, don't forget the freshmen of the workforce, the unpaid kids doing menial and administrative work: the interns. Blow the whistle on illegal situations you've experienced or witnessed or heard about. Stand up for people's right to get paid for an honest day's work, whoever those people may be—7,000 miles away or just next door.

"How can you be the first to speak up?" writes the anonymous author of the long-time blog "Unfair Internships," which chronicles the hypocrisies of the Intern Economy—adding that what interns face is "a simple collective action problem."[6] Internships pass by quickly, and few interns are experienced enough to know the levers of power. "Internships are just a transitional situation," as the blogger points out. "Students suck it up for a year or two and then get a job and move on. It's not like some major issues of unfairness, such as gender and race, where it follows you all your life and, at any point, you have an interest in addressing the unfairness of the situation." And so it always goes with injustices faced by the young—

you forget about them as you grow older, then you perpetuate them, and the cycle repeats itself …

Legal protection for interns is not a pipe dream—it's a reality within reach, a set of rights waiting to be claimed. Learning about a profession should include learning about the nature of work itself and issues such as fairness, compensation, protection, and solidarity. Interns *can* and *should* organize, as interning becomes near universal, and schools, employers, and governments continue not to do the right thing. Large-scale student organizations, the anti-precarity groups, and platforms for contingent workers such as WashTech and the Freelancers Union all represent possible models, though organizing interns represents a special challenge, given the diversity and transience of internship situations.

What has to change is more than a policy or a law—it's a mindset. We are the future of work. The internship explosion is not an emergency, yet—it's a slow boil, a simmering injustice, a glass ceiling half-built which there's still time to tear down. This is more than just a phase or a fluke: when working for free becomes the norm, everyone loses, except at the very top. We've trusted too much. We've been free for the taking. When will our hours matter?

Afterword

ENTHUSIASM *n.*, a distemper of youth, curable by small doses of repentance in connection with outward applications of experience.
—Ambrose Bierce, *The Devil's Dictionary*

A fledgling writer's first effort is always a kind of apprenticeship—the bright-eyed novice sticks his proverbial foot in the publisher's door (and often enough in his own mouth), learns the ropes on the fly from editors and readers, and unwittingly becomes a jack-of-all-trades. Likewise, a book is a little like a startup, only minus the big bucks and silicon glory. You find yourself glad-handing countless strangers and murmuring elevator pitches in your sleep. You invest everything up front, gambling on an expansive horizon, and learn how to fail better next time.

Five years ago, simple curiosity led me to start asking questions about internships—utterly ordinary questions (How many are there? What's their larger impact?) that no one had answered, or even tried to answer. Taking the advice of art critic Harold Rosenberg, I loitered in the neighborhood of the problem, waiting for a solution to stroll by, and soon found myself immersed in a substantial, mushrooming project, with connections to history, sociology, educational theory, economics, business, law, and digital culture. Now, half a year since *Intern Nation* first came out, the bigger picture surrounding the rise of internships is clearer than ever. Its suddenness has been uncanny, but a long overdue, remarkably robust debate about youth and work is finally underway, both in America and around the globe.

From Tahrir Square to Zuccotti Park, people in their twenties and thirties have been emerging at the forefront of new political movements, exposing a generational rift wider than anything seen since the 1960s. Internships are surfacing as a central issue facing young people—not just as a personal concern but as a political question—along with the soaring costs of higher education, onerous student loans, youth unemployment, and downward mobility.

"Screw Your Unpaid Internships" was among the posters I saw at a massive Occupy Wall Street march across the Brooklyn Bridge on an extraordinary day of dissent when tens of thousands, above all the young and precarious, marched and spoke out against corporate greed and economic injustice. That same day, several thousand striking students were loudly and enthusiastically chanting, "Fuck internships!" in New York City's Union Square—an unprecedented condemnation. Among the protesters' others messages: "Occupy Unpaid Internships," "I Will Never Own My Own House," "Middle Class and Sinking Fast," "Lost My Job, Found an Occupation."

New numbers, based on Census Bureau data, substantiate the outrage, laying to rest any gripes about "entitled" youth: 37 percent of American households headed by someone under thirty-five now have a net worth of zero or less; households headed by a person over sixty-five have a net worth forty-seven times greater than younger households; the incomes of young people have fallen over 10 percent since 2000, even as the cost of living has risen; and starting salaries are frozen or down for those lucky few who do find jobs. Also according to the Census Bureau, 5.9 million young Americans, aged twenty-five to thirty-four, are now living with their parents, up from 4.7 million before the recession—if calculated separately from their parents, 45 percent of these young people would fall below the poverty line. Although some degree of inequality based on age is inevitable and natural, these statistics are the highest on record—by far.

Meanwhile, the political system has been utterly mute, aside from emitting the usual hot air about the shining promise of future generations. Funding for education and youth programs disappears while Medicare and social security remain sacrosanct, at least for now. Young people—whose parents and grandparents attended university virtually for free, never had to work unpaid, could afford home ownership, enjoyed inexpensive healthcare, and received pensions and social security at a reasonable retirement age—can expect none of these things themselves.

Meanwhile, the American Association of Retired Persons (AARP) stands as one of the most powerful lobbying organizations in America, publishing the most widely circulated periodical in the country (far eclipsing the *New York Times*, *Newsweek*, *Time*, and several other publications, combined). While AARP zealously defends the rights and privileges of those over age fifty, nothing comparable exists for the young—and simple demographics determine that retirement communities matter more than university campuses for any politician. Even when young people turn up to the polls in droves and power a campaign with their organizational and financial contributions (as in 2008), the result is nearly always deep disappointment.

Unlike the "ageism" which affects some older workers, the closure of the workplace to young people without "experience" has become absolute and systemic, the disappearance of the entry-level job a primary symptom. The paradox raised in *Intern Nation* remains unanswered: how can we get experience if we don't already have experience? There may be sound personal and financial reasons for older people to remain in the workforce later and later in life, and important public policy reasons to encourage (or require) this, but we ignore the collateral damage at our peril: a generation of young people left perpetually precarious, treading water during what should be the crucial years of career-building.

Intern Nation represents a first word on the subject, by no means the last. In covering a sprawling topic long overlooked, the best metric of success may be paradoxical: to cause enough of a ruckus (research, writing, discussion, and concrete action) so that the original book ultimately becomes obsolete or, at best, quaint. Every modern society, in every generation, will continue to struggle with the basic, underlying question at stake here—"How do we move young people from school to the workplace?"—but internships themselves are just one particular, recent manifestation, characteristic of our time, our politics, and the nature of our economy. With a cluster of exciting internship-related projects now in the offing—academic, artistic, journalistic, commercial, and nonprofit—it's clear that the conversation is only just beginning. Major issues of substance, such as the connection between internships and gender and the degree to which internships are replacing regular jobs (and entry-level jobs in particular), still remain to be illuminated.

Despite their own notorious reliance on unpaid intern labor, media outlets around the world respectfully reviewed *Intern Nation* and its arguments. Everyone seems to agree, at least, that internships are worth talking about and that the discussion is long overdue. Indeed, most journalists seemed to "get" the issue instantly because of their own past experiences, and a number of outlets (CBS and the *Washington Post*, among others) assigned their current interns to cover the issues raised in the book, with personal anecdotes sprinkled in liberally along the way. (Usually that was as far as the self-awareness went—few of the news organizations publicly divulged, let alone questioned, their own internship policies.)

But aren't internships still a fair deal for most people? Don't they represent the free market in action? These two basic critiques, both anticipated and addressed in the book, are well worth taking into account. Of course it's true that for some people, even disingenuous illegal internships may seem to represent a "fair deal"—the ends justifying the means, and "fairness" existing principally in the eye of the beholder—if they ultimately lead to a job or else pay off in some other abstract but substantive enough way. The problem is that fewer and fewer do, and that training-focused internships and paid internships are demonstrably *more likely* to lead to such benefits. Pretty soon this argument devolves into the insistence, no longer really an argument, that beggars can't be choosers. Almost everyone has an internship story to tell these days, and certainly some situations do work out well. Internships can launch careers and also nip them in the bud. Arguing that it worked out for you (or for your progeny, your friend, or your co-worker) is light years away from arguing that the internship system *overall* is working.

As for the role of the free market, there remains no protection against workers getting caught in a race to the bottom. A broad consensus exists that the adoption of minimum wage laws and various workplace protections has brought decent living conditions, sustained prosperity, and social stability. Besides, the rise of internships has hardly been inevitable—schools, companies, and governments have actively created and promoted this new category of job, originally because of technocratic worries about talent and training and later with cost savings in mind. Readers and reviewers have been right to note that having "something like internships" is probably unavoidable, but I hope that the discussions of apprenticeship, cooperative education, and ethical internships in the book have highlighted real, existing alternatives to the status quo, tested by time and experience. And the most consequential problem with internships today, as I will reemphasize below, still centers on social mobility and access to the professional world for the non-interns who can't afford to pay to play.

Beyond debate and criticism, there has been action too—starting with the book's publisher, Verso, where previously unpaid interns now earn a living wage. Nor is Verso alone: several organizations are remedying or at least reconsidering their internship policies in light of the book's arguments and the resulting publicity. On an industry level, the Public Relations Society of America released an advisory containing guidance about the ethical use of interns in that profession, following the example of architecture. Some college career centers have changed direction too, declining to list or promote illegal internships (and at least at one such school, California State University–San Bernardino, is seeing a substantial uptick in paid positions). As for the government, an official from the Department of Labor stated unequivocally for the first time, at a book-related panel, that illegal internships are "a spreading cancer" and that an increasing number of interns are filing formal complaints.

In perhaps the most remarkable turn of events, two former interns, Eric Glatt and Alex Footman, have courageously taken on Fox Searchlight, the Hollywood studio behind the film *Black Swan*. Although the movie earned over $300 million at the box office, some one hundred interns have received no compensation whatsoever from the production company, despite performing essential administrative and accounting work, among other tasks, that would otherwise have required the hiring of regular workers. The open class-action lawsuit filed by Glatt and Footman, with the help of their lawyers at the New York firm Outten & Golden, is notable for going beyond back wages to announce a larger critique. The ongoing case, to date probably the most high-profile legal challenge to internship culture, represents a historic stand against an entire industry which has exploited and continues to exploit thousands of people.

The ripple effects could spread far. In another, even more recent suit, five young plaintiffs are seeking back wages from the developers of Brooklyn's multibillion dollar Atlantic Yards project, alleging that their "pre-apprentice training" was in effect a kind of unpaid internship—two months spent renovating a private home while receiving no compensation and little training. Meanwhile, hundreds of foreign students bravely protested an abusive internship-like arrangement at a Hershey's plant in Pennsylvania, which appears to closely resemble the Disney International College Program described in Chapter 1. Brought to the U.S. under dubious J-1 "exchange visitor" visas, like many Disney interns, the students found themselves forced into backbreaking factory work, often on the night shift, deprived of expected opportunities to improve their English and learn about America, and barely taking home a salary after mandatory deducted expenses.

In the UK, where internships are a comparatively recent arrival (replacing an older tradition of very short-term job shadowing known as "work experience"), the last two years have seen an intense backlash. The political sensitivity surrounding youth unemployment and crime, the involvement of trade unions, and a strong sense of fairness surrounding work and social class have all played a part in putting internships squarely on the political agenda.

The Conservative Party provided the spark with an act of stupendous hypocrisy: talking up issues of social mobility and then brazenly auctioning off prestigious internships, American-style, at a tony fundraiser. Deputy Prime Minister Nick Clegg, seeking to differentiate himself from his Conservative coalition partners, stepped in with a prominent proposal to make internships "about what you know, not who you know." The proposal included a promise to end informal internships in Britain's civil service by the end of 2012, thus ensuring a fair and transparent application process, as well as the introduction of a number of paid model internship programs at well-known employers such as the *Guardian* and consulting firm KPMG.

Clegg's hypocrisy—he and his party have continually used unpaid interns, and his own career once received a crucial boost from a privileged, insider internship—soon drowned out the policy substance. Yet the U.K. publication of *Intern Nation* coincided fortuitously with a flurry of inspiring activity, including the launch of Parliament's first ethical internship program, supported by several outspoken legislators. A "cashback for interns" initiative, developed by the National Union of Journalists, has made it simple and straightforward for interns to claim their deserved back wages under the law, and over a hundred are already lining up to do so. Most recently, Her Majesty's Revenue and Customs, the government body charged with enforcing the minimum wage law, has taken the bold and unprecedented step of convening a twelve-member task force to raid fashion companies that use interns illegally. Judging from polls, opinion articles, and other sources, there is strong support across the U.K. for these efforts. The challenge now lies in enforcement and perseverance.

On the whole, internship mania is still alive and well, seemingly as frenzied as ever. The backlash is only just beginning. The pressure to intern is at an all-time high, the number of illegal internships appears to be more or less undiminished, colleges remain compromised collaborators, and a legion of new businesses scheme about buying and selling the free labor of young people. Nepotism, cronyism, and lack of transparency remain the order of the day in filling many internship positions, even as people quietly admit that the situation is out of control.

Here are the absurd new heights lately reached by the internship racket: as a PR stunt, an internship-hawking company (Internships.com) pays a loose-cannon, abusive celebrity (Charlie Sheen) six figures to hire an intern to manage his tweets and status updates, and it becomes the most sought-after internship in history. A total of 82,148 people from around the world applied for a single spot to be a "TigerBlood intern" for The Machine, helping to "leverage the social network" of a self-immolating celebrity known for bizarre tirades, cocaine and alcohol addiction, threesomes with porn stars, and domestic violence.

Nor is Sheen the only intern employer capable of giving you a gunshot wound along with your letter of reference. Earlier this year, Chelsea soccer star Ashley Cole, "larking around" with a .22-caliber air rifle, fired at team intern Tom Cowan from five feet away and left the twenty-four-year-old seriously wounded. Meanwhile, the globalization of internships is proceeding faster than ever. In one more harrowing example, anthropologist Thaddeus Blanchette explained to National Public Radio how many interns in Rio de Janeiro are supporting themselves through dangerous sex work. Many young Brazilians "have to spend a year, maybe two, in a free internship after they leave university in order to get a good job in a profession," says Blanchette. "And there are a lot of men and women who turn tricks to make ends meet during that internship as well."

Beyond the horror stories lurks something even more sinister. The trials faced by unpaid interns are real but temporary. For those on the other side of the divide, who can't afford an unpaid work credential, internships represent a more lasting, pernicious injustice—a new prerequisite for entering the professional world, to which access is drastically unequal. Many readers of *Intern Nation*, and even more so those who have only eavesdropped on its arguments (some of whom asked me to help them land an internship), have been fixated on the question of whether internships are good or bad, in and of themselves. Perhaps I failed before to make the internship divide clear enough. Requiring unpaid work is functionally equivalent to charging an entrance fee to the white-collar world, or at least to particular fields, making them no better than exclusive clubs for a well-heeled, well-connected elite unworthy of a land of opportunity.

Intergenerational social mobility—living better than your parents did, on the basis of merit and hard work—remains at the heart of our social contract. Yet to have a shot at the American dream (or its equivalent elsewhere) increasingly requires earning a college degree and struggling through unpaid, or low-stipend, internships. Although some can still succeed without these credentials, many more will remain trapped in dead-end, low-wage jobs, unable to enter the white-collar workforce. Access to higher education is an issue widely acknowledged, already mitigated by a million (endangered) efforts: public universities, Pell Grants, widespread financial aid, and so on. Even if similar measures for internships were feasible, they would miss the point: firms should pay for work.

Is this simply a call to restore meritocracy in the working world—a worry, as Tim Barker wrote in *Dissent*, that internships "gum up the pipes of meritocratic mobility"? Barker pointedly charges *Intern Nation* with "reproducing the competitive logic that drives the internship craze" by failing to do battle with "the idea that kids need to exercise constant scrutiny of themselves and their time to be employable, or with the snobbish concept of 'second-tier' careers as a pit to be avoided." Without attempting a full-on discussion of hyper-credentialing and careerism, the evidence gathered in *Intern Nation*, seen in tandem with ongoing changes in the working world, does indeed raise more fundamental questions about merit, inequality, and the nature of work.

A new dogma has taken hold, recently expressed in its purest form by no less a New Economy superhero than Mark Zuckerberg: "Someone who is exceptional in their role is not just a little better than someone who is pretty good. They are 100 times better." With the same triumphalist imprecision, Netscape co-founder and prominent venture capitalist Marc Andreessen has said the same thing in a slightly different way: "The gap between what a highly productive person can do and what an average person can do is getting bigger and bigger. Five great programmers can completely outperform 1,000 mediocre programmers."

Quietly and not-so-quietly this "talent myth" has become an underlying justification for massive and growing inequality, runaway executive compensation, a winner-take-all economy, and an intense focus on superstars—not to mention multibillion-dollar companies hiring unpaid interns. We're meant to welcome a master race of hyper-talented free-agent heroes who destroy the jobs of others to fatten their own bonuses, make a quick killing with unsustainable business models, leverage themselves to the point where they're too big to fail, and insure themselves by capturing the corridors of power. Meanwhile, they cloak themselves in meritocracy at a time when social mobility is shrinking and the role of privilege is on a continual increase.

By now the corollaries should sound disturbing familiar. "Ordinary" workers are virtually worthless (perhaps not even worth paying), training them has become meaningless (since any "real talent" is inherent—and doesn't stick around anyway), and proximity to stardom is worth virtually any price. Those left behind (because they didn't graduate from college, couldn't afford an internship, lost their way to the fast track etc.) are relegated to the dust, hardly worth noting.

Those employed work longer and longer hours, despite stubbornly high unemployment. Companies complain of a record number of job vacancies, even with "plenty of people out there who *could* step into jobs with just a bit of training—even recent graduates who don't have much job experience," as Peter Cappelli, a professor of management at Wharton, recently wrote in the *Wall Street Journal*. "Unfortunately, American companies don't seem to do training anymore," he adds, and won't take a chance on unproven young people, even with their ever more specialized vocational degrees (Cappelli cites pharmaceutical marketing and retail logistics).

Besides being unscientific and self-serving, the talent myth radically undervalues the importance of cooperative work, the contributions of a so-called supporting cast, and the fact that our individual successes are in reality collective projects of family, community, culture, and environment. Inequality sanctioned in the economy seeps into our neighborhoods, our laws, our politics, our values.

The world of work is chronically unstable, drastically unequal, utterly undemocratic. At the boundaries, we barely know what counts as work—just look at childcare, housekeeping, or volunteering. And yet work is virtually the only legitimate way to secure a foothold of dignity and security in the world—for some of us, it may even be "the best prize that life has to offer," as Theodore Roosevelt called it. As far into the future as anyone can imagine, the demand for dignified and fairly compensated work—and for fair and equitable access to that work—is not going to disappear.

Ross Perlin
Brooklyn, New York
November 22, 2011

Notes

There are few, if any, experts on the sprawling subject of internships, and little research is available. One-on-one interviews—conducted in person, by phone, and via email between 2008 and 2010—form the core of this book. I've talked to hundreds of people across the U.S., indeed around their world, about internships they've participated in, managed, witnessed, and heard about. It was inevitably what a sociologist would call a convenience sample, and I hope that this initial look at internships—wide-ranging but still impressionistic, empirically minded but still lacking in rigorously collected data—will prompt further work.

Many people I spoke with, especially former interns, were reluctant to use their real names or the real name of their employer—completely understandable, given that so many interns leave their work with little more besides precarious references and weak relationships. Real names are generally used for noninterns; first names that appear in quotation marks are inventions, and in some cases other identifying information has been obscured as well. Besides interviews, I've also drawn on a wide range of other materials, including traditional sources such as media reports and academic papers, but also online forums, guidebooks, video materials, pop culture references and so on.

PREFACE

1 For a hair-raising account of an absurd war-zone internship, see Willem Marx, "I Was a PR Intern in Iraq," *Harper's Magazine*, September 18, 2006, reprinted by Alternet at alternet.org/story/41479.

2 BNO News, "Dutch teenage girls take 'internship' as prostitutes," December 15, 2010, channel6newsonline.com.

3 Jeffrey Tucker, "War on Internships: Should Unpaid Internships Be Regulated?", *The Christian Science Monitor*, April 7, 2010.

4 The number of students attending four-year colleges and universities in the U.S. is drawn from the Census Bureau's "Current Population Survey" (CPS), October 2008. There are no authoritative statistics for the percentage of college students involved in internships, or the number of internships undertaken each year. But 75 percent of student participation is based on impressionistic surveys conducted by two career information websites, Vault and Quintessential Careers, and the comments of Phil Gardner of the College Employment Research Institute, all discussed in Chapter 2. The figure of between 1 and 2 million internships in the U.S. each year is my own, calculating that the current enrolled population will account for some 6 million internships (perhaps 75 percent of the 8 million enrolled students). Divided evenly over four or even five years of school, that means 1.2 to 1.5 million undergraduate internships each year.

5 For middle-aged interns, see Elizabeth Pope, "Testing the Waters with Internships," *New York Times*, April 21, 2008 and Amy Farnsworth, "Rise of the 40-Something Intern," *The Christian Science Monitor*, June 26, 2009. See Steven Greenhouse, "Growth of Unpaid Internships May Be Illegal," *New York Times*, April 2, 2010 and "Fact Sheet #71: Internship Programs Under the Fair Labor Standards Act" issued by the U.S. Department of Labor's Wage and Hour Division in April 2010 and accessible at dol.gov/whd/regs/compliance/whdfs71.htm.

1 THE HAPPIEST INTERNS IN THE WORD

1 Baudrillard's comment, from his 1983 essay "Simulacra and Simulations," refers to the original Disneyland in southern California, but if anything it applies with even greater force to the more complete universe of Disney World in Orlando.

2 Wesley Jones, *Mousecatraz: The Walt Disney World College Program*, 2006, Lulu.com.

3 "Disney Internships Draw Students, Criticism," The Associated Press, July 5, 2005.

4 For Goffman's classic formulation of the "total institution," see Erving Goffman, *Asylums: Essays on the Condition of the Social Situation of Mental Patients and Other Inmates*, Harmondsworth: Penguin, 1961.

5 For a recent introduction to "Disney Studies"—and there's a lot out there—see Thomas Doherty, "The Wonderful World of Disney Studies," *The Chronicle of Higher Education*, July 21, 2006.

6 For more on the Reedy Creek Improvement Distrcit, see Joshua Wolf Shenk, "Hidden Kingdom: Disney's Political Blueprint," *The American Prospect*, March 21, 1995.

7 NACE Executive Director Marilyn Mackes would not comment on her involvement with the Disney program, other than to write: "I would recommend more research through Disney directly to learn the scope and depth of the experiences offered."

8 Bruce Nissen, Eric Schutz, and Yue Zhang, "Walt Disney World's Hidden Costs: The Impact of Disney's Wage Structure on the Greater Orlando Area," Research Institute on Social and Economic Policy, Center for Labor Research and Studies, Florida International University, March 19, 2007.

9 See Jane Kuenz, Susan Willis, Shelton Waldrep, Stanley Fish, eds., *Inside the Mouse: Work and Play at Disney World*, Durham: Duke University Press, 1995, pp. 110–63.

2 THE EXPLOSION

1 Michael True, director of the Internship Center at Messiah College, also runs the Internship-Net listserv, an active email forum, primarily for college career counselors, from which this proposed definition of "academic internship" is drawn.

2 The American figures are drawn from *The Debate Over Unpaid College Internships*, published by Intern Bridge in 2010. The U.K. research, announced in mid-2010, was produced by the Chartered Institute of Personnel and Development and included a recommendation for paying interns at least a low training wage. The German figure, published in 2008, comes by a survey undertaken by the country's International Institute for Empirical Socioeconomics (INIFES).

3 Stone's results are described in Jim Frederick, "Internment Camp: The Intern Economy and the Culture Trust," *Baffler*, no. 9, 1997: 51–8. The numbers concerning game design and law enforcement internships come from "2010 Internship Salary Report," published by Intern Bridge.

4 For the Michigan State study, see Philip Gardner, Georgia Chao, and Jessica Hurst, "*Ready for Prime Time? How Internships and Co-ops Affect Decisions on Full-time Job Offers*, White Paper, Fall 2008, MonsterTRAK.com.

5 The NACE figure is found in their *Job Outlook 2009*.

6 See Rosemary Stevens, "Graduate Medical Education: A Continuing History," *Journal of Medical Education*, vol. 53, January 1978: 1–18.

7 For education, see Anonymous, "Intern System Urged for Schools," *The Science News-Letter*, vol. 14, no. 403, Dec. 29, 1928, Reports of AAAS New York Meeting, 399–400. For accounting, S. G. Winter, "The Next Decade in Accounting," *The Accounting Review*, vol. 3, no. 3, September 1928, 311–22. For marketing, See D. J. Duncan, "The Teaching of Advanced Marketing Courses in Specialized Programs," *The Journal of Marketing*, vol. 1, no. 4, April 1937: 379–82.

8 There are three detailed and illuminating accounts of the National Institute for Public Affairs' pioneering internship program, written by its directors in the early years: Otis Theodore Wingo, "Internship [sic] Training in the Public Service," *Annals of the American Academy of*

Political and Social Science, vol. 189, January 1937: 154–8; Otis Theodore Wingo, "Training for Public Administration," *The Journal of Higher Education*, vol. 8, no. 2, February 1937: 84–8; and Henry Reining, Jr., "Internship Training for Public Service", *Journal of Educational Sociology*, vol. 14, no. 5, January 1941: 286–91. There is also a useful account from the intern perspective, written a half-century after the fact, contained in Herbert Kaufman, "Music of the Squares: A Lifetime of Study of Public Administration," *Public Administration Review*, vol. 56, no. 2, March–April 1996: 127–38.

9 Anne E. Polivka and Thomas Nardone, "On the Definition of 'Contingent Work,'" *Monthly Labor Review*, vol. 112, 1989. Freedman first described "contingent employment arrangements" at a 1985 conference on employment security. See also Andrew Ross, *Nice Work If You Can Get It: Life and Labor in Precarious Times*, New York: NYU Press, 2009.

10 James N. Baron, Frank R. Dobbin, and P. Devereaux Jennings, "War and Peace: The Evolution of Modern Personnel Administration in U.S. Industry," *American Journal of Sociology*, vol. 92, issue 2, September 1986: 350–83. Pamela S. Tolbert and Lynne G. Zucker, "Institutional Sources of Change in the Formal Structure of Organizations: The Diffusion of Civil Service Reform, 1880–1935," *Administrative Science Quarterly* 28, 1983: 22–39.

3 LEARNING FROM APPRENTICESHIPS

1 For more details and stories on modern apprenticeships in the U.S., see the Registered Apprenticeship website (21stcenturyapprenticeship .workforce3one.org). Bob Lerman, Lauren Eyster, and Kate Chambers, *The Benefits and Challenges of Registered Apprenticeship: The Sponsors' Perspective*, The Urban Institute Center on Labor, Human Services, and Population, March 2009, makes a case for the program's usefulness to employers.

2 The Washington State info comes from "Washington State Workforce Board 2008 Evaluation of Apprenticeship," available at 21stcentury apprenticeship.workforce3one.org/view/2000911459872740346/info.

3 See Ilana Krausman Ben-Amos, "Failure to Become Freemen: Urban Apprentices in Early Modern England," *Social History*, vol. 16, no. 2, May 1991: 155–72; Margaret Pelling, "Apprenticeship, Health, and Social Cohesion in Early Modern London," History Workshop Journal Issue 37, 1994; and Gillian Hamilton, "The Decline of Apprenticeship in North America: Evidence from Montreal," *The Journal of Economic History*, vol. 60, no. 3, September 2000.

4 Robert Darnton, *The Great Cat Massacre*, New York: Vintage Books, 1985.

5 Media Monkey, "Grazia Staffers in a Froth," *Guardian*, December 21, 2009.

6 Benjamin Franklin, *The Autobiography of Benjamin Franklin*, New York: Dover Publications, 1996.

7 See W. J. Rorabaugh, *The Craft Apprentice: From Franklin to the Machine Age in America*, New York: Oxford University Press, 1988.

8 See Daniel Jacoby, "The Transformation of Industrial Apprenticeship in the United States," *The Journal of Economic History*, vol. 51, no. 4, December 1991: 887–910, and Bernard Elbaum, "Why Apprenticeship Persisted in Britain but Not in the United States," *The Journal of Economic History*, vol. 49, no. 2, June 1989: 337–49.

9 Joan Lane, *Apprenticeship in England 1600–1914*, London: UCL Press, 1996, p. 19.

4 A LAWSUIT WAITING TO HAPPEN

1 For the attempt to replace regular staff with interns at *The Point Reyes Light*, the newspaper in question, see Josh Chin's blog post "Point Reyes Light: Appalling Hubris of a Young Editor (OR Take this Internship and Shove It Right Up Your Ass)," chinfamous.com.

2 David C. Yamada, "The Employment Rights of Student Interns," 35 Conn. L. Rev. 215, 217, 2002 is the most comprehensive treatment of the legal issues bearing on internships.

3 Elena de Lisser, "Firm in Atlanta Settles Dispute over Interns," *Wall Street Journal*, March 1, 1995.

4 Avakian's comments were made on the Oregon Public Broadcasting show *Think Out Loud*, which ran a segment called "Internships 101" on April 26, 2010.

5 Chevalier's estimate is reported in Jethro Mullen, "Interns in French Firms Stage Protest," *New York Times*, November 24, 2005.

6 The national survey on wage theft and pervasive FLSA violations is by the National Employment Law Project, *Just Pay: Improving Wage and Hour Enforcement at the United States Department of Labor*, New York: NELP, 2010.

7 Michael Walsh's blog is at californiawagelaw.com.

8 Wiley's corporate communications director notes that the company pays those students who are not receiving academic credit, adding that a "key benefit (for interns and the company) is that internships frequently lead to full-time permanent jobs."

9 See Cynthia Grant Bowman and MaryBeth Lipp, "Legal Limbo of the Student Intern: The Responsibility of Colleges and Universities to Protect Student Interns Against Sexual Harassment," *Harvard Women's Law Journal*, vol. 23, 2000. The economics professors at Bates is quoted in Sara Lipka, "Would You Like Credit with that Internship?", *Chronicle of Higher Education*, May 9, 2010.

10 Craig J. Ortner, "Adapting Title VII to Modern Employment Realities: The Case for the Unpaid Intern," *Fordham Law Review*, vol. 66, 1998.

11 James LaRocca, "*Lowery v. Klemm*: A Failed Attempt at Providing Unpaid Interns and Volunteers with Adequate Employment Protections," *Public Interest Law Journal*, Vol. 16, 2006.

5 CHEERLEADERS ON CAMPUS

1 Lipka, "Would You Like Credit with that Internship?"

2 Donald T. O'Connor, "The Price of Free Labor: Companies Using Interns as Unpaid Employees May Run Afoul of Wage Laws," *ABA Journal*, January 1997.

3 David Gregory, "The Problematic Employment Dynamics of Student Internships," *Notre Dame Journal of Law, Ethics and Public Policy*, vol. 12, 1998: 227–64.

4 See Tom Peter, "Unpaid Interns Struggle to Make Ends Meet," *The Christian Science Monitor*, March 5, 2007. The survey of 713 colleges was conducted by the National Association of Colleges and Employers (NACE) in May 2010.

5 Lipka, "Would You Like Credit With That Internship?"

6 Lindsey Gerdes, "Goldman Picks Former Interns for Jobs as Hiring Drops," Bloomberg.com, December 11, 2009.

7 G. Jeffrey MacDonald, "International Internships Propel Students," *USA Today*, April 26, 2007. Jonelle Marte, "Creating Internships Out of Thin Air," *Wall Street Journal*, May 18, 2010.

8 Paul Hager, "Conceptions of Learning and Understanding Learning at Work," *Studies in Continuing Education*, vol. 26 (1), 1994.

9 Luc Boltanski and Eve Chiapello, *The New Spirit of Capitalism*, London: Verso, 2005.

10 Figures drawn from Bill Ferris, "Cooperative Education: Neglected Winner," *Journal of Higher Education*, vol. 40, no. 6, June 1969, pp. 480–3, and Ann Carlson, "Co-op Planet: Organizations at NU Plant Co-op's Seeds Far and Wide," *Northeastern University Magazine* 24 (5), May 1999. See also Richard Walter, "The Rebirth of Cooperative Education," *Journal of Industrial Teacher Education*, vol. 32, no. 1, Fall 1994.

6 NO FEE FOR SERVICE

1 Politico Staff, "D.C. Interns by the Numbers," July 14, 2009, politico.com.

2 Andrew Morton, *Monica's Story*, New York: St. Martin's Press, 1999, p. 70.

3 The memoir by JFK's former intern Mimi Beardsley Alford is reportedly being published by Random House. Sullivan's comment can be found in Andrew Sullivan, "Sex and this City: Even Without the Harsh Glare of Scandal, Washington's Sexual Dynamic Has Always Had a Uniquely Predatory Cast," *New York Times Magazine*, July 22, 2001.

4 For a discussion of interns in the British Parliament, see Rowenna Davis, "House of Poshos," *New Statesman*, February 18, 2010.

5 Joe Davidson, "Obama to Shut Down Federal Career Intern Program," *Washington Post*, December 26, 2010.

6 Sharlet discussed the intern's situation on "The Rachel Maddow Show" in April 2010. See "C Street House Used Interns as Servants, Author Tells Rachel Maddow," huffingtonpost.com.

7 Rob Reich, Lacey Dorn, and Stefanie Sutton, *Anything Goes: Approval of Nonprofit Status by the IRS*, Stanford University Center on Philanthropy and Civil Society, 2009.

8 Karen Gieselman and Wendy Smith, "Do Your Internships Comply with Wage-Hour Law?", *Education Labor Letter*, Fisher and Phillips' Education Practice Group, November–December 2007.

7 THE ECONOMICS OF INTERNSHIPS

1 Anya Kamenetz, "Take This Internship and Shove It," *New York Times*, May 30, 2006.

2 Chris Anderson, *Free: The Future of a Radical Price*, New York: Hyperion, 2009.

3 Gary S. Becker, *Human Capital: A Theoretical and Empirical Analysis, with Special Reference to Education*, Chicago: University of Chicago Press, 1964.

4 Controversy rages on about the size of the "college bonus": for a recent, skeptical overview, see Mary Pilon, "What's a Degree Really Worth?", *Wall Street Journal*, February 2, 2010.

5 Michael Spence's famous paper on this subject is "Job Market Signaling," *Quarterly Journal of Economics*, vol. 87, no. 3, 1973: 355–74.

6 See Derek Neal, "The Complexity of Job Mobility among Young Men," *Journal of Labor Economics*, vol. 17, issue 2, April 1999: 237–61. For more detail on "delayed adulthood," see the website of the Network on Transitions to Adulthood, based at the University of Pennsylvania: transad.pop.upenn.edu/. See also Tony Doukopil, "Why I Am Leaving Guyland," *Newsweek*, September 8, 2008 and Don Peck "How a New Jobless Era Will Transform America," *Atlantic Monthly*, March 2010.

7 Bibi S. Watson, "The Intern Turnaround," *Management Review*, 9–12, June 1995.

8 Dustin Walsh, "Internships on Front Lines in Fight to Keep College Grads in Michigan," *Crain's Detroit*, June 6, 2010.

9 The 21 percent drop in mostly paid internships was registered by NACE in March 2009. See their press release, "Internship Hiring Falls 21 Percent," naceweb.org.

10 The global surge in higher education has been documented by the U.S. Department of Education, the Census Bureau, and UNESCO. See: chronicle.com/article/Chart-More-College-Students/48516/.

11 David Card's major contributions to the minimum wage literature include "Do Minimum Wages Reduce Employment? A Case Study of California, 1987–89," *Industrial and Labor Relations Review* 46, October 1992; "Using Regional Variation in Wages to Measure the Effects of the Federal Minimum Wage," *Industrial and Labor Relations Review* 46, October 1992; and "Minimum Wages and the Teenage Labor Market: A Case Study of California, 1987–89," *Annual Proceedings of the Industrial Relations Research Association*, December 1990. In addition, there are "A Re-analysis of the Effect of the New Jersey Minimum Wage with Representative Payroll Data," *American Economic Review* 90, December 2000; "Time-Series Minimum Wage Studies: A Meta-Analysis," *American Economic Review* 85, May 1995; "Minimum Wages and Employment: A Case Study of the Fast Food Industry in New Jersey and Pennsylvania," *American Economic Review* 84, September 1994—all three written with Alan Krueger. See also Barbara Kiviat, "Why Do People Care So Much about the Minimum Wage?", *Reuter's*, 20 October 2010. The estimate from EPI is in Laura Fitzpatrick, "A Brief History of the Minimum Wage," *Time*, July 24, 2009.

12 Madeline Zavodny, "Why Minimum Wage Hikes May Not Reduce Employment," *Federal Reserve Bank of Atlanta Economic Review*, Second Quarter 1998, pp. 18–28. The popularity of the minimum wage is discussed in Adam Cohen, "Could the Courts Outlaw the Minimum Wage?," *Time*, October 20, 2010.

8 FUTURES MARKET

1 The comments by Menlo Provost James Kelly are in Sara Lipka, "Dream Internships and Dubious Academic Credit for Sale: $9,500," July 18, 2008.

2 Don Peck, "How a New Jobless Era Will Transform America," *Atlantic Monthly*, March 2010.

3 The $42,500 *Vogue* internship was widely reported. For a broader look at intern auctions in the U.S., see Sue Shellenbarger, "Do You Want an Internship? It'll Cost You," *Wall Street Journal*, January 28, 2009; for the U.K., see Harriet Meyer and Graham Snowdon, "What Price Work Experience," *Guardian*, December 5, 2009.

4 The CEO of CharitzBuzz.com is quoted in Beth Harpaz, "Thank You, Mom and Dad, for Landing My Internship," *The Ledger*, May 10, 2010.

9 WHAT ABOUT EVERYBODY ELSE?

1 These anecdotes are drawn from a reader comment in Greenhouse, "The Unpaid Intern, Legal or Not"; Amita Parekh, "Invaluable experience has a price tag," *Daily Trojan*, February 25, 2010; a reader comment to Oregon Public Broadcasting's "Internships 101" segment; Liz Seasholtz, "Unpaid Internships: No Pay, No Gain," Wetfeet.com, wetfeet.com/undergrad/internships/articles/unpaid-internships.aspx; and Julie Halpert, "Can You Afford to Be a Summer Intern?", *Newsweek*, April 5, 2010.

2 Ben Yagoda, "Will Work for Academic Credit," *Chronicle of Higher Education,* March 21, 2008.

3 The full title of the Milburn Report is *Unleashing Aspiration: The Final Report of the Panel on Fair Access to the Professions*, released in July 2009 and available at cabinetoffice.gov.uk/accessprofessions.

4 Daniel Brook, *The Trap: Selling Out to Stay Afloat in Winner-Take-All America*, New York: Henry Holt, 2007.

5 David Graeber, "Army of Altruists: On the Alienated Right to Do Good," *Harper's Magazine*, January 2007.

6 Laura Vanderkam, "With Interns, You Get What You Pay For," *USA Today*, April 19, 2004.

7 To get more sense of the "Nachtwey Intern Ad Kerfuffle," as one photographer blog called it, see the discussion at Jamie's List: jamieslist.wordpress.com/2009/12/15/the-james-natchwey-internship-follow-up-harrington-smith/.

8 For more on Spielberg and Lucas's internships, see Jim Windolf, "Keys to the Kingdom," *Vanity Fair*, February 2008. For Matt Singer's horror stories, see Matt Singer, "Mr. Coffee," *Village Voice*, January 3, 2006.

9 David Robb, "Commentary: Prod'n Assistants Need Pay," *Hollywood Reporter*, April 7, 2010.

10 Jennifer 8. Lee, "Crucial Unpaid Internships Increasingly Separate Haves from the Have-Nots," *The New York Times*, August 10, 2004.

11 Adelle Waldman, "Intern or Die," *New Republic*, June 25, 2008, tnr.com/article/politics/intern-or-die.

12 David W. Chen and Michael Barbaro, "To Get an Internship at City Hall, It's Not Always What You Know," *New York Times*, July 19, 2010.

10 THE GLOBAL INTERN

1 Jethro Mullen, "Interns in French Firms Stage Protest," *New York Times*, November 24, 2005. Tommie Ullman, "135,000 unemployed Swedes will be offered internships," *Stockholm News*, February 26, 2010. "Youth Ministry to Launch Internship Programme," *Nation* (Pakistan), April 8, 2009. Ha Jung-yun, "The Internship Illusion," *The Yonsei Annals*, August 9, 2010. Caroline Milburn, "Push for Intern Scheme," *The Age* (Australia) April 26, 2010. Luke Harding, "A Merry Band," *Guardian*, May 17, 2006. For more on the Infosys program, visit the official InStep site: infosys.com/InStepWeb/default.asp.

2 "The Intern Trap—Graduate Job Seekers Cheated and Exploited by Employers," China Labour Bulletin, January 26, 2010, china-labour.org.hk/en/node/100662.

3 Andrew Ross, *Nice Work If You Can Get It: Life and Labor in Precarious Times*, New York: NYU Press, 2009.

4 On Foxconn's internship, see Hu Yinan, "Students 'Forced' to Work at Foxconn," *China Daily*, June 26, 2010, as well as Liu Linlin, "Foxconn 'Abuses, Kidnaps' Interns: Universities' report," *Epoch Times*, October 9, 2010, and Kathleen McLaughlin, "Silicon Sweatshops: Foxconn Refutes Accusations," *Global Post*, October 12, 2010.

5 See Marcello Tari and Ilaria Vanni, "On the Life and Deeds of San Precario, Patron Saint of Precarious Workers and Lives," *Fibreculture*, vol. 5, December 1, 2005. More on the Chainworkers at chainworkers .org/faq.

6 The documentary is Charlotte Buchen and Singeli Agnew, "France: The Precarious Generation," FRONTLINE/World, April 19, 2007; see pbs.org/frontlineworld/rough/2007/04/france_the_prec.html.

7 See Anonymous, "Labor Minister Scholz Wants to Help a Bit" [in German], *Der Spiegel*, March 18, 2008, spiegel.de/unispiegel/ jobundberuf/0,1518,542233,00.html.

8 Merijn Oudenampsen and Gavin Sullivan, "Precarity and N/European Identity: An Interview with Alex Foti," *Metamute*, October 5, 2004, metamute.org/en/Precarity-european-Identity-Alex-Foti-Chain Workers. See also Stevphen Shukaitis, "Whose Precarity Is It Anyway?," December 29, 2006, precariousunderstanding.blogsome.com/2006/ 12/29/whose-precarity-is-it-anyway/#more-43, August 8, 2010.

11 NOTHING TO LOSE BUT YOUR CUBICLES

1 See David Brooks, "The Organization Kid," *Atlantic*, April 2001.

2 See Athena Merritt, "Phila. City Council OKs Tax Credit for Internships," *Philadelphia Business Journal*, June 17, 2010. The legislation, which could come into effect as early as 2012, would allow businesses that hire interns and pay them at least $8 an hour to claim tax credits of up to 40 percent of the compensation paid.

3 See Thomas Fisher, "The Intern Trap: How the Profession Exploits Its Young," *Progressive Architecture*, 1994, p. 69–73.

4 Rebecca Delaney, "About Those Unpaid Internships," *American Prospect*, July 16, 2010.

5 Kathryn Anne Edwards and Alex Hertel-Fernandez, "Paving the Way Through Paid Internships: A Proposal to Expand Educational and Economic Opportunities for Low-Income College Students," *Demos and Economic Policy Institute*, March 23, 2010.

6 The "Unfair Internships" blog is at unfairinternships.wordpress.com.

The Intern Bill of Rights

Given that the word "intern" has no strict definition and covers a broad range of actual roles,

Given that most interns are workers, performing work of operational and economic importance,

Given that the laws and regulations pertaining to internships are often unclear, vary by jurisdiction, and rarely reference interns specifically,

Given that internships are of increasing, global importance and have broad social implications,

Given that some internships are legal, just, and beneficial, while others are illegal, unethical, and even exploitative,

Given that it is inequitable to require people to work for free to enter the workforce,

We proclaim this INTERN BILL OF RIGHTS as a common standard by which to evaluate and improve internships for the benefit of interns, employers, and society as a whole:

Article 1: All interns deserve fair compensation for their work, usually in the form of wages and sometimes in the form of dedicated training.

Article 2: Interns are entitled to the same legal protections as all other workers, and should not be subject to discrimination, harassment, or arbitrary dismissal. Under these circumstances, interns should have the same standing in court and the same recourse to the law as all other workers.

Article 3: Interns should enjoy the same basic workplace benefits guaranteed to all other workers, including sick days, vacation time, worker's compensation, and extra pay for overtime.

Article 4: The hiring of interns should be as transparent and nondiscriminatory as the hiring of full-time employees.

Article 5: No one should be forced to take an unpaid internship or required to pay in order to work.

Article 6: Any internships subsidized with public funds should meet exemplary legal and ethical standards.

Article 7: Internships are a category of work that should be defined, recognized by policy makers and officials, studied, monitored, and improved.

Article 8: Interns must be treated with dignity and respect by co-workers and supervisors.

Article 9: The word "intern" should be applied ethically and transparently to opportunities that involve substantial training, mentoring, and getting to know a line of work.

APPENDIX B

Internships and the Law

M any legal issues relating to internships remain unclear, partly because the word "intern" itself is rarely used in the relevant laws and regulations and partly because court precedents are few. In general, doing substantive work without pay for any meaningful length of time is illegal in most countries; on the other hand, many countries also have exemptions for legitimate student trainees. What's offered below is not formal legal advice, but simply a very general guide.

UNITED STATES

The single best source of information for American internships and the law is David C. Yamada, "The Employment Rights of Student Interns," 35 Conn. L. Rev. 215, 217, published in 2002.

The basic law pertaining to the status of interns is the Fair Labor Standards Act (see Chapter 4), under which most interns are entitled to minimum wage and "time-and-a-half" for overtime. The law is enforced by the Wage and Hour Division (WHD) of the Department of Labor and applies to all but the very smallest firms. Based on the 1947 Supreme Court decision in *Walling v. Portland Terminal Co.*, WHD only considers an unpaid internship legal if it meets all of the following criteria:

1. The training, even though it includes actual operation of the facilities of the employer, is similar to that which would be given in a vocational school;
2. The training is for the benefit of the trainee;
3. The trainees do not displace regular employees, but work under close observation;
4. The employer that provides the training derives no immediate advantage from the activities of the trainees and on occasion the employer's operations may actually be impeded;
5. The trainees are not necessarily entitled to a job at the completion of the training period; and
6. The employer and the trainee understand that the trainees are not entitled to wages for the time spent in training.

The latest word on how these criteria are interpreted for internships can be found in "Fact Sheet #71: Internship Programs Under the Fair Labor Standards Act," issued by WHD in April 2010.

Also:

- Just because you agreed to an unpaid or underpaid internship does *not* mean you signed away your right to fair pay.
- Just because you received academic credit and the approval of your school does not mean you lost the right to be paid.
- Interns have won cases against their employers on numerous occasions and received "double damages" (double the amount of backpay owed) as well as the reimbursement of legal fees.
- Unless you are a paid intern, you may not have the right to challenge discrimination, harassment and other abuses in the workplace (see the discussion of *O'Connor v. Davis* in Chapter 4).
- Several states have laws that make it even harder for organizations not to pay.
- Nonprofit internships seem to be a gray area.

If you believe that you are taking part, or have recently taken part, in an illegal internship, the first step is to talk to interns past and present who have worked in the same office and see if a group of you share the same complaints. Whether or not you form a group, contact the department of labor in your home state (it will probably have a website) and make a minimum wage complaint. You can also go straight to the federal level by contacting WHD in Washington online or by phone. Talking to your employer directly is another solution. If none of these works, contact an employment lawyer in your area—an easy way to find one is to visit nela.org, the website of the National Employment Lawyers Assocation (NELA).

CANADA

Unlike in the U.S., there is no relevant federal legislation like the FLSA—interns must look to the relevant legislation about employment standards for the province where they're working. For instance, according to Sara Parchello, a lawyer in the Labour, Employment, and Human Rights Group at Canadian firm Fasken Martineau, the province of Ontario defines an intern as an employee "if he or she is being trained in a skill used by the company's other employees, unless the intern:

- is receiving training similar to training given in a vocational school;
- benefits from the training and the employer doesn't;
- doesn't replace other "employees"; and
- doesn't automatically become an "employee" when the training has finished."

As in the U.S., interns deemed to be employees are fully entitled to pay and other workplace rights. Contact the relevant provincial ministry of labor to file a claim about an illegal situation (sometimes it can even be done online), and look to employment lawyers if need be.

UNITED KINGDOM

With more and more illegal opportunities recently on offer, awareness about internship practices (or "work experience," as it's sometimes called) is growing. Although the legal situation is still somewhat unclear, and knowledge of the law is not widespread, a government employment tribunal in Reading recently ordered London Dreams Motion Pictures to pay more than £2,000 to a former unpaid intern who sued with the help of BECTU, the union for British workers in the film, TV and other audio-visual industries. According to the *Financial Times*, the U.K. government has provided guidance that interns "should be paid if they have a list of duties and work set hours," as per the National Minimum Wage of 1998.

If you want to report an illegal situation and get justice, one option is to contact the Pay and Work Rights Helpline or the National Minimum Wage Helpline associated with HM Revenue and Customs: both provide confidential help. You should also consider contacting the Low Pay Commission and reporting your experience on some of the relevant websites that have recently sprung up in the U.K., including Intern Aware, Interns Anonymous, and Rights for Interns.

Acknowledgments

Above all, a deep and serious gratitude to all those who have trusted me with their stories, opinions, leads, and expertise. This book was conceived in London in conversation with fellow interns; became a serious endeavor over meals with Nicholas Casey in Pasadena and Jack Chung in San Francisco; and matured during a crucial meeting with Jin Auh in New York. I researched the book in a dozen different cities and wrote it primarily in Brooklyn and Kunming, China, especially in the tolerant coffee houses of Wenlin Jie and Wenhua Xiang. Particular thanks are due to Steve Greenhouse, Mark Granovetter, Brad Trushin, Tom Wolf, Aleksey Dubilet, Anya Kamenetz, Greg Kaplan, Ben Knelman, Rob Wilkins, Ned Farmer, Rich Bottner, Nathaniel Rich, and Dave Glauber. Andy Hsiao, Audrea Lim, and their colleagues at Verso made it happen. Clara Heyworth was a star and a dynamo behind this book: it's still unthinkable that she's gone. Karan Mahajan has been a tireless champion, an intoxicating co-conspirator, and a virtuoso editor. And in this, as in all things, JFA has journeyed with me from first to last.

Index

A. Brown-Olmstead Associates, 68
ABC, 175
academic credit
  covering costs of, 175
  Disney, 6–10
  legal issues of, 61–62
  Menlo College, 148
  statistics on, 188
  student interns, 84–88
  University of Dreams, 146
  using to justify unpaid labor,
      156–157, 217
  value of, 209
  Washington Center, 110
academic majors, 27, 35–36
Accreditation Council for Graduate
      Medical Education, 31
Administrative Management Division
      of the Bureau of the Budget, 33
adolescence, 53
Agriculture, Department of, 176
AIA (American Institute of Architects),
      212–214
AIAS (American Institute of
      Architecture Students), 213–215
AIESEC, 189, 190
Alford, Mimi Beardsley, 232n3
Alpert, Eugene, 34, 105
AMA (American Medical Association),
      30
American Cancer Society, 120
American Council on Education, 10

American Federation of Government
      Employees, 108
American Institute of Architects (AIA),
      212–214
American Institute of Architecture
      Students (AIAS), 213–215
American Medical Association (AMA),
      30
American Prospect (magazine), 216
American Red Cross, 149
American Revolution, 51–52
American Society of News Editors
      (ASNE), 179
American University, 111, 157
AmeriCorps, 116–118
Amherst College, 90
Anderson, Chris, 125
Anderson, Wes, *xiii*
apprenticeships
  American, 51–54
  compared with internships, 25, 58–59
  English, 47–51
  history of, 46–54
  overview, 43–46
  registering, 54–56
  revival of, 56–57
  statistics on, 44–45
  Western Europe, 187
ApprentiCorps, 152
architecture internships, 208, 212–215
Ariely, Dan, 126
Asia Society, 113–114

ASNE (American Society of News Editors), 179
Association for International Practical Training, 188
Atlantic Media company, 211
Aufstand der Praktikanten (Uprising of the Interns), 200
Autobiography (Franklin), 51
Avakian, Bob, 69
Ayefour Corporation, 5

Backstage (*newspaper*), 151
Baldwin, Michael, 43
BankAtlantic, 139
Bates College, 88
Becker, Gary, 56, 127, 128, 130
BECTU (Broadcasting, Entertainment, Cinematograph and Theatre Union), 244
Ben-Amos, Ilana Krausman, 48
Bennett, Matthew, 103, 104
BETI (Businesses for the Ethical Treatment of Interns), 152
Bill of Rights (U.S.), 64
Black, Hugo, 64–65
Blackstone Group, 180
Bloomberg, Michael, 180
BLS (Bureau of Labor Statistics), 29, 36, 133
Boltanski, Luc, *vi*, 37, 95
Boston City Hospital, 30
Boston University, 111
Bottner, Richard, 153
Bousquet, Marc, 134
Bouvier, Jackie, 35
Bowman, Cynthia Grant, 78, 80, 82
Boy Scouts, 54
Bradley, Stewart, *xii*
Broadcasting, Entertainment, Cinematograph and Theatre Union (BECTU), 244
Brook, Daniel, 164
Brown Internship Award Program, 90
Brownley, John, 5
Bullock, John, 57
Bureau of Labor Statistics (BLS), 29, 36, 133
Bureau of the Budget, 33
Businesses for the Ethical Treatment of Interns (BETI), 152

California, University of, 111
californiawagelaw.com (blog), 231n7
campus representatives, 8
Canada, legal issues, 243
Card, David, 142, 143, 234n11
career centers (college)
    cost of, 147–148
    origins of, 157–158
    overview, 87
    rise in, 193
career coaches, 153–155
career development centers. *See* career centers (college)
career services, 24, 87, 118. *See also* career centers (college)
Careerealism (blog), 153
Carnegie, Andrew, 53
Caro, Robert, 180
Carpenters Training Committee, 57
Carr, Frank C., 182
Carson, Kit, 52
Cartoon Brew, 69
Cartoon Network, 68–69
CBS, 180
celebrity interns, *xii*. *See also* glamor industries
Census Bureau, 29, 226n4
Center for Integrative Body Therapies, 81
Central Michigan University, 8
Chainworkers, 197
Chambers, Ed, 10, 12, 13
CharityBuzz.com, 155–156
Charles, John, 157
Chartered Institute of Personnel and Development, 228n2
Chastain, Je'Nen, 213–215
Cheh, Mary, 81–82
Cheselden, William, 58
Chevalier, Jean-Marie, 71
Chiapello, Eve, *vi*, 37, 95
Chicago School, 127
Children's Nature: The Rise of the American Summer Camp (Paris), 54
China, internships in, 191–196
China Labour Bulletin, 194, 195
China Student Internship Program, 192
Cincinnati, University of, 96
Civil Rights Division, 112
Civil Service Commission, 33

Claremont McKenna, 111
clerkships, 168
Clinton, Bill, 105, 109
Clinton, Eric, 11–13, 15, 16
Clinton, Jennifer, 109–110
Cockerell, Lee, 10
Code of Federal Regulations, 15
Code of Hammurabi, 46
College Confidential, 20
College Employment Research Institute, 26, 226n4
CollegeGrad.com, 27
College Program, 6
CollegeRecruiter.com, 139
Columbia University, 74
Come Recommended, 153
Commission on Medical Education, 30–31
Committee of Interns and Residents, 31
Committee on Civil Rights, 33
Compass East Corporation, 5
competition for internships, 91–93
Congressional Accountability Act (1995), 105
Congressional Reorganization Act (1974), 34
Conley, Dalton, 216
Connecticut College, 90, 92
Conrad, Lauren, xii
Contat, Nicolas, 50
contingent labor
    organization of, 198
    origin of, 36
    rise in, 26, 38–39, 207, 222
cooperative education
    movement, 95–98
    overview, 6–7
    rise of, 56
Cooperative Education and Internship Association, 7
Cornell University, 111
Council on Foreign Relations, 114
Council on Medical Education, 30
CPE (First Employment Contract), 199
Craigslist, 174
"Current Population Survey" (Census Bureau), 226n4
Curtis, Howard, 137, 138

Darnton, Robert, 49–50
Dartmouth College, 111

Davis, Don, 57
D.C. Human Rights Act (DCHRA), 81
Dean Witter, 176
The Debate Over Unpaid College Internships (Intern Bridge), 26–27, 28, 228n2
Defense, Department of, 109
degree programs. *See* education
Delaware, University of, 161
Deloitte & Touche, 28, 137
Denmark, internships in, 201
Department of Agriculture, 176
Department of Defense, 109
Department of Interior, 109
Department of Labor
    on academic credit, 217
    definition of internship, *xvii*
    empowerment of, 55
    enforcement of law by, 219
Department of Mental Hygiene (California), 33
Department of the Treasury, 106, 109
Department of Transportation, 12, 109
Dewey, John, 94
Dickens, Charles, 53
Dickson, Duncan, 5, 6, 7, 9, 14
Director's Internships (Harvard), 90
discrimination, 80–81
Disney. *See* Walt Disney Corporation
Disney, Walt, 4
Disney Career Start Program, 4
Disney College Program, 8
Disney Dreamers Academy, 4
Disney Institute, 4
Disney Learning Centers, 10
Disney Look, 20–21
Disney University, 3
Disneyspeak, 21
Division of Labor Standards Enforcement, 67
Dream Careers, Inc. *See* University of Dreams
Dreams, University of, 145–150, 188, 189, 190, 217
Drexel University, 96
Duggal Color Projects, Lipphold v., 80

Economic and Social Council, 199
economic inequalities, 163
Economic Policy Institute (EPI), 143, 211, 220

economics of internships
  human capital theory, 127–136
  investment view, 136–140
  overview, 123–127
  supply and demand, 140–144
education. *See also* academic credit;
    specific types
  academic majors, 27, 35–36
  Federal Work-Study Program,
      183–184, 220
  inflation of supply of interns, 217
  potential changes in, 215–221
Edwards, Kathryn, 220
Eisenberg, Ross, 211
Eisenman, Peter, 214
Eisner, Michael, 13
Elbaum, Bernard, 48–49, 52–53
Elizabethan Statute of Artificers (1563), 48
"The Employment Rights of Student
    Interns" (Yamada), 241
Energy Corps, 117
Ensign, John, 113
Enterprise, 28
EPA (Environmental Protection
    Agency), 109
EPCOT (Experimental Prototype
    Community of Tomorrow), 5, 22
EPI (Economic Policy Institute), 143,
    211, 220
EuroMayDay, 197
experiential education, 7, 22, 25–26,
    93–95
Experimental Prototype Community of
    Tomorrow (EPCOT), 5, 22
externs, 26
ExxonMobil, 138, 207

"Fact Sheet #71: Internship Programs
    Under the Fair Labor Standards
    Act" (WHD), 242
Fair Labor Standards Act. *See* FLSA (Fair
    Labor Standards Act)
Fasken Martineau, 243
Fast Company (Kamenetz), 177
Fast Track Internships, 154
Faulkner, William, 221
FCIP (Federal Career Intern Program),
    108–109
Federal Poverty Line, 220
Federal Work-Study Program, 183–184,
    220

Feldman, Michael, 86
First Employment Contract (CPE), 199
Fisher, Thomas, 212–213
Fitzgerald, Kevin, 212, 214
Fitzgerald Act (1937), 54–57, 221
flexicurity, 201–202
Florida Project, 4–5
FLSA (Fair Labor Standards Act)
  application of, 74
  exemption from, 219, 220
  non-enforcement of, 207
  protection of interns under, 62
  Roosevelt on, 64–65
  student interns under, 83
  violations of, 72–74
Footlik, Jay, 103
Ford, Henry, 142
Ford Coppola, Francis, 171
Foti, Alex, 197, 198, 200
Foxconn, 195–196
France, internships in, 198–199
Franklin, Benjamin, 51, 52
Franzen, Willy, 70, 74, 92, 149
Free Agent Nation, 37
Free: The Future of a Radical Prize
    (Anderson), 125
Freedman, Audrey, 36
freelancers, 24, 26, 198, 222
Freelancers Union, 223
Fulbright, J. William, 105

GAO (Government Accountability
    Office), 37, 72
Gap, 136
Gardner, Phil
  on academic credit, 85
  on cooperative movement, 97–98
  on Federal Work-Study Program, 220
  Intern Bridge and, 175
  on internships, *xiv*, 90–91
  statistics, 226n4
  on understanding of student interns,
      89
  on use of labor terns, 26
Gates, A. I., 32
Gates, Bill, 138
Gawker (website), 156
General Electric, 124, 174–175
Generation Debt, 126–127
Generation Debt (Kamenetz), 132
Generation Free, 125

Generation Précaire, 198
George Washington University, 35, 81, 94
Germany, internships in, 199–200
Gieselman, Karen, 118–119
gift economies, 124
glamor industries, 92, 137, 151, 168–169, 179–180
Global Experiences, 188
Global Intern, 188
global interns, rise and rebellion of, 185–202
Global Placement, 188
Goff, Bruce, 212
Goldman Sachs, 91–92, 180
Google, 181
Gothic Europe, 46
Government Accountability Office (GAO), 37, 72
Graeber, David, 164–165
Granovetter, Mark, 29, 39–40, 132
Grazia (magazine), 50–51
Great Depression, 64
Great Expectations (Dickens), 53
Great Recession, 138
The Great Cat Massacre (Darnton), 49–50
Greenhouse, Steven, *xvii*, 68
Gregory, David, 86
Grossfeld, Jim, 39
Grunewald, Mark, 37
Gurtman, Stephanie, 92

H2B "seasonal work" visas, 7, 15
Hager, Paul, 94
Hall, G. Stanley, 53
Hamburg, Rebecca, 81, 118
Hamilton, Gillian, 51, 52
Hard Hatted Women (Martin), 44
Harper's (magazine), 177
Harvard University, 90, 111
HCIA (Hong Kong China Internship Association), 194
Health and Human Services Department, 112
Hertel, Alex, 220
hierarchy of political internships, 99–100
higher education. *See* education
Hispanic Association of Colleges and Universities, 182–183
Hispanic Heritage Foundation, 183

HM Revenue and Customs, 244
home office internships, 209
Hong Kong China Internship Association (HCIA), 194
House Foreign Affairs Committee, 106–107
housing (Disney), 15–17
How the University Works (Bousquet), 134
Hoyer, Steny, 99
Huffington Post, 156
Hughes, James, 88
Huhman, Heather, 153
human capital theory, 127–136
human resources, 28, 39–41, 89, 127

IBM, 181
ICE (Immigration & Customs Enforcement), 15
ICPs (International College Program interns), 7
IDP (Intern Development Program), 213
illegal internships
    growth of, 62–63
    media attention on, 166–167
    unfairness of, 85
    variations on, 70–71
ILO (International Labor Organization), 133
Immigration & Customs Enforcement (ICE), 15
independent contractors, 38, 71
industry
    domination, 167–171
    reforms, 212
industry of internships
    career coaches, 153–155
    growth of, 156–158
    Intern Guru, 152
    Intern Lady, 152–153
    Intern Queen, 151–152
    internship auctions, 155–156
    University of Dreams, 145–150
INROADS, 181–182, 207
insourcing, 11
Institute on Business and Government Affairs, 111
Interior, Department of, 109
Intern Anti-Discrimination Act (2009), 81
Intern Aware, 200, 244

Intern Bill of Rights, 220, 221, 239–240
Intern Bridge, 26–29, 61, 86, 108, 175, 228n2
Intern Development Program (IDP), 213
Intern Economy, 222
"Intern Edition" (NPR), 219
Intern Ethiks, 151
Intern Guru, 152
Intern Lady, 152–153
"Intern or Die" (Waldman), 179
Intern Queen Inc., 151–155
intern satisfaction, 29
International College Program interns (ICPs), 7
International Labor Organization (ILO), 133
International Meeting of the Precariat (Berlin), 198
Interns Anonymous, 200, 244
internship auctions, 155–156, 200
Internship Center, 228n1
internship explosion, 26, 36–41, 186
Internship Institute, 152
Internship Readiness Centers, 152
internship search engines, 154–155
internship tax code, 212
Internship-Net listserv, 228n1
Internships International, 188
Internships.com, 154
interns/internships. *See also* illegal internships; industry of internships; nonprofit organization interns; political interns; student interns
  access to, 165–166
  ambiguity of, 23
  architecture, 208, 212–215
  as barrier to entry, 163–165
  broad spectrum of, 26
  changing structure of, *xiv–xv*
  China, 191–196
  compared with apprenticeships, 58–59
  compared with regular jobs, 24–25
  conclusions, 206–212
  consensus, 221–223
  current day, *xi–xv*
  defined, *xvi*, 209
  Denmark, 201
  economics of, 123–144
  financial pressures of, 174–176

France, 198–199
Germany, 199–200
home office, 209
journalism, 131, 176–179
law and, 241–244
medical, 30–34, 82
Milan, 196–198
Municipal-level, 33
Netherlands, 201
Northern Europe, 201–202
origins of, *x–xi*
overview, 203–204
radio, 28, 179
requiring, 36–37, 218
research of, *xv–xviii*
role of, 163
serial, 113
shortfalls of, 205
state-level, 33
United Kingdom, 200
views on, 25
virtual, 209
Western Europe, 201
Intrax Internships Abroad, 188, 189, 190
Issa, Darrell, 105–106

J-1 Exchange Visitor Program, 7, 8, 15, 217
Jacoby, Dan, 45, 58, 95
Jamie's List, 169
Jamieson, Adrienne, 101, 111–112
Job Placement Centers, 152
Jobnob, 154
John Wiley & Sons, 77–78, 231n8
Johns Hopkins University, 31, 96
Johnson, Andrew, 52
Johnson, Melanie, 43
Johnson and Wales College, 5
Jones, Wesley, 2, 10, 17–19, 22
Journal of Cooperative Education, 98
Journal of Cooperative Education and Internships, 98
Journal of Higher Education, 97
Journal of Marketing, 32
journalism internships, 131, 176–179

Kahn, Lisa, 135
Kaiser Permanente, 181
Kamenetz, Anya, 88, 91, 119–120, 124–127, 132, 161, 177

Kaplan, Greg, 37, 128–129, 131, 135–136, 141
Kaufman, Herbert, 32–33
Kaye, Walter, 103
Kazanka, 189, 190
Kelley, Colleen, 108
Kelly, James, 148
Kennedy, Jackie, 35
Kennedy, John Fitzgerald, 105
Kerr, Clark, 90
King, Martin Luther, 182
Kirk, Claude, Jr., 4
Klemm, Lowery v., 80–81
Korematsu v. United States, 64
Krogh, Ryan, 140, 177
Krueger, Alan, 142
Ku Klux Klan, 11, 64
Kuenz, Jane, 21

Labor, Department of. *See* Department of Labor
Labour, Employment, and Human Rights Group, 243
Ladd, John, 44, 45–46, 54, 55
Lady Gaga, *xii*
Lakeland Regional Medical Center, 11
Landers Group, 70
Lane, Joan, 58
LaRocca, James, 80–81
Late Night With Conan O'Brien (TV show), 172
Latin-American Development and Management Corporation, 5
Latinos on the Fast Track (LOFT), 183
lawsuits
    Korematsu v. United States, 64
    Lipphold v. Duggal Color Projects, 80
    Lowery v. Klemm, 80–81
    Walling v. Portland Terminal Co., 65, 241
Le Corbusier, 212
legal issues
    Canada, 243
    examples, 68–71
    Fair Labor Standards Act, 64–67
    internships and, 241–244
    loopholes, 74–78
    overview, 61–64
    protection for interns, 223
    student interns, 78–82
    student internships, 86–87

United Kingdom, 243–244
United States, 241–243
Wage and Hour Division, 71–74
legislation
    Congressional Accountability Act (1995), 105
    Congressional Reorganization Act (1974), 34
    D.C. Human Rights Act, 81
    Fitzgerald Act (1937), 54–57, 221
    Intern Anti-Discrimination Act (2009), 81
    Legislative Reorganization Act (1946), 33
    Smith-Hughes Act (1917), 56
    Statute of Artificers (1563), 48
Legislative Reorganization Act (1946), 33
Letterman, David, 82
Levy, Chandra, 82
Lewinsky, Monica, 25, 82, 103
The Life Aquatic with Steve Zissou (film), *xiii*
Lim, Susan, 175
LinkedIn, 27
Lipp, MaryBeth, 78, 80, 82
Lipphold v. Duggal Color Projects, 80
Little Airplane, 68–69
Lochtefeld, Eric, 146–147, 148, 188
Lockheed Martin, 28
LOFT (Latinos on the Fast Track), 183
London Dreams Motion Pictures, 200, 244
Low Pay Commission, 244
Lowell, 111
Lowery v. Klemm, 80–81
The L Word (TV show), 151
Lucas, George, 171
Lundsteen, Natalie, 24–25, 35–36, 93, 136, 200

Mackes, Marilyn, 227n7
Mademoiselle (magazine), 35
Magic Kingdom. *See* Walt Disney Corporation
Magic Kingdom College Program, 6
Management Leadership for Tomorrow, 183
Martin, Molly, 44
Marymount College, 79
Masa Israel, 188

maximalism, 90
Mayo, William, 31
Mayo Clinic, 31
McCaslin, Teri, 137
medical interns, 30–34, 82
Members of Parliament (U.K.), 106
Menlo College, 148
Mental Hygiene, Department of
 (California), 33
Merrill Lynch, 69–70, 138, 149
Metropolitan Museum, 120
Michigan State University, *xiv*, 85
Microsoft, 38, 138
middle-aged interns, 226n5
Milan, internships in, 196–198
Milburn, Alan, 163
Miles, Bud, 8
minimum wage
 Disney, 2, 13–14
 earning less than, 134
 enforcing rights to, 141–143
 establishment of, 64–66
 law, 73–74
 Metropolitan Museum, 120
 NBC, 174–175
 results of paying, 167
 statistics on, 28, 61–62, 72–73, 210
 United Kingdom, 106, 200
Minnesota, University of, 212
Missouri, University of, 28
Monsanto program, 137
Monster.com, 74
MonsterTRAK, 154
Montclair State University, 8
Montgomery, Jerry, 9
Morgan-Jaffe, Cindy, 152–153
Morton, Andrew, 103
Mouse Trap (Yee), 17–18
Mousecatraz (Jones), 2, 10, 17–19, 22
MP3.com, 153–154
MTV, 151, 175
multidiversity, 90
multi-level marketing, 70
Municipal-level internships, 33
Musambacine, Kunda, 181–182
Myers-Briggs tests, 98

NACE (National Association of Colleges
 and Employers), 8, 26, 227n7
Nachtwey, James, 169
National Archives, 109

National Association of Colleges and
 Employers (NACE), 8, 26, 227n7
National Center for Charitable Statistics
 (NCCS), 116
National Civil Service League, 33
National Employment Law Project
 (NELP), 72
National Employment Lawyers
 Association (NELA), 81, 118, 243
National Institute of Public Affairs,
 32–33, 228n8
National Internship Program, 111
National Minimum Wage (1998), 244
National Public Radio, 219
National Society for Experiential
 Education, 26, 34
National Theatre (Beijing), 195
National Treasury Employees Union,
 108
National Union of Journalists, 163
*The National Longitudinal Survey of
 Youth 1997* (NLSY97), 27
Nature Conservancy (TNC), 117
NBC, 86, 151, 174, 176
NCCS (National Center for Charitable
 Statistics), 116
Neal, Derek, 135
Neal, Michelle, 181–182
Neff, Gina, 37, 85, 89, 90, 131, 169–170,
 207
NELA (National Employment Lawyers
 Association), 81, 118, 243
NELP (National Employment Law
 Project), 72
Netherlands, internships in, 201
New Deal, 207
New Economy, 125–126, 204
New York Life, 28
New York University, 86
Nickelodeon, 68–69
Nissen, Bruce, 14
non-interns, 159–163
nonprofit organization interns
 AmeriCorps, 116–118
 compared with volunteers, 118–119
 example, 120–121
 importance of, 119–120
 statistics on, 116
Normington, Eric, 145–150
North, Oliver, 113
North Carolina, University of, 8

Northeastern University, 96, 98
Northern Europe, internships in, 201–202
Northwestern, 218
Northwestern Mutual Life Insurance Company, 35
Northwestern University, 124–125, 177, 218

OA (Office of Apprenticeship), 44, 51, 55
Obama, Barack, 104, 107–109, 201–202
O'Connor, Bridget, 79, 220
O'Connor, Donald T., 84
O'Donnell, J. P., 153
Office of Apprenticeship (OA), 44, 51, 55
Office of the Chief of Staff, 103
Office of the First Lady, 104
One Day One Internship, 69, 70, 74, 92, 149
OneCubicle, 151
Ortner, Craig, 80
Outside (magazine), 140, 177
Outward Bound, 94
overseas labor, 15
Oxford University, 200

PA (production assistant), 173
Palladino, Grace, 53
Parchello, Sara, 243
Paris, Leslie, 54
Partnership for Public Service, 106
part-timers, 26
Paul Smith's College, 5
"Paving the Way Through Paid Internships" (EPI), 220
Pay and Work Rights Helpline, 244
Peggy Guggenheim Interns Society, *xii*
Peking University, 193
Pelling, Margaret, 48–49
Pencavel, John, 128
Pennsylvania, University of, 86
pension plan (Disney), 13
permalancers, 26
permatemps, 26, 38
permed, 21–22
Philadelphia City Council, 212, 237n2
Phillips, Kent, 7
Pink, Daniel, 37
Plath, Sylvia, 35

Pleitez, Emanuel, 183
political interns
    educational institution programs, 111–112
    examples, 113–115
    FCIP (Federal Career Intern Program), 108–109
    nonprofit organizations, 112–113
    overview, 99–100
    prevalence of unpaid, 105–108
    roles of, 101–103
    statistics on, 100–101
    Washington Center, 109–111
    White House internship program, 103–105
Polsby, Nelson, 33
Ponzi scheme, 74
Port, Whitney, *xii*
Portland Terminal Co., Walling v., 65, 241
Praxis program, 90
Precair Forum (Amsterdam), 198
Precarias a la Dervia (Precarious Women Adrift), 198
precarity, 197–201
Precarity Ping Pong, 198
Precogs, 198
Predictably Irrational: The Hidden Forces that Shape Our Decisions (Ariely), 126
printer's devils, 51
production assistant (PA), 173
Prunty, Kim, 20
Publix, 15
Purchase, Harry, 5
Purdue University, 8
The Pursuit of Happyness (film), 176
pyramid selling, 70

Quintessential Careers, 26, 226n4

radio interns, 28, 179
RCID (Reedy Creek Improvement District), 4, 5, 17
Reagan, Ronald, 128
Reedy Creek Improvement District (RCID), 4, 5, 17
Registered Apprenticeship (website), 229n1
regular jobs, *xiii–xiv*
Reich, Rob, 116

Renmin University, 194
resident, 31
Richards, Robin, 153–154
Rights for Interns, 244
Robb, David, 173–174
Robert F. Kennedy Center for Justice
    and Human Rights, 156
Robin Hood gang, 199
Robinson, James, 57
Rockefeller Center, 91
Rockland Psychiatric Center, 79
Rodems, Steve, 154
Roeth, Brett, 215
Rorabaugh, William, 52
Rosen College, 7
Ross, Andrew, 3, 36, 37, 39, 195, 198
Roth, Mark, 108
Rothberg, Steven, 139
Ruckelshaus, Catherine, 72, 73
Russert, Tim, 180

Salem State, 111
Salvation Army, 149
San Precario, 196, 197
Saturday Night Live (TV show), 172
Schneider, Herman, 96
Schneider, Howard, 177
scholarships, for student internships,
    90–91
Scholz, Olaf, 199
Schutz, Eric, 14
SEO (Sponsors for Educational
    Opportunity), 182
serial interns, 113
Service Employees International Union,
    31
Service Trades Council, 10, 12
Seventeen (magazine), 151
sexual harassment, 64, 80–82, 178
Sharlet, Jeff, 112–113
Showtime, 151
Shukaitis, Stevphen, 200
signal theory, 130–132
Simon, Neil, 180
"Simulacra and Simulations"
    (Baudrillard), 227n1
Singer, Matt, 171
situated learning, 93
Smith, Adam, 49
Smith, Michael, 110–111, 148
Smith, Wendy, 118–119

Smith, Will, 176
Smith Barney, 138, 149
Smith College, 90
Smith-Hughes Act (1917), 56
Snow White Village Campground, 6
social inequalities, xv, 162–163, 206, 216
Spence, Michael, 130
Spielberg, Steven, 170–171
Sponsors for Educational Opportunity
    (SEO), 182
Stanford University, 24, 96, 111, 112,
    200
Stanford-in-Washington program, 101
State Department, 106–107
state-level internships, 33
Statute of Artificers (1563), 49, 51
Stevens, Rosemary, 30, 31
Stone, Vernon, 28
student interns. See also academic credit;
    career centers; cooperative
    education; experiential education
    competition, 91–93
    under FLSA, 83
    internship requirements, 89–90
    legality of internships, 86–87
    overview, 78–84
    paying for internships, 85–86
    scholarship and subsidization, 90–91
    views on, 93–96
subsidization, for student internships,
    90–91
Sullivan, Andrew, 105
summer jobs, xi, 8, 24, 54, 147
SUNY-Stony Brook, 177
supply and demand, 140–144, 208
Syracuse University, 111
Szillagi, Beth, 43–44

Taliesin Fellowship, 212
Target, 36, 181
Tari, Marcello, 197
Teachers College at Columbia
    University, 32
Teenagers: An American History
    (Palladino), 53
temps/temporary workers, 24, 26, 193,
    198–199, 203, 209, 222
Thyne, Tone, 68
Tickets.com, 153–154
Time Warner, 118
TNC (Nature Conservancy), 117